Solicitors' Accounts—
A Practical Guide

Solicitors' Accounts— A Practical Guide

Dale Kay

Solicitor (Hons)

and

Janet Baker

LLB (Hons), Solicitor

OXFORD

UNIVERSITY PRESS

OXFORD
UNIVERSITY PRESS

Great Clarendon Street, Oxford OX2 6DP

Oxford University Press is a department of the University of Oxford.
It furthers the University's objective of excellence in research, scholarship,
and education by publishing worldwide in

Oxford New York

Auckland Cape Town Dar es Salaam Hong Kong Karachi
Kuala Lumpur Madrid Melbourne Mexico City Nairobi
New Delhi Shanghai Taipei Toronto

With offices in

Argentina Austria Brazil Chile Czech Republic France Greece
Guatemala Hungary Italy Japan Poland Portugal Singapore
South Korea Switzerland Thailand Turkey Ukraine Vietnam

Oxford is a registered trade mark of Oxford University Press
in the UK and in certain other countries

Published in the United States
by Oxford University Press Inc., New York

First edition 1997
Second edition 1998
Third edition 1999
Fourth edition 2000
Fifth edition 2001
Sixth edition 2002
Seventh edition 2003
Eighth edition 2004
Ninth edition 2005

British Library Cataloguing in Publication Data
Data available

Library of Congress Cataloging in Publication Data
Data available

Typeset by Newgen Imaging Systems (P) Ltd., Chennai, India
Printed in Great Britain
on acid-free paper by
Antony Rowe Limited, Chippenham

ISBN 0-19-928137-8

1 3 5 7 9 10 8 6 4 2

OUTLINE CONTENTS

DETAILED CONTENTS

PREFACE

I would like to thank Janet Baker, whose original book still forms the basis of this Guide. My thanks also go to my husband, Roger and son, Richard, to all my students, my colleagues and ex-colleagues, to all at Oxford University Press, and in particular Rebecca Webb.

Dale Kay
April 2005
Manchester

Introduction to solicitors' accounts and basic bookkeeping

1.1 Introduction

This chapter includes:

1. an introduction to accounts;
2. the purpose of keeping accounts;
3. an explanation of the double entry bookkeeping system with worked examples;
4. practical self test exercises in drawing up accounts using the double entry system.

1.2 Overview of accounts

Accounts on the Legal Practice Course is regarded as a pervasive subject, although it is separately assessed. A word of encouragement at the start. Although initially Accounts can seem daunting, most students do well, and even manage to enjoy the time they spend on Accounts. Do not worry if you did not enjoy GCSE maths; the only maths involved here is very basic arithmetic.

Do practice using the exercises in the book and those given to you on your course. This is the best way to come to grips with the subject. The questions at the end of each chapter are graded, starting with easier exercises and working up to more challenging questions.

The following web sites may be useful to you, and will also be mentioned in the relevant chapters:

www.lawsociety.org.uk in respect of solicitors accounts;
www.companieshouse.gov.uk in respect of company accounts;
www.dti.gov.uk in respect of company accounts;
www.hmrc.gov.uk Customs and Excise in respect of VAT, Inland Revenue.

1.2.1 Why study Accounts?

You may think that Accounts is the last subject a prospective solicitor needs to know. However, there are very good reasons why it is included. Solicitors can be struck off as solicitors if they breach the Solicitors' Accounts Rules—have a look in the *Law Society Gazette* and see how often this is a reason. They look after large sums of money on behalf of their clients, and must be trusted to do so. They are ultimately responsible and cannot totally rely on the skill or honesty of others.

Solicitors are running a business, they must also be able to understand how the accounts are kept, and, as partners, be able to read their Profit and Loss accounts and Balance sheets each year.

Solicitors need some understanding of accounts when giving advice, whether to corporate clients, or for example to matrimonial clients when advising on asset distribution.

1.2.2   How to study Accounts

Accounts is a practical subject, it involves understanding the principles and applying them. The best way to do this is by reading the explanation and then working through the exercises. Only when you are satisfied that you understand what you are doing should you move on to the next section. Repetition of exercises will consolidate your understanding. Once you understand the basic principles the later sections should fall into place.

1.2.3   The main areas of study

Accounts on this course falls into two main sections:

1. Business Accounts
2. Solicitors' Accounts

Business Accounts

This includes basic double entry bookkeeping, the Trial Balance, and preparation of Final Accounts, being the Profit and Loss and Balance Sheet. The Final Accounts can be prepared for a sole owner, a partnership or a company.

Solicitors' Accounts

This covers the Solicitors' Accounts Rules, the difference between office and client account, controlled trust money, and the bookkeeping entries required. It also covers how to prepare a simple Financial Statement for a client, and the particular bookkeeping entries required for certain types of work, for example property or probate work.

1.3   The purpose of keeping accounts

All businesses need to keep a day-to-day record of all their financial transactions, so that they can see what is happening. From these records they will be able to draw up final accounts.

These fall into two main sections:

The Profit and Loss account

This will record all income less expenses, to give the profit or loss for the period.

The Balance Sheet

This will show what the business OWNS—its assets and what the business OWES—its liabilities.

Different people will use the accounts for different purposes, for example:

The owners—will need to know what is happening financially, this will help them with planning for the business.

The Inland Revenue or Customs and Excise—for tax purposes

Any person or company that has lent money to the business, for example the bank

A buyer of the business

A new partner coming into a partnership.

1.4 An introduction to double-entry bookkeeping

A basic account is a record or a history of financial transactions.

To record monies received and monies paid out, a simple single entry cash account could be drawn up as follows:

EXAMPLE

Roger receives £500 salary (income) during the week and pays out £200 rent (expense) and £100 on food (expense).

Cash account

	Received	Paid	Balance
Wages (Income)	500		500
Rent (expense)		200	300
Food (expense)		100	200

Although this may appear to be an adequate record, it does not show, for example, any goods or services received or supplied on credit, nor how much food was left in the cupboard. It would also be difficult to extract information on the breakdown of expenses and income if many entries were made.

To maintain a complete and accurate record of financial transactions, the double-entry system of bookkeeping is used.

1.4.1 The principle of double entry bookkeeping

The principle of double-entry bookkeeping is that there are two aspects to every single financial transaction:

(a) the benefit received;

(b) the consideration given.

Thus two entries are made for each single transaction.

In the example above Roger received £500 cash, but £500 worth of work was given by him in return for this cash.

Thus the entries would be:

Cash account

	Benefit received	Consideration given	Balance
Salary	500		500

Income account (Value of work done)—names the source of the income

	Benefit received	Consideration given	Balance
Cash		500	500

When Roger paid for the rent he received the benefit of £200 worth of accommodation, and £200 cash was given by him.

Thus the entries would be:

Rent account (names the source of the loss) Expense

	Benefit received	Consideration given	Balance
Cash	200		200

Cash account

	Benefit received	Consideration given	Balance
Balance			500
Rent paid		200	300

When Roger paid for the food the entries would be:

Food account Expense

	Benefit received	Consideration given	Balance
Cash	100		100

Cash account

	Benefit received	Consideration given	Balance
Balance			300
Food		100	200

The benefit received is shown on the left hand side of the account and called the **DEBIT** entry, the consideration given is shown on the right hand side of the account, and called the **CREDIT** entry.

DEBIT   CREDIT
BENEFIT RECEIVED   CONSIDERATION GIVEN

This may seem strange or wrong at this stage, as you may associate credit with receipts, and debit with payments out, usually based on your bank statement sent out from the bank, where payments out of your account are shown as debit entries and receipts are shown as credit entries.

EXAMPLE

Jane pays £1,000 into her bank account with the Northern Bank PLC. The Northern Bank will draw up its accounts as follows:

Northern Bank PLC cash account

	Benefit received DEBIT	Consideration given CREDIT	Balance
Jane	1,000		1,000 DR

Jane account

	Benefit received DEBIT	Consideration given CREDIT	Balance
Cash		1,000	1,000 CR

The bank has followed the rules given above, but all Jane sees is her account which is one part of the double entry. From Jane's point of view the credit entry records a receipt. From the Bank's point of view the receipt was recorded on the Bank's cash account and Jane's account shows that Jane has given the cash. Jane is a creditor of the Bank—see later.

Remember that the two entries made *do* record the same *single* transaction. The principle of double-entry bookkeeping is therefore: *for every debit entry in one account there must be a corresponding credit entry in another account.*

1.4.2 The layout of an account

There are several methods of drawing an account. The method adopted in this book is as follows.

Name of account

Date	Details	DR	CR	Balance

Note the following:

(a) This layout has five columns.

(b) There is one column each for date and details. Note that the details column must indicate clearly the name of the account which forms the other part of the double entry.

(c) The column headed 'DR' (abbreviation of debit) is always on the LEFT. Debit entries, the meaning of which will be explained later in the chapter, are made in this column.

(d) The column headed 'CR' (abbreviation of credit) is always on the RIGHT. Credit entries are made in this column.

(e) There is a balance column which gives a running balance on the account after each transaction is completed. The balance is the difference between the debit and credit entries. If the debit side is heavier than the credit side then there is a debit balance, and vice versa.

Note that for solicitors, Rule 32(5) of the Solicitors' Accounts Rules 1998 imposes an obligation to show the current balance on each client's ledger, or the balance must be readily ascertainable from the records kept.

1.5 Classification of accounts

All financial transactions will therefore be recorded by double entry in the ledger accounts of a business. These ledger accounts can be divided into three types:

(a) *PERSONAL ACCOUNTS* These will be DEBITED when the individual, firm or company dealing with the business receives goods, cash or services from the business, and CREDITED when the individual, firm or company gives goods, cash or services to the business.

(b) *ASSET/REAL ACCOUNTS*   These will be DEBITED when the business receives an asset, or assets are increased and CREDITED when the business disposes of an asset, or assets are reduced.

(c) *INCOME/EXPENSE ACCOUNTS*   Expense accounts are DEBITED with the loss/money paid out—they name the source of the loss by showing nominally what the business has received in return for its loss.

Income accounts are CREDITED with the gain/money received—they name the source of the gain by showing nominally what the business has given in return for the gain.

NB: each account drawn up will have a balance column which will show the difference between all the debit entries made and all the credit entries made. For example, if an account has debit entries totalling £10,000 and credit entries totalling £8,000 it will have a debit balance of £2,000.

1.5.1   Personal accounts

The following should be noted with regard to personal accounts:

(a) They record transactions involving individuals, firms or companies.

(b) A separate account must be kept for each person, firm or company with which the business has dealings, for example, each debtor and creditor.

The rule for making entries in a personal account is:

DEBIT   When goods, cash or services are received by that person or company from the business
        (They are then a DEBTOR)

CREDIT   When that person or company gives goods, cash or services to the business
        (They are then a CREDITOR)

1.5.2   The personal accounts of the business owner

The accounts look at a transaction from the point of view of the business. For accounting purposes the business and its owner are treated as separate entities. This principle holds good for a solicitor's practice. The accounts which record transactions between the business and its owner are personal accounts. These accounts are:

1.5.2.1   Capital account

When a solicitor sets up in practice he or she will introduce assets, e.g., money, premises, car and equipment. When this happens:

(a) DEBIT the asset account.

(b) CREDIT the Capital account showing the amount due to the owner.

EXAMPLE

On 1 January Harry starts up in practice as a sole practitioner. He introduces £8,000 cash, a car valued at £5,000 and office equipment worth £2,000. These opening entries will be recorded as follows:

Cash account

Date	Details	DR	CR	Balance
		(Received)	(Paid)	
1 Jan	Capital introduced by Harry	8,000		8,000 DR

Car account

Date	Details	DR	CR	Balance
1 Jan	Capital introduced by Harry	5,000		5,000 DR

Office equipment account

Date	Details	DR	CR	Balance
1 Jan	Capital introduced by Harry	2,000		2,000 DR

Capital account

Date	Details	DR	CR	Balance
1 Jan	Cash		8,000	8,000 CR
	Car		5,000	13,000 CR
	Office		2,000	15,000 CR
	equipment			

1.5.2.2   Drawings account

From time to time the owner will take money out of the business either in cash or by paying private expenses, for example, a home gas bill. These are called drawings and are usually recorded in a personal account, the drawings account.

The drawings account will always be DEBITED.

EXAMPLE

On 31 January Harry draws £1,000 out of the firm's bank account for his own use and pays his personal tax of £500. The entries to record these transactions are as follows:

Drawings account

Date	Details	DR	CR	Balance
31 Jan	Cash—drawings	1,000		
31 Jan	Cash—personal tax	500		1,500 DR

Cash account

Date	Details	DR	CR	Balance
	Balance			8,000 DR
31 Jan	Drawings—cash		1,000	7,000 DR
	Drawings—personal tax		500	6,500 DR

The credit balance on the capital account shows the amount which the business owes to its owner, i.e., the amount he has invested. The debit balance on the drawings account shows the amount the owner owes the business.

1.5.3 Asset/real accounts

These will show the assets at the price paid for them (cost price).

It is not always easy to decide whether a purchase should be recorded as an asset, or as an expense. For example if the business buys office furniture, this is likely to last for some time and so will be recorded as an asset. However, if the business buys stationery, this will be used up in a fairly short time, and so it will be recorded as an expense.

The cash account

This is not only a real account it is also a personal account with the bank.

The business will usually place most of its cash in the bank, it will pay all cheques received into the bank, and make most payments out by cheque or transfer. Any cash in the bank will be an asset. However if the business went overdrawn at the bank, then the overdraft would be a liability.

The petty cash account

This deals with cash payments made by the firm. A cash sum will be taken out of the bank each week as a cash float. This can be used to make payments out, and topped up when required.

The rule for making entries in an asset account is:

DEBIT   receipt of an asset
CREDIT   reduction of an asset

EXAMPLE *ASSET ACCOUNTS*

Assume that a firm has £10,000 cash in the bank.
The firm purchases office furniture for £2,000.
DEBIT the increase on the office furniture account
CREDIT the decrease on the Cash Account

Office furniture account

Date	Details	DR	CR	Balance
	Cash	2,000		2,000 DR

Cash account

Date	Details	DR	CR	Balance
	Balance			10,000 DR
	Office Furniture		2,000	8,000 DR

The balances on the accounts show the shift in assets from cash to office furniture; at first the firm had £10,000 cash, now it has £8,000 cash and office furniture worth £2,000.

1.5.4 Income and Expense Accounts

(a) INCOME ACCOUNTS. These record the receipt of income by the firm. The following are examples of income accounts kept by a solicitor:

(i) *Profit costs account*   This account shows the profit costs charged to clients. It is based on the bills sent to clients.

(ii) *Interest received account*   This account shows interest received by the firm on money held in a deposit account.

(iii) *Rent received account*   This account shows rent received by the firm if it leases out any of its surplus office accommodation.

Income accounts are CREDITED with income received and will therefore always have CREDIT balances.

EXAMPLE

A firm lets its surplus office premises for which it receives rent of £800 per month. On 1 January the firm receives the first month's rent.

CREDIT   Rent received account
DEBIT   Cash Book

Rent received account

Date	Details	DR	CR	Balance
1 Jan	Cash		800	800 CR

Cash account

Date	Details	DR	CR	Balance
1 Jan	Rent received	800		800 DR

EXAMPLE

The firm does work for Basil, for which the charge is £500. When the bill is sent to Basil, the income (work done) account will be credited; it shows what the business has given in return for the gain. Note that in solicitors' firms the income account based on the bills sent out is usually called the Profit Costs account. Basil's personal account will be debited, showing that Basil has received £500 worth of services. The debit balance will show that Basil is a debtor of the firm; he owes £500.

CREDIT   Profit Costs Account
DEBIT   Basil Account

Profit Costs account (work done account)
Income

Date	Details	DR	CR	Balance
	Basil—bill		500	500 CR

Basil account (personal account)

Date	Details	DR	CR	Balance
	Profit costs—bill	500		500 DR

When Basil pays the bill, the entries will be:

DEBIT   The Cash account (real account)
CREDIT   Basil's Account

Cash account

Date	Details	DR	CR	Balance
	Balance say			8,000 DR
	Basil	500		8,500 DR

Basil account

Date	Details	DR	CR	Balance
	Balance			500 DR
	Cash you		500	—

The debt of £500 due from Basil has been paid and converted into cash.

Note: the balance on Basil's account was £500 debit, the balance is now nil as the amount owed has been paid.

    (b) EXPENSE ACCOUNTS. These record the payment of business expenses.

        (i)   A separate expense account is opened for each type of expense which the firm has; for example, most firms will have rent, council tax, electricity, telephone and salaries accounts.

        (ii)   An expense account is DEBITED each time the firm pays a business expense.

EXAMPLE

On 30 November the firm pays an office electricity bill of £500.

DEBIT   Electricity account
CREDIT   Cash account

Electricity account

Date	Details	DR	CR	Balance
30 Nov	Cash	500		500 DR

Cash account

Date	Details	DR (Received)	CR (Paid out)	Balance
	Balance say			5,000 DR
30 Nov	Electricity		500	4,500 DR

Payments made under any leasing or rental agreement are business expenses and are recorded in an expense account.

EXAMPLE

A firm leases word processors from Computer Supplies Ltd. The quarterly rental is £100. On 1 April the first instalment is paid. Assume the firm has a cash balance of £5,000 at the bank.

DEBIT   Rental account
CREDIT   Cash account

Word processors rentals account

Date	Details	DR	CR	Balance
1 Apr	Cash	100		100 DR

Cash account

Date	Details	DR	CR	Balance
1 Apr	Balance Word processors rentals		100	5,000 DR 4,900 DR

Expense accounts will always have DEBIT balances.

1.5.5   Trading accounts

Manufacturing and trading accounts are dealt with in more detail in **Chapter 7**, where the same principles apply. Where goods are purchased as part of the trading cycle, e.g. goods are purchased for £6,500 cash, the entries would be:

CREDIT the cash account £6,500
DEBIT the Purchases (expense account) £6,500

On the assumption that the firm starts with £16,500 cash then the accounts would be as follows:

Cash account

Date	Details	DR	CR	Balance
	Balance Purchases		6,500	16,500 DR 10,000 DR

Purchases account

Date	Details	DR	CR	Balance
	Cash	6,500		6,500 DR

When the goods are sold a separate sales account will be opened. This will be CREDITED.

EXAMPLE

Assume the business has £10,000 Cash.
Goods are sold for £9,000 cash.

DEBIT   The cash account £9,000
CREDIT   The sales account (an income account) £9,000

Cash account

Date	Details	DR	CR	Balance
	Balance			10,000 DR
	Sales	9,000		19,000 DR

Sales account (nominal income account)

Date	Details	DR	CR	Balance
	Cash		9,000	9,000 CR

1.5.6 Solicitors and accounts

Note that as solicitors will usually be holding large sums of money on behalf of clients they will have at least two bank accounts, one dealing with the firm's own money, called OFFICE ACCOUNT and the other dealing with clients' money called CLIENT ACCOUNT. For further details see Chapter 11 onwards.

1.6 Worked example on double entry

Fiona, a sole practitioner, sets up her practice on 1 February with £10,000 cash, office equipment worth £1,000 and premises valued at £140,000.

During the month of February the practice engages in the following transactions:

1. It pays her secretary's salary of £1,300.
2. It receives one month's rent from the tenant occupying part of the office premises—£800.
3. It buys a desk for £500.
4. It buys a car on credit from Karsales Ltd for £9,000.
5. Fiona draws £1,000 out of the bank for her own use.
6. The firm sends a bill to Jim for £500, re profit costs for work done.
7. Jim pays the bill of £500.

Cash account

Date	Details	DR	CR	Balance
Feb	Capital introduced	10,000		10,000 DR
	Salaries		1,300	8,700 DR
	Rent received	800		9,500 DR
	Office furniture		500	9,000 DR
	Drawings (cash)		1,000	8,000 DR
	Jim	500		8,500 DR

A real account/personal account with the bank.

Office equipment account

Date	Details	DR	CR	Balance
Feb 1	Capital introduced	1,000		1,000 DR

A real/asset account.

Premises account

Date	Details	DR	CR	Balance
Feb 1	Capital introduced	140,000		140,000 DR

A real/asset account.

Capital account

Date	Details	DR	CR	Balance
Feb	Cash		10,000	10,000 CR
	Office equipment		1,000	11,000 CR
	Premises		140,000	151,000 CR

A personal account.

Salaries account

Date	Details	DR	CR	Balance
Feb	Cash (secretary)	1,300		1,300 DR

A nominal expense account.

Rent received account

Date	Details	DR	CR	Balance
Feb	Cash		800	800 CR

A nominal income account.

Office furniture account

Date	Details	DR	CR	Balance
Feb	Cash (desk)	500		500 DR

A real/asset account.

Motor vehicles account

Date	Details	DR	CR	Balance
Feb	Karsales Ltd (car)	9,000		9,000 DR

A real/asset account.

Karsales Ltd account

Date	Details	DR	CR	Balance
Feb	Motor vehicles (car)		9,000	9,000 CR

A personal account.

Drawings account

Date	Details	DR	CR	Balance
Feb	Cash (drawings)	1,000		1,000 DR

A personal account.

Profit costs income account

Date	Details	DR	CR	Balance
	Jim—bill		500	500 CR

A nominal income account.

Jim

Date	Details	DR	CR	Balance
	Profit Costs—bill	500		500 DR
	Cash—you		500	—

A personal account.

1.7. Check list

By the end of this chapter you should be able to:

1. Appreciate that for ONE financial transaction there will be TWO entries—A DEBIT ENTRY on one account; and A CREDIT ENTRY on another account.
2. Identify the main types of account being: INCOME accounts and EXPENSE accounts; ASSET (REAL) accounts; PERSONAL accounts.
3. Understand which of these accounts will be debited or credited.
4. Complete all the self test exercises at the end of the chapter.

1.8 Exercises on double-entry bookkeeping

1 State the double entry that would be made in the following transactions:
   (a) Kirk starts a business and introduces cash of £5,000.
   (b) Little and Co. receive cash of £600 in payment of work done.
   (c) North pays out £300 in respect of an electricity bill.
   (d) Fishwick pays an employee's salary of £500.
   (e) Grayling draws £1,000 from her business for her own use.
   (f) Morris purchases a car for his business for £15,000 on credit from Stockton Garage Ltd.

2   Blears starts in business on 1 January as a solicitor, and introduces cash of £6,000 and office furniture worth £4,000. Show the accounts to record this.

3   Latter starts a business with £5,000 cash on 10 November. He then buys a computer for £800 on 11 November. He sends a bill for £1,000 to a customer Howard for work done on 20 November.

Show the accounts to record this.

4   Paula starts in practice as a solicitor on 1 July with cash of £10,000, a car worth £16,000 and premises worth £128,000. During the month of July the following transactions occur:

1 July	Pays council tax £900.
3 July	Buys office furniture £1,800. Pays by cheque.
8 July	Pays secretary's salary £1,500.
10 July	Receives £12,500 as a loan from her brother-in-law Ted, to be repaid in three years without interest.
14 July	Draws £2,500 for her own use.

Prepare accounts to record the above transactions.

1.9   Suggested answers to exercises on double-entry bookkeeping

1

(a) DEBIT the Cash Account £5,000
     CREDIT the Capital Account (for Kirk) £5,000

(b) DEBIT the Cash Account £600
     CREDIT the Profit Costs (work done) account (income account) £600

(c) CREDIT Cash Account £300
     DEBIT Electricity account (expense account) £300

(d) CREDIT Cash Account £500
     DEBIT Salaries account (expense account) £500

(e) CREDIT Cash Account £1,000
     DEBIT Drawings account (personal account) £1,000

(f) DEBIT Car account (asset account) £15,000
     CREDIT Stockton Garage Ltd account (personal account) £15,000

2   Cash account

Date	Details	DR	CR	Balance
1 Jan	Capital	6,000		6,000 DR

Office furniture account

Date	Details	DR	CR	Balance
1 Jan	Capital	4,000		4,000 DR

Capital account

Date	Details	DR	CR	Balance
1 Jan	Cash Office furniture		6,000 4,000	6,000 CR 10,000 CR

3 **Cash account**

Date	Details	DR	CR	Balance
10 Nov 11 Nov	Capital Computer	5,000	 800	5,000 DR 4,200 DR

Capital account

Date	Details	DR	CR	Balance
10 Nov	Cash		5,000	5,000 CR

Computer account

Date	Details	DR	CR	Balance
11 Nov	Cash	800		800 DR

Howard account

Date	Details	DR	CR	Balance
20 Nov	Profit costs –bill	1,000		1,000 DR

Profit costs

Date	Details	DR	CR	Balance
20 Nov	Howard–bill		1,000	1,000 CR

4 **Cash account**

Date	Details	DR	CR	Balance
1 July	Capital	10,000		10,000 DR
	Council tax		900	9,100 DR
3 July	Office furniture		1,800	7,300 DR
8 July	Salary		1,500	5,800 DR
10 July	Loan: Ted	12,500		18,300 DR
14 July	Drawings		2,500	15,800 DR

Car account

Date	Details	DR	CR	Balance
1 July	Capital	16,000		16,000 DR

Premises account

Date	Details	DR	CR	Balance
1 July	Capital	128,000		128,000 DR

Capital account

Date	Details	DR	CR	Balance
1 July	Cash		10,000	10,000 CR
	Car		16,000	26,000 CR
	Premises		128,000	154,000 CR

Council tax account

Date	Details	DR	CR	Balance
1 July	Cash	900		900 DR

Office furniture account

Date	Details	DR	CR	Balance
3 July	Cash	1,800		1,800 DR

Salaries account

Date	Details	DR	CR	Balance
8 July	Cash (secretary)	1,500		1,500 DR

Loan account: Ted

Date	Details	DR	CR	Balance
10 July	Cash		12,500	12,500 CR

Drawings account

Date	Details	DR	CR	Balance
14 July	Cash	2,500		2,500 DR

The Trial Balance

2.1 The Trial Balance

This is only a LIST of all the balances at the end of each account—it is not an account.

2.1.1 Purpose of the Trial Balance

The Trial Balance is used:

1. to check the accuracy of the double entry bookkeeping;
2. as a first stage in drawing up the Final accounts.

2.1.2 Preparation of the Trial Balance

As two entries are always made for each single transaction, one debit and one credit, then all the debit entries must equal all the credit entries. Provided all the entries are correct, then all the debit balances at the end of the accounts should equal all the credit balances at the end of the accounts.

To check the accuracy of the double entries that have been made a Trial Balance is drawn up. This will be done regularly, and also before the final accounts are prepared. All the balances at the end of each account are listed. There will be one column for all the debit balances and one column for all the credit balances. Each column will be added up.

On the Trial Balance

The DEBIT column will show EITHER assets OR expense accounts.
The CREDIT column will show EITHER liabilities OR income accounts.

2.1.3 Suspense Accounts

If the debit and credit columns do not agree, even after checking all the entries, it may be necessary to adjust for the difference by opening a Suspense account until the difference can be found. Thus, if the credit balances exceed the debit balances by £100 a Suspense account can be opened with a debit balance of £100.

EXAMPLE TRIAL BALANCE

On 31 October the bookkeeper extracts the following balances from the accounts of A. Solicitor:

Profit costs	16,000
Capital account	15,000
Motor cars account	20,000
Office furniture account	5,000
Rent paid account	1,300
General expenses account	200

Council tax account	1,250
Postage account	100
Stationery account	80
Salaries account	1,600
Drawings account	800
Cash account	4,500 DR
Petty cash account	170
Loan account	4,000

The following trial balance is then prepared.

A. Solicitor: Trial Balance as at 31 October

Name of account	DR	CR
Profit costs		16,000
Capital amount due to owner		15,000
Motor cars—asset/real account	20,000	
Office furniture—asset/real	5,000	
Rent—expense	1,300	
General expenses—expense	200	
Council tax—expense	1,250	
Postage—expense	100	
Stationery—expense	80	
Salaries—expense	1,600	
Drawings—amount taken out by owner—personal	800	
Cash—asset/real	4,500	
Petty cash—asset/real	170	
Loan—liabiity		4,000
Totals	35,000	35,000

You can see from the above that the DEBIT balances show either ASSET accounts or EXPENSE accounts. The CREDIT balances show either LIABILITIES (e.g. due to the owner of the business or creditors) or INCOME accounts.

2.1.4   Errors not revealed by the Trial Balance

The fact that the total debit and total credit balances agree does not mean that the bookkeeper has not made any mistakes. There are some errors which will not be revealed by the trial balance, for example:

(a) Errors of entry—the same incorrect entry is made in both accounts used to record the transaction.

EXAMPLE

The firm buys a typewriter for £500. The bookkeeper inadvertently makes a debit entry in the office equipment account of £50 and a credit entry of £50 in the cash account.

(b) Compensating errors—the bookkeeper makes two separate errors which cancel each other out.

EXAMPLE

The bookkeeper incorrectly totals one account by £100 too much on the credit side and another by £100 too much on the debit side.

(c) Errors of omission—the bookkeeper leaves out both parts of the double entry from the accounts.

(d) Errors of commission—the bookkeeper makes the right entry but in the wrong account.

EXAMPLE

The firm buys office equipment costing £1,000. Instead of debiting the office equipment account with £1,000 the bookkeeper debits the office furniture account.

(e) Errors of principle—the bookkeeper makes an entry in the wrong type of account.

EXAMPLE

The purchase of office equipment is shown in the general expenses account, i.e., a nominal instead of a real account. If this error remains undetected at the time the firm's final accounts are prepared the business expenses will be overstated in the profit and loss account and the value of the assets will be understated in the balance sheet.

2.2 Check list

By the end of this chapter you should:

1. understand the nature of the Trial Balance and its limitations;
2. be able to categorise the types of accounts listed on the Trial Balance;
3. identify which accounts would have a debit balance and which a credit balance (note for those accounts which could have either a credit or a debit balance you will be told whether it is a debit or a credit balance);
4. have completed all the self test exercises at the end of the chapter.

2.3 Exercises on double-entry bookkeeping and Trial Balance

1 The bookkeeper has extracted the following balances from the accounts of Hooper, a sole practitioner, on 30 September. From the balances you are asked to prepare a Trial Balance. State what each account is, for example an asset account, a personal account, or an income or expense account.

Salaries	1,000
Leasehold property	15,000
Capital	35,000
Drawings	2,000
Administration expenses	4,000
Motor cars	12,500
Cash account	500 DR

2 From the following information, extracted as at 30 June, prepare a trial balance for Timothy, a sole practitioner.

General expenses	200
Salaries	1,200
Drawings	4,000
Rent	1,250
Council tax	150
Electricity	800
Creditors	2,500
Office furniture	7,000
Bank overdraft	2,300
Loan account	9,000
Car	7,700
Capital	8,500

3 The bookkeeper has extracted the following balances from the accounts of Sally Jones, a sole practitioner, on 31 January. From the balances you are asked to prepare a Trial Balance.

Salaries	3,000
Office equipment	15,000
Freehold property	235,000
Capital	220,000
Drawings	13,200
Midshire Bank—loan account	20,000
Cash—office account	1,000 DR
Cash—client account	125,000 DR
Council tax	900
General expenses	1,400
Debtors	2,000
Creditors	1,500
Rent received	2,000
Profit costs	30,000
Due to clients	125,000
Bank interest paid	2,000

2.4 Suggested answers to exercises on double-entry bookkeeping and Trial Balance

1 **Hooper: Trial Balance as at 30 September**

Name of account	DR	CR
Salaries—expense	1,000	
Leasehold property—asset	15,000	
Capital—personal		35,000
Drawings—personal	2,000	
Administration expenses—expense	4,000	
Motor cars—asset	12,500	
Cash account—asset/personal	500	
Totals	35,000	35,000

2 Timothy: Trial Balance as at 31 June

Name of account	DR	CR
General expenses	200	
Salaries	1,200	
Drawings	4,000	
Rent	1,250	
Council tax	150	
Electricity	800	
Creditors		2,500
Office furniture	7,000	
Cash		2,300
Loan account		9,000
Car	7,700	
Capital		8,500
Totals	22,300	22,300

3 Sally Jones: Trial Balance as at 31 January

Name of account	DR	CR
Salaries	3,000	
Office equipment	15,000	
Freehold property	235,000	
Capital		220,000
Drawings	13,200	
Loan account		20,000
Cash (office)	1,000	
Cash (client)	125,000	
Council tax	900	
General expenses	1,400	
Debtors	2,000	
Creditors		1,500
Rent received		2,000
Profit costs		30,000
Due to clients		125,000
Bank interest paid	2,000	
Totals	398,500	398,500

2.5 Full exercise on double-entry bookkeeping and Trial Balance

Allow around 45 minutes to complete this exercise.

Jane starts in practice as a solicitor on 1 January. She introduces £15,000 into the firm's bank account and a car worth £8,200. She leases her office premises and pays rent of £1,000 per month. During the month of January the following transactions take place:

4 January	Pays first month's rent.
5 January	Pays salary £1,200 to secretary.
6 January	Buys a computer costing £650 on credit from Wylie Ltd.
9 January	Pays office telephone bill £25.
11 January	Pays council tax £150.
18 January	Pays legal executive's salary £1,500.
22 January	Buys stationery for £80.
23 January	Pays office electricity bill £45.
24 January	Pays instalment of £65 to Wylie Ltd.
25 January	Draws £1,600 for her own use.

Prepare accounts to record the above transactions, and prepare a trial balance as at 31 January.

2.6 Suggested answers to exercise on double-entry bookkeeping and Trial Balance

Cash account

Date	Details	DR	CR	Balance
1 Jan	Capital	15,000		15,000 DR
4 Jan	Rent		1,000	14,000 DR
5 Jan	Salaries		1,200	12,800 DR
9 Jan	Telephones		25	12,775 DR
11 Jan	Council tax		150	12,625 DR
18 Jan	Salaries		1,500	11,125 DR
22 Jan	Stationery		80	11,045 DR
23 Jan	Electricity		45	11,000 DR
24 Jan	Wylie Ltd		65	10,935 DR
25 Jan	Drawings		1,600	9,335 DR

Capital account

Date	Details	DR	CR	Balance
	Cash		15,000	15,000 CR
1 Jan	Car		8,200	23,200 CR

Car account

Date	Details	DR	CR	Balance
1 Jan	Capital	8,200		8,200 DR

Rent account

Date	Details	DR	CR	Balance
4 Jan	Cash	1,000		1,000 DR

Salaries account

Date	Details	DR	CR	Balance
5 Jan	Cash (secretary)	1,200		1,200 DR
18 Jan	Cash (legal executive)	1,500		2,700 DR

Office equipment account

Date	Details	DR	CR	Balance
6 Jan	Wylie Ltd (computer)	650		650 DR

Wylie Ltd

Date	Details	DR	CR	Balance
6 Jan	Office equipment		650	650 CR
24 Jan	Cash	65		585 CR

Telephone account

Date	Details	DR	CR	Balance
9 Jan	Cash	25		25 DR

Council tax account

Date	Details	DR	CR	Balance
11 Jan	Cash	150		150 DR

Stationery account

Date	Details	DR	CR	Balance
22 Jan	Cash	80		80 DR

Electricity account

Date	Details	DR	CR	Balance
23 Jan	Cash	45		45 DR

Drawings account

Date	Details	DR	CR	Balance
25 Jan	Cash	1,600		1,600 DR

Jane: Trial Balance as at 31 January

Name of account	DR	CR
Cash	9,335	
Capital		23,200
Motor cars	8,200	
Rent	1,000	
Salaries	2,700	
Office equipment	650	
Wylie Ltd		585
Telephones	25	
Council tax	150	
Drawings	1,600	
Stationery	80	
Electricity	45	
Totals	23,785	23,785

Final accounts

3.1 Introduction

Basic final accounts consist of:

(1) the Profit and Loss Account;

(2) the Balance Sheet.

Final accounts are usually prepared annually at the end of the firm's financial year.

Immediately before the final accounts are prepared a trial balance is drawn up listing the balances on the accounts. Each balance shown on the trial balance will EITHER be:

(a) transferred to the Profit and Loss account;

OR

(b) shown on the Balance Sheet.

3.1.1 Profit and Loss account

Note that this is a double-entry account, i.e., it is part of the double-entry system.

Its function is to calculate the net profit or loss made by the practice during the financial year.

3.1.2 Balance Sheet

The Balance Sheet is a statement of the firm's assets and liabilities on a given date, usually the last day of the financial year.

The Balance Sheet is NOT an account and is therefore not part of the double-entry system. It is a list of the balances on the asset and liability accounts.

At any time the assets of a business should equal its liabilities. This is because each time the business acquires something of value it gives consideration.

EXAMPLE

X, a solicitor, commences in practice with £2,000 in cash which is placed in the firm's bank account. Immediately X has a balance sheet; it is:

Liability		**Asset**	
Capital	2,000	Cash at bank	2,000

X's practice is thus shown to own £2,000 cash (an asset) all of which is owed to X, the owner of the practice (a liability).

3.2 Closing the accounts

(a) Before preparing the final accounts the Income and Expense accounts are closed by transferring the balance on each account to the Profit and Loss account.

(b) Expense accounts have DEBIT balances and so to transfer from an expense account to the Profit and Loss account, the bookkeeping entries are:
   (i)   CREDIT the nominal expense account.
   (ii) DEBIT the profit and loss account.

All you have done is move the debit balance to the Profit and Loss account.

EXAMPLE

At the end of the year the firm's salaries account has a debit balance of £15,000. The balance is transferred to the Profit and Loss account on 31 December.

Salaries account

Date	Details	DR	CR	Balance
	Balance			15,000 DR
31 Dec	Profit and loss account: transfer		15,000	—

(c) Income accounts have CREDIT balances and so to transfer from an income account to the Profit and Loss account, the bookkeeping entries are:
   (i)   DEBIT the income account.
   (ii) CREDIT the Profit and Loss account.

EXAMPLE

At the end of the year the firm's Profit Costs account has a credit balance of £300,000. On 31 December the balance is transferred to the Profit and Loss account.

Costs account

Date	Details	DR	CR	Balance
	Balance			300,000 CR
31 Dec	Profit and loss account: transfer	300,000		—

(d) These transfer entries close the Income and Expense accounts.

(e) The Balance Sheet, unlike the Profit and Loss account, is not an account of double entry and so the balances on the asset and liability accounts are not transferred to the Balance Sheet. They are merely listed on the Balance Sheet. The asset and liability accounts are ongoing and will be kept open for as long as the asset is owned by the firm or for as long as the liability remains unsettled.

3.3 Presentation of final accounts

3.3.1 Vertical format: Profit and Loss account

There are two methods of presenting final accounts: the horizontal format and the vertical format. In this book, the vertical format will be used. A basic vertical format Profit and Loss account is shown in the following example:

Sally Jones: Profit and Loss account for the year ended 30 September 200—

INCOME		
Profit costs	300,000	
ADD rent received	20,000	
TOTAL INCOME		320,000
LESS EXPENDITURE		
Salaries	60,000	
Rates	9,000	
General expenses	14,000	
Bank interest charged	2,000	85,000
NET PROFIT		235,000

This is a very simple example of a profit and loss account. You will see in the next chapter that adjustments will be made to give a more accurate picture of the profit or loss.

3.3.2 Notes on the Profit and Loss account

(a) At the end of the financial year the Income and Expense accounts are closed. The credit balances from the Income accounts are transferred to the Income part of the Profit and Loss account. The debit balances from the Expense accounts are transferred to the Expenses part of the Profit and Loss account.

(b) The balance left after deducting total Expenses from total Income is net profit (or loss). If a profit is made this is credited to the Capital account in the case of a sole owner. If a loss is made this is debited to the Capital account. For the position in the case of a partnership see **Chapter 6**.

(c) Note that Drawings made by the owner are appropriations of profit, NOT business expenses. Thus the balance on the Drawings account is NOT transferred to the Profit and Loss account, but will be shown on the Balance Sheet.

3.4 The Balance Sheet

3.4.1 Definitions

3.4.1.1 Assets

A business may own all kinds of assets, for example:

    Premises—freehold or leasehold

    Office furniture

Office equipment

Machinery

Stocks of goods

Cars

Work in Progress (the value of work done but not yet billed)

Debtors (they will pay and convert the debts into cash)

Cash at the Bank

Cash in hand (petty cash)

Note that assets are split into two groups:

FIXED ASSETS

CURRENT ASSETS

Fixed Assets

These are assets which are held long term, they are not part of the day to day working cycle. Examples would be:

Premises

Factory Machinery

Office equipment

Office furniture

Library

Cars

Current assets

Also known as circulating assets. These arise from the day-to-day trading or working cycle of the business, they represent cash, or are intended for conversion into cash, or they have a short life, e.g., stationery. They include: cash at the bank, petty cash, debtors, work in progress and payments in advance (see later). If the firm is a trading one, then goods (stock) intended for resale will be a current asset.

Those assets which are cash, or assets which can be easily converted into cash, e.g. debtors, are known as liquid assets.

3.4.1.2 Liabilities

Money owed by the business in respect of loans to the business, e.g. capital, bank loans, mortgages, or money owed for goods or services supplied to the firm, i.e. creditors.

Like assets liabilities can be broken down into groups:

(a) Capital;

(b) Long-term liabilities;

(c) Current liabilities.

3.4.1.3 Capital

This is the amount due to the owner of the business. It will include the value of any assets the owner introduced to the business. Any profit made will also belong to the owner, less any drawings that the owner has taken out over the year.

This will be shown as follows:
For a sole owner

> CAPITAL
>
> PLUS PROFIT
>
> LESS DRAWINGS
>
> equals AMOUNT DUE TO OWNER

Note that the Drawings account is a personal account, showing that the proprietor is a debtor of the business. It is not an expense account and should never be shown on the Profit and Loss account. Think of it as a personal account which will reduce the amount due to the owner.

Long-term liabilities

Usually some formal loan from an individual, bank or other financial institution, repayable over, or after, a stated number of years. These would include long-term bank loans (not usually overdrafts), private loans, mortgages.

Current liabilities

If a liability has to be settled in the short term, then it is a current liability. Current liabilities include: creditors, bank overdrafts, outstanding expenses.

3.4.2   The form of the Balance Sheet

The form more commonly used now is the vertical form. The Balance Sheet is in two halves.

The first half will show   NET ASSETS
The second half will show THE AMOUNT DUE TO THE OWNER
The two totals should be equal.

3.4.3   Listing assets and liabilities on the Balance Sheet

There is a common set order in listing the assets and liabilities on the balance sheet.

Assets

Fixed assets are shown first and then Current assets. The general rule is that you start at the top with the most permanent asset and work down to the least permanent. The top asset on the list will be the most difficult to turn into cash, the bottom will be the most liquid asset, e.g. cash itself. (The order of liquidity is reversed.)

For example, fixed assets may start with premises, which are usually the most permanent fixed asset belonging to the firm, and end with motor cars which are usually the least permanent fixed asset. Current assets start with work in progress which is the least liquid current asset, as it needs two stages to be converted into cash; first it would have to be billed, then the debtors will have to pay.

Current liabilities are deducted from the Current Assets, to give a figure known as Net Current Assets, or Working Capital, being that part of the capital invested in the business which is left to run the business after providing the Fixed Assets. This important figure is then added to the Fixed Assets.

Long-term liabilities will then be deducted from this total, which gives the total Net Assets.

The total achieved should equal the Capital due to the owner of the business.

The vertical form Balance Sheet will look as follows:

NAME OF BUSINESS

BALANCE SHEET as at 31 December 200—

FIXED ASSETS	
ADD	
NET CURRENT ASSETS	
(BEING CURRENT ASSETS	
LESS CURRENT LIABILITIES)	
	TOTAL
LESS LONG-TERM LIABILITIES	
	FINAL TOTAL, i.e., NET ASSETS
CAPITAL EMPLOYED	
CAPITAL	
PLUS PROFIT	
SUB TOTAL	
LESS DRAWINGS	
	FINAL TOTAL—AMOUNT DUE TO OWNER(S)

3.4.4 The solicitor and client money

When a solicitor handles money on behalf of his/her clients, it is the client's money and not the solicitor's. The Solicitors' Accounts Rules 1998 say that a solicitor must keep the records showing dealings with this money totally separate from the solicitor's own money. To do this the solicitor must have a separate bank account (or accounts) for clients' money called the Client Account. The money held in the client bank account(s) must always equal the amount that is shown due to clients.

This can be shown at the end of the balance sheet.

3.4.5 Example vertical format: Balance Sheet

Sally Jones: Balance Sheet as at 30 September 200—

FIXED ASSETS			
Freehold property	235,000		
Office equipment	15,000		
			250,000
CURRENT ASSETS			
Debtors	20,000		
Cash (office bank account)	10,000		
		30,000	
LESS CURRENT LIABILITIES			
Creditors		15,000	

NET CURRENT ASSETS			15,000
			265,000
LESS LONG TERM LIABILITIES			
Midshire Bank loan			40,000
TOTAL NET ASSETS			225,000
CAPITAL EMPLOYED			
Capital at start of year	200,000		
Add net profit	64,000		
		264,000	
Less drawings		39,000	
TOTAL DUE TO OWNER			225,000
CLIENT ACCOUNT			
Cash at bank client current account	300,000		
deposit account	200,000	500,000	
Due to clients		500,000	

3.5 Check list

By the end of this chapter you should be able to:

1. understand the functions of a Profit and Loss account and a Balance Sheet;

2. identify which accounts on a Trial Balance will go to Profit and Loss account and which accounts will be shown on the Balance Sheet;

3. appreciate the Profit and Loss account shows the total income for the period less the total expenses;

4. understand the vertical form Balance sheet shows the total net assets of a business which should equal the amount due to the owner or owners of the business;

5. draw up a simple Profit and Loss account showing the total income and total expenditure and the resulting net profit;

6. draw up a Balance sheet in vertical form;

7. complete all the self test exercises at the end of the chapter.

3.6 Exercises on basic final accounts

1 From the following Trial Balance dated 31 December 200— draw up a Profit and Loss account and Balance Sheet for the owner, Smith.

	DR	CR
Profit costs		82,500
General expenses	24,000	
Wages	22,000	
Drawings	34,000	
Cash at Bank	5,250	

Freehold premises	150,000	
Capital		154,000
Creditors		2,950
Debtors	4,130	
Petty cash	70	
	239,450	239,450

2 From the Trial Balance of North drawn up on 31 December 200— and set out below, draw up a Profit and Loss account and a Balance Sheet.

	DR	CR
Freehold premises	140,000	
Profit costs		62,920
Office furniture	5,000	
Car	15,000	
Interest received		1,450
Creditors		1,200
Cash at bank	2,500	
Petty Cash	150	
Salaries	20,000	
Drawings	25,000	
Capital		110,000
General expenses	10,578	
Administrative expenses	4,642	
Debtors	1,700	
Long-term loan		49,000
	224,570	224,570

3 From the following balances extracted from the accounts of Alexandra on 30 September 200— prepare:

(a) a Trial Balance;

(b) a Profit and Loss account;

(c) a Balance Sheet.

Profit costs	130,000
Light and heat	3,600
Drawings	55,000
Creditors	4,969
Cash at bank (office)	19,230 DR
Cash at bank (client)	750,000 DR
Premises	220,000
Insurance commission received	3,000
Council tax	1,700
Salaries	48,000
Stationery	2,000
Capital	100,400
Bank loan	120,000
Debtors	7,960
Petty cash	879
Due to clients	750,000

3.7 Suggested answers to exercises on basic final accounts

1 Smith Profit and Loss account for the year ending 31 December 200—

Income		
Profit costs		82,500
Less expenses		
General expenses	24,000	
Wages	22,000	
Total expenses		46,000
Net profit		36,500

Smith Balance Sheet as at 31 December 200—

FIXED ASSETS			
Freehold premises			150,000
CURRENT ASSETS			
Debtors	4,130		
Cash at bank	5,250		
Petty cash	70		
		9,450	
LESS			
CURRENT LIABILITIES			
Creditors		2,950	
NET CURRENT ASSETS			6,500
TOTAL			156,500
less long term liabilities			—
TOTAL			156,500
CAPITAL EMPLOYED			
CAPITAL	154,000		
ADD NET PROFIT	36,500		
	190,500		
LESS DRAWINGS	34,000		
TOTAL DUE TO OWNER			156,500

2 North Profit and Loss account for the year ending 31 December 200—

Income		
Profit costs		62,920
Add		
Interest received		1,450
		64,370
less expenses		
General expenses	10,578	
Administrative expenses	4,642	
Salaries	20,000	
		35,220
Net profit		29,150

North Balance Sheet as at 31 December 200—

FIXED ASSETS
Freehold premises	140,000	
Office furniture	5,000	
Car	15,000	
		160,000

CURRENT ASSETS
Debtors	1,700	
Cash at bank	2,500	
Petty cash	150	
	4,350	

LESS CURRENT LIABILITIES
Creditors	1,200	
NET CURRENT ASSETS		3,150
TOTAL		163,150

LESS LONG TERM LIABILITIES
Long-term loan		49,000
TOTAL		114,150

CAPITAL EMPLOYED
Capital	110,000	
plus net profit	29,150	
	139,150	
less drawings	25,000	
TOTAL		114,150

3 **Alexandra: trial balance as at 30 September 200—**

Name of account	DR	CR
Profit costs		130,000
Light and heat	3,600	
Drawings	55,000	
Creditors		4,969
Cash at bank (office)	19,230	
Cash at bank (client)	750,000	
Premises	220,000	
Insurance commission received		3,000
Council tax	1,700	
Salaries	48,000	
Stationery	2,000	
Capital		100,400
Bank loan		120,000
Debtors	7,960	
Petty cash	879	
Due to clients		750,000
Totals	1,108,369	1,108,369

Profit and Loss account for the year ended 30 September 200—

INCOME		
Profit costs	130,000	
Add		
ADDITIONAL INCOME insurance commission received	3,000	133,000
LESS EXPENDITURE		
Light and heat	3,600	
Council tax	1,700	
Salaries	48,000	
Stationery	2,000	55,300
NET PROFIT		77,700

Alexandra: Balance Sheet as at 30 September 200—

FIXED ASSETS			
Premises			220,000
CURRENT ASSETS			
Debtors	7,960		
Cash (office bank account)	19,230		
Petty cash	879		
		28,069	
LESS CURRENT LIABILITIES			
Creditors		4,969	
NET CURRENT ASSETS			23,100
TOTAL ASSETS LESS CURRENT LIABILITIES			243,100
LESS LONG TERM LIABILITIES			
Bank loan			120,000
TOTAL NET ASSETS			123,100
CAPITAL EMPLOYED			
Capital at start of year	100,400		
Add Net Profit	77,700		
		178,100	
Less drawings		55,000	
TOTAL DUE TO OWNER			123,100
CLIENT ACCOUNT			
Client bank balance	750,000		
Less: due to clients	750,000		

Adjustments to final accounts

4.1 The need for adjustments

The balances on the income and expenses accounts do not show all the income earned, or all the expenses actually incurred during the year. Adjustments are made to make sure:

1. that income includes the value of work done during the current year, even though it has not yet been billed;
2. that expenses include those which have been incurred in the current year, even though they have not yet been billed or paid;
3. that expenses do not include those which have been paid in the current year but which relate to the next year.

In this chapter we will look at the following adjustments:

(a) Outstanding expenses;

(b) Payment in advance;

(c) Closing stock;

(c) Work in progress.

4.2 Outstanding expenses adjustment

There are expenses incurred during the current financial year but payment will not be made until the next financial year, for example, gas, electricity and telephone charges.

At the end of the financial year, a provision is made for this. If a bill has not already been received the provision will be an estimate. The relevant expense will be INCREASED by the provision to give the true expense for the year.

Thus the adjustment is made on the relevant expense account by:

1. DEBITING the expense for the current year
2. CREDITING the expense for the next year.

These entries will shift the expense from one year to the next, increasing this year's expense and reducing next year's expense.

The effect on the Profit and Loss Account and the Balance Sheet for the current year will be:

1. Profit and Loss account—INCREASE expenses
2. Balance Sheet—show as a CURRENT LIABILITY.

EXAMPLE

A solicitor prepares final accounts on 31 October. At that date the telephone account has a debit balance of £600. This represents cash paid for telephone charges over the year. It is decided to make provision of £200 for telephone charges due but unpaid. The telephone account will appear as follows:

Telephone account

Date	Details	DR	CR	Balance
31 Oct	Balance Provision carried down (c/d)	200		600 DR 800 DR

The balance on the expense account, including the provision made at the end of the financial year, is transferred to the Profit and Loss account and the nominal expense account is closed. Continuing the example:

Telephone account

Date	Details	DR	CR	Balance
31 Oct	Balance Provision c/d Profit and loss account: transfer	200	800	600 DR 800 DR —

The provision is carried down as a credit entry in the expense account at the start of the next financial year. The provision will be set off against payment of the bill in the next financial year. Continuing the example, on 10 November the bill of £200 is paid.

Telephone account

Date	Details	DR	CR	Balance
31 Oct	Balance Provision c/d Profit and loss account: transfer	200	800	600 DR 800 DR —.
1 Nov 10 Nov	Provision brought down (b/d) Cash	200	200	200 CR —

Profit and Loss account for the year ended 31 October

EXPENSES

Telephones	600
Add outstanding expenses	200
	800

The provision brought down for outstanding expenses is shown on the Balance Sheet as a current liability because on the date on which the Balance Sheet is prepared, it is expenditure incurred but not yet paid. Continuing the example:

Balance Sheet as at 31 October

FIXED ASSETS		XX
CURRENT ASSETS	XX	
LESS CURRENT LIABILITIES		
Outstanding expenses—telephone	200	
		XX
		XX
CAPITAL EMPLOYED		
		XX

4.3 Payment in advance

If a payment is made in the current financial year for a service which will not be used until the next financial year, for example, council tax, then, at the end of the financial year, the appropriate expense account is credited with the amount paid in advance. This has the effect of REDUCING the expenses and increasing the profit. The corresponding debit entry is made in the same account at the start of the next financial year. This time the double entry shifts the expense out of the current year into the next year.

The adjustment is made on the relevant expense account by:

1. CREDITING the expense for the current year (reducing expenses);

2. DEBITING the expense for the next year (increasing next year's expenses).

The effect on the Profit and Loss account and the Balance Sheet for the current year will be:

The Profit and Loss account

REDUCE expenses

The Balance Sheet

Show as a CURRENT ASSET.

EXAMPLE

A solicitor pays council tax of £4,000 per annum by two equal instalments, in advance, on 31 March and 30 September each year. Final accounts are prepared on 31 December each year. Thus a payment in advance of £1,000 for council tax is being made because the £2,000 paid on 30 September is for council tax from 1 October to 31 March.

Council tax account

Date	Details	DR	CR	Balance
31 Mar	Cash	2,000		2,000 DR
30 Sept	Cash	2,000		4,000 DR
31 Dec	Payment in advance c/d		1,000	3,000 DR

The balance on the expense account is transferred to the Profit and Loss account at the end of the year. Continuing the example:

Council tax account

Date	Details	DR	CR	Balance
31 Mar	Cash	2,000		2,000 DR
30 Sept	Cash	2,000		4,000 DR
31 Dec	Payment in advance c/d		1,000	3,000 DR
	Profit and loss account: transfer		3,000	—

Note that the firm is charging to the Profit and Loss account as a business expense only the amount spent on council tax from 1 January to 31 December, i.e. in the current financial year.

The payment in advance is brought down as a debit entry on the expense account at the start of the next financial year, which is when the service that has been paid for in the current financial year will be used. Continuing the example:

Council tax account

Date	Details	DR	CR	Balance
31 Mar	Cash	2,000		2,000 DR
30 Sept	Cash	2,000		4,000 DR
31 Dec	Payment in advance c/d		1,000	3,000 DR
	Profit and loss account: transfer		3,000	—
1 Jan	Payment in advance b/d	1,000		1,000 DR

Profit and Loss account for the year ending 31 December

EXPENSES
Council tax   4,000
Less payment in advance   1,000
                                               ─────
                                                            3,000

The payment in advance is shown on the Balance Sheet as a current asset. In theory the person to whom the payment has been made is a debtor of the firm for the service which is to be supplied. Continuing the example:

Balance Sheet as at 31 December

FIXED ASSETS   XX
CURRENT ASSETS
Payments in advance
Council tax   1,000
                                               ─────
                                                            XX
LESS CURRENT LIABILITIES
                                                            XX
                                                            ──
                                                            XX
CAPITAL EMPLOYED
                                                            XX

4.4 Closing stocks

Where a business has paid for items used over the year, for example stationery or pens, then only the cost of the items actually used during the year should be shown as an expense. Thus the value of any items left will be DEDUCTED from the relevant expense account, to give the true expense.

The adjustment is made on the relevant expense account by:

CREDITING expense for the current year (thus reducing expenses).

DEBITING the expense for the next year (increasing next year's expenses).

Again this shifts the expense from the current year to the next year.
The effect on the Profit and Loss account and the Balance Sheet will be:

The Profit and Loss account;

REDUCE expenses;

The Balance Sheet;

show as a CURRENT ASSET.

EXAMPLE

During the year the firm pays the following amounts for stationery:

31 March	£40
16 October	£25
8 December	£35

Final accounts are prepared on 31 December. On 31 December the firm has a stock of stationery paid for but unused, valued at £30.

Stationery account

Date	Details	DR	CR	Balance
31 Mar	Cash	40		40 DR
16 Oct	Cash	25		65 DR
8 Dec	Cash	35		100 DR
31 Dec	Closing stock c/d		30	70 DR

At the end of the year the nominal expense account is closed and the balance on it is transferred to the Profit and Loss account. Continuing the example:

Stationery account

Date	Details	DR	CR	Balance
31 Mar	Cash	40		40 DR
16 Oct	Cash	25		65 DR
8 Dec	Cash	35		100 DR
31 Dec	Closing stock c/d		30	70 DR
	Profit and loss account: transfer balance		70	—

Note that only the cost of stationery used during the current financial year is transferred to the Profit and Loss account as a business expense.

The value of the closing stock is brought down as a debit entry in the expense account at the start of the next financial year. Continuing the example:

Stationery account

Date	Details	DR	CR	Balance
31 Mar	Cash	40		40 DR
16 Oct	Cash	25		65 DR
8 Dec	Cash	35		100 DR
31 Dec	Closing stock c/d		30	70 DR
	Profit and loss account: transfer		70	—
1 Jan	Opening stock b/d	30		30 DR

Note that at the start of the next financial year the closing stock from the previous year becomes opening stock.

Profit and Loss account for the year ending 31 December

EXPENSES
Stationery   100
Less closing stock   30

                                                              70

On the Balance Sheet the value of the closing stock is shown as a current asset. Continuing the example:

Balance Sheet as at 31 December

FIXED ASSETS   XX
CURRENT ASSETS
Closing stock of stationery   30

                                                  XX
LESS CURRENT LIABILITIES
                                                  XX

                                                  XX
CAPITAL EMPLOYED
                                                  XX

4.5   Work in progress

For solicitors, the main source of income is from bills delivered in respect of work done for clients. However at the end of the year the firm will have done work for clients, which has not yet been billed. As this work has been carried out in the current year it can be valued and shown as income earned during the year. This will be added to the current year's income and deducted from the next year's income.

The adjustment will be made to Profit Costs by:

CREDITING the account for the current year (increasing income);

DEBITING the account for the next year (reducing next year's income).

The effect on the Profit and Loss account and the Balance sheet will be as follows:

The Profit and Loss account;

INCREASE the Profit Costs by the Work in Progress for the end of the year;

On the Balance Sheet;

Show the Work in Progress at the end of the year as a CURRENT ASSET.

The next year

As shown above the Work in Progress brought forward reduces the Profit Costs income. Thus the Profit and Loss account would show:

Profit Costs

LESS Work in Progress at the START of the year

PLUS Work in Progress at the END of the year.

This gives the VALUE OF WORK DONE during the year.

The Balance Sheet would show:

the Work in Progress at the END of the year as a CURRENT ASSET.

EXAMPLE

The firm prepares its final accounts on 31 December each year. On 31 December the Profit Costs account has a credit balance of £30,000. Work in progress is valued at £5,000.

Profit costs account

Date	Details	DR	CR	Balance
31 Dec	Balance			30,000 CR
	Closing work in progress c/d		5,000	35,000 CR

At the end of the financial year the Profit Costs account is closed and the balance on the account is transferred to the Profit and Loss account. At the start of the new financial year the closing work in progress is brought down on the DR side as opening work in progress. Continuing the example:

Profit costs account

Date	Details	DR	CR	Balance
31 Dec	Balance			30,000 CR
	Closing work in progress c/d		5,000	35,000 CR
	Profit and loss account: transfer	35,000		—
1 Jan	Opening work in progress b/d	5,000		5,000 DR

The value of the closing work in progress is shown on the balance sheet as a current asset. Continuing the example:

Balance Sheet as at 31 December

FIXED ASSETS		XX
CURRENT ASSETS		
Work in progress at the end of year	5,000	
		XX
LESS CURRENT LIABILITIES		XX
		XX
CAPITAL EMPLOYED		
		XX

In the following year the Profit Costs account begins with the debit entry for opening work in progress. This reduces the income from profit costs in that year (as the profit costs figure includes bills delivered which include costs for work carried out in the previous year). The movement on the Profit Costs account will be shown in the Profit and Loss account, which will give the value of work done during the year.

EXAMPLE

Work in progress at start of year 1 January 200—	£15,000
Profit costs as at 31 December 200—	£125,000
Work in progress at end of year 31 December 200—	£20,000

Profit and loss account for the year ended 31 December 200—

INCOME		
Profit costs (based on bills delivered)	125,000	
Add closing work in progress at 31 Dec	20,000	145,000
Deduct opening work in progress at 1 Jan		15,000
VALUE OF WORK DONE DURING THE YEAR		130,000

Note: only the closing work in progress figure is shown in the Balance Sheet.

Note: you should show each subtotal after adding the closing work in progress and then deducting the opening work in progress. Any additional income, e.g. rent received, interest received, insurance commission received, should be shown after the work in progress adjustments have been made.

4.5.1 Worked example on closing work in progress adjustment

A firm of solicitors prepares its final accounts on 30 June each year. The firm's profit costs account shows an opening debit balance on 1 July 2004 of £35,000. During the year ending 30 June 2005, bills have been delivered to clients totalling £175,000. The firm estimates that the value of work done during the year ending 30 June 2005, in respect of which bills have not yet been delivered, is £45,000. The accounts to record the above will appear as follows:

Profit Costs account

Date	Details	DR	CR	Balance
2004 1 July	Opening work in progress b/d	35,000		35,000 DR
2005 30 June	Sundry profit costs		175,000	140,000 CR
	Closing work in progress c/d		45,000	185,000 CR
	Profit and loss account: transfer	185,000		—
1 July	Opening work in progress b/d	45,000		45,000 DR

Profit and Loss account for the year ended 30 June 2005

INCOME

Profit costs	175,000	
Add: Closing work in progress	45,000	
	220,000	
Less: Opening work in progress	35,000	
Value of work done during the year		185,000

Note: by convention the detailed movement on the profit costs account is shown on the Profit and Loss account.

Balance Sheet as at 30 June 2005

FIXED ASSETS		XX
CURRENT ASSETS		
Closing work in progress	45,000	
		XX

4.6 Summary adjustments

Outstanding expenses:

>   Profit and Loss account;
>
>   INCREASE expenses;
>
>   Balance Sheet;
>
>   CURRENT LIABILITY.

Payments in advance:

>   Profit and Loss account;
>
>   REDUCE expenses;
>
>   Balance Sheet;
>
>   CURRENT ASSET.

Closing stock:

> Profit and Loss account;
>
> REDUCE expenses;
>
> Balance Sheet;
>
> CURRENT ASSET.

Work in progress:

> Profit and Loss account;
>
> DEDUCT Work in Progress at the START of the year from Profit Costs;
>
> ADD Work in Progress at the END of the year to Profit Costs;
>
> The Balance Sheet;
>
> Show Work in Progress at the END of the year as a CURRENT ASSET.

4.7 Check list

By the end of this chapter you should be able to:

1. understand the reasons for adjustments;
2. appreciate that adjustments made will affect both the Profit and Loss account and the Balance Sheet and that they will also be carried forward to the next accounting period;
3. know the effect of each adjustment in this chapter on the Profit and Loss account and the Balance sheet;
4. use entries on a Trial Balance together with information supplied in respect of adjustments to draw up a Profit and Loss account and a Balance sheet;
5. complete all the self test exercise at the end of the chapter.

4.8 Exercises on adjustments and final accounts

1 On 31 October 200— the firm's light and heat account has a debit balance of £5,000. The firm estimates that a further £250 worth of gas has been used.

Show the state of the light and heat account on 1 November 200— and the entries which you would make in the final accounts which are prepared on 31 October 200—.

2 The firm pays council tax of £1,000 on 1 April and 1 October 2004 for the following six months. The firm's final accounts are prepared on 31 December each year.

Show the rates account at 1 January 2005 and the entries you would make in the final accounts for the year ended 31 December 2004.

3 Final accounts are prepared on 30 June each year. On 30 June 2005 the stationery account shows a debit balance of £800. On checking the stationery it is discovered that there is £200 worth left.

Show the stationery account at 1 July 2005 and the entries in the final accounts for the year ended 30 June 2005.

4 At the end of its financial year, 31 December 2003, Grace & Co. had profit costs of £180,000 and its work in progress was valued at £18,000. At the end of its second year, 31 December 2004, the firm had delivered bills totalling £220,000 and its work in progress was valued at £25,000.

Show the profit costs account and also the final accounts for the year ended 31 December 2004.

5   The Trial Balance of Torr, a solicitor, is set out below.

	31 December 200—	
	DR	CR
Capital		65,000
Office equipment	6,330	
Car	14,900	
Leasehold property	95,000	
General expenses	38,290	
Rent paid	4,800	
Salaries	27,000	
Mortgage		45,000
Drawings	30,570	
Cash at bank office account	2,210	
Cash at bank client account	67,900	
Amount due to clients		67,900
Creditors		3,650
Amount due from clients (debtors)	2,000	
Profit costs		110,000
Work in progress at 1 Jan 200—	5,000	
Commission received		2,450
	294,000	294,000

Work in Progress as at 31 December 200— is £6,000. Payments in advance are £1,200, and outstanding expenses are £540. Draw up the Profit and Loss Account for the year ending 31 December 200— and the Balance Sheet as at that date.

4.9   Suggested answers to exercises on adjustments and final accounts

1   Light and heat account

Date	Details	DR	CR	Balance
200— 31 Oct	Balance Provision: Gas c/d Profit and loss: transfer	250	5,250	5,000 DR 5,250 DR —
1 Nov	Provision: Gas b/d		250	250 CR

Profit and Loss account for the year ended 31 October 200—

INCOME			XX
LESS EXPENDITURE			
Light and heat	5,000		
Add provision	250	5,250	

Balance Sheet as at 31 October 200—

FIXED ASSETS		XX
CURRENT ASSETS	XX	

LESS CURRENT LIABILITIES
Provision for light and heat   250
                                                                                    XX
                                                                                                          XX

CAPITAL EMPLOYED
                                                                                    XX

2 Council tax account

Date	Details	DR	CR	Balance
2004				
1 Apr	Cash	1,000		1,000 DR
1 Oct	Cash	1,000		2,000 DR
31 Dec	Payment in advance c/d		500	1,500 DR
	Profit and loss: transfer		1,500	—
2005				
1 Jan	Payment in advance b/d	500		500 DR

Profit and Loss account for the year ended 31 December 2004

INCOME   XX
LESS EXPENDITURE
Council tax   2,000
Less paid in advance   500   1,500

Balance Sheet as at 31 December 2004

FIXED ASSETS   XX
CURRENT ASSETS
Council tax paid in advance   500
                                                                                    XX
LESS CURRENT LIABILITIES
                                                                                    XX
                                                                                    XX
CAPITAL EMPLOYED
                                                                                    XX

3 Stationery account

Date	Details	DR	CR	Balance
2005				
30 June	Balance			800 DR
	Closing stock c/d		200	600 DR
	Profit and loss: transfer		600	—
1 July	Opening stock b/d	200		200 DR

Profit and Loss account for the year ended 30 June 2005

INCOME   XX
LESS EXPENDITURE

| Stationery | 800 | |
| Less closing stock | 200 | 600 |

Balance Sheet as at 30 June 2005

FIXED ASSETS		XX
CURRENT ASSETS		
Closing stock of stationery	200	
		XX

4 **Profit costs account**

Date	Details	DR	CR	Balance
2003				
31 Dec	Balance (bills delivered)			180,000 CR
	Closing work in progress c/d		18,000	198,000 CR
	Profit and loss: transfer	198,000		—
2004				
1 Jan	Opening work in progress b/d	18,000		18,000 DR
31 Dec	Profit costs		220,000	202,000 CR
	Closing work in progress c/d		25,000	227,000 CR
	Profit and loss: transfer	227,000		—
2005				
1 Jan	Opening work in progress b/d	25,000		25,000 DR

Grace & Co: Profit and Loss account for the year ended 31 December 2004

INCOME		
Profit Costs	220,000	
Add closing work in progress	25,000	
	245,000	
Less opening work in progress	18,000	227,000
LESS EXPENDITURE		XX

Grace & Co: Balance Sheet as at 31 December 2004

FIXED ASSETS		XX
CURRENT ASSETS		
Closing work in progress	25,000	
		XX

5 **Torr Profit and Loss account for the year ending 31 December 200—**

INCOME	
Profit costs	110,000
Less work in progress at start of year	5,000
	105,000
ADD	
Work in progress at end of year	6,000
Value of work done	111,000

ADDITIONAL INCOME

Commission received		2,450
TOTAL INCOME		113,450

LESS EXPENSES

General expenses	38,290	
Salaries	27,000	
Rent paid	4,800	
Outstanding expenses	540	
	70,630	
Less payments in advance	1,200	
Total expenses		69,430
Net profit		44,020

Torr Balance Sheet as at 31 December 200—

FIXED ASSETS

Leasehold premises	95,000		
Office equipment	6,330		
Car	14,900		
			116,230

CURRENT ASSETS

Work in progress	6,000		
Debtors (due from clients)	2,000		
Cash at bank	2,210		
Payment in advance	1,200		
		11,410	

LESS CURRENT LIABILITIES

Creditors	3,650		
Outstanding expenses	540		
		4,190	
NET CURRENT ASSETS			7,220
TOTAL			123,450

LESS LONG TERM LIABILITIES

Mortgage			45,000
TOTAL NET ASSETS			78,450

CAPITAL EMPLOYED

Capital	65,000		
plus net profit	44,020		
		109,020	
less drawings		30,570	
TOTAL			78,450

CLIENT ACCOUNT

Cash at bank client account		67,900
Amount due to clients		67,900

Further adjustments to final accounts

5.1 Introduction

In this chapter we will look at:

(a) Bad and doubtful debts;

(b) Depreciation and sale of assets.

5.2 Bad debts and doubtful debts adjustments

5.2.1 Writing off bad debts

Debts owed to a business are assets. When the debtors pay the debts are converted into cash. However, some debtors will never pay and so the debts will be worthless. If a business knows that a particular debtor is never going to pay, e.g. the debtor has disappeared or is bankrupt, then the business will write off the bad debt, showing that it is worthless. The firm has lost that debt and it will be recorded as an expense.

To write off a bad debt:

CREDIT the debtor's account (this wipes out the debt).

DEBIT the Bad Debts account (this shows the expense).

The effect on the Profit and Loss account and the Balance sheet will be as follows:

On the Profit and Loss account

Show the Bad Debts as an EXPENSE.

On The Balance Sheet

If the Trial Balance shows a figure for Bad debts then the Debtors figure will already have been reduced by the bad debts written off.

Note

If, however, you are asked to write off a bad debt—AFTER the Trial Balance has been drawn up, then you would have to reduce the Debtors figure, as well as showing the Bad Debt as an expense on the Profit and Loss account above.

EXAMPLE

A bill delivered to Jack for £235 (including £35 VAT) has not been paid. At the end of the financial year 31 October the debt was written off.

Jack's account

Date	Details	DR	CR	Balance
31 Oct	Balance: amount due Bad debt: written off		235	235 DR —

Bad debts account

Date	Details	DR	CR	Balance
31 Oct	Jack: debt written off	235		235 DR

5.2.2 Recovery of a debt that has been written off

When a debt that has previously been written off as a bad debt is recovered, the following entries will be made in the account:

(a) DEBIT cash account.

(b) CREDIT Bad Debts account.

Continuing the example, assume that in the year after the debt has been written off, Jack pays his bill.

Cash account

Date	Details	DR	CR	Balance
15 Jan	Bad debts (recovered from Jack)	235		235 DR

Bad Debts account

Date	Details	DR	CR	Balance
15 Jan	Cash (debt recovered from Jack)		235	235 CR

No entry is made in Jack's account, although a note that he has paid could be made.

5.2.3 Making a provision for doubtful debts

As well as writing off bad debts a business will also make provision for the debts that are unlikely to be paid. This provision is an estimated loss.

The provision is usually calculated as a percentage of the debtors figure, after bad debts have been written off.

Effect on Profit and Loss account:

INCREASE expenses by this year's provision for doubtful debts

Effect on Balance Sheet.

REDUCE the Debtors figure by this year's provision for doubtful debts.

(1) DEBIT the Bad Debts account with the provision at the end of the current financial year.

(2) CREDIT the Bad Debts account with the provision at the start of the next financial year.

Note that the provision brought forward to the next year will reduce the expense of bad debts.

EXAMPLE

A. Solicitor prepares final accounts on 31 October. On that date the bad debts account has a debit balance of £1,500 in respect of bad debts written off during the year. Total debts owed to the practice amount to £20,000 and A. Solicitor decides to make a provision for doubtful debts of 5% of the total.

Bad Debts account

Date	Details	DR	CR	Balance
31 Oct	Balance—bad debts previously written off			1,500 DR
	Provision: doubtful debt c/d	1,000		2,500 DR

5.2.4 Effect of bad debts on final accounts

At the end of the financial year the Bad Debts account will be closed and the balance will be transferred to the Profit and Loss account. If, at the end of the financial year, the Bad Debts account has a debit balance this will be transferred to the Profit and Loss account as an expense by making the following entries in the accounts:

(a) CREDIT the Bad Debts account.

(b) DEBIT the Profit and Loss account.

Continuing the example of A. Solicitor:

Bad Debts account

Date	Details	DR	CR	Balance
31 Oct	Balance			1,500 DR
	Provision: doubtful debts c/d	1,000		2,500 DR
	Profit and Loss account: transfer		2,500	—

Profit and Loss account for the year ended 31 October 200—

INCOME   ___

Less EXPENSES
Bad debts   1,500
Provision for doubtful debts   1,000
                                 _____

                                                         2,500

At the start of the next financial year the provision will be carried down as a credit entry on the Bad Debts account. Continuing the example of A. Solicitor:

Bad Debts account

Date	Details	DR	CR	Balance
200—	Balance			1,500 DR
31 Oct	Provision: doubtful debts c/d	1,000		2,500 DR
	Profit and loss account: transfer		2,500	—
1 Nov	Provision for doubtful debts b/d		1,000	1,000 CR

The provision for doubtful debts made at the end of the financial year is shown as a deduction from the debtors figure on the current assets part of the Balance Sheet. Continuing the example of A. Solicitor:

Balance Sheet as at 31 October 200—

FIXED ASSETS   XX
CURRENT ASSETS
Debtors   20,000
Less: Provision for doubtful debts   1,000
                                               _____
                                                         19,000
                                                         XX

Note: If the Bad Debts account has a credit balance at the end of the year because the firm has overestimated its provision for doubtful debts in previous years, the credit balance is transferred to the profit and loss account as income by making the following entries:

(a) DEBIT Bad Debts account.

(b) CREDIT Profit and Loss account.

EXAMPLE

At the start of the financial year, 1 January 200—, a provision of £3,000 is brought down from the previous year. During the year bad debts of £5,000 are written off. At the end of the financial year, 31 December 200—, total debtors amount to £40,000. It is decided to make a provision for doubtful debts of 10%.

Bad Debts account

Date	Details	DR	CR	Balance
200—				
1 Jan	Last year's Provision		3,000	3,000 CR
	Bad debts written off	5,000		2,000 DR
31 Dec	This year's Provision c/d	4,000		6,000 DR
	Profit and loss account:			
	transfer		6,000	—

Profit and Loss account for the year ended 31 December 200—

EXPENSES		
Bad debts	5,000	
Add: this year's provision	4,000	
	9,000	
Less: last year's provision	3,000	6,000

Balance sheet as at 31 December 200—

FIXED ASSETS			XX
CURRENT ASSETS			
Debtors	40,000		
Less this year's provision	4,000	36,000	

Only one method of providing for bad debts and doubtful debts has been shown in this book. There are other, equally acceptable methods in use.

5.3 Depreciation

5.3.1 Introduction

The asset accounts show the cost price of the assets. Over time the cost price of an asset is unlikely to be its true value, as most assets go down in value, through wear and tear or obsolescence. Instead of waiting until the asset is sold to find out the loss, the business will spread the fall in value over time, showing an expense of depreciation each year.

Calculating depreciation

There are different ways of doing this, the simplest is known as the straight-line method. Depreciation can be calculated as a percentage of the cost price each year, for example if a car cost £20,000, the business could calculate depreciation at 20% each year, being £4,000 a year.

Alternatively the formula for calculating depreciation by the straight line method is:

$$\frac{\text{Cost of asset} - \text{value of asset at end of its life}}{\text{life expectancy of asset}}$$

EXAMPLE

A firm buys a car for £5,500. The car has an estimated life of five years, at the end of which its sale value will be £500. The annual provision for depreciation using the straight-line method of calculating depreciation will be:

$$\frac{£5,500 - £500}{5} = £1,000 \text{ p.a.}$$

A separate depreciation account is opened for each class of fixed assets to be depreciated.

Using the straight-line method, depreciation may be calculated as a percentage of the cost price of the asset.

EXAMPLE

A firm buys a car for £16,000. Depreciation is calculated at 15% per annum on the cost price. Thus each year the depreciation will be £2,400.

A further alternative is to depreciate on the reducing balance of the asset rather than the cost price.

EXAMPLE

A firm buys a car for £16,000. Depreciation is calculated at 15% per annum on the reducing balance of the car. Thus in year 1 depreciation will be £2,400. In year 2 the reduced balance of the car will be:

Cost price	£16,000
Less depreciation	£2,400
	£13,600

Thus depreciation in year 2 will be £2,040.

In year 3 the reduced balance of the car will be £11,560. Depreciation in year 3 will be £1,734.

5.3.2 Recording depreciation in the accounts

To record depreciation in the accounts at the end of the financial year, the following entries are made:

(a) CREDIT the appropriate accumulated depreciation account with depreciation charged on the fixed asset.

(b) DEBIT the Profit and Loss account with the current year's depreciation, as an expense.

Note that if an asset is bought during the year it is usual to depreciate it for a full year. Do this unless you are told otherwise.

EXAMPLE

The firm buys a car for £6,000 in March 200—. Depreciation on the car is 20% a year.
The firm's financial year ends on 31 December 200—.

Accumulated depreciation (Cars) account

Date	Details	DR	CR	Balance
200— 31 Dec	Profit and Loss		1,200	1,200 CR

Accumulated depreciation is shown on the Balance Sheet as a deduction from the cost price of the asset. Continuing the example:

Profit and Loss account for year ended 31 December 200—

INCOME   —

LESS EXPENDITURE
Depreciation: motor cars

        1,200

Balance Sheet as at 31 December 200—

FIXED ASSETS
Motor cars at cost   6,000
Less: accumulated depreciation   1,200

        4,800

In year 2 the accounts would be shown as follows

Accumulated depreciation (Cars) account

Date	Details	DR	CR	Balance
Year 1 31 Dec	Profit and Loss		1,200	1,200 CR
Year 2 31 Dec	Profit and Loss		1,200	2,400 CR

Profit and loss account for year 2

INCOME   —

LESS EXPENDITURE
Depreciation: motor cars

        1,200

Balance Sheet as at end year 2

FIXED ASSETS   XX
Motor cars at cost   6,000
Less: accumulated depreciation   2,400

        3,600

5.4   Sale of assets

When an asset is sold an asset disposal account will be opened. The cost price of the asset and its accumulated depreciation to date will be transferred to this account, and the sale price will be recorded. From this account you will be able to see whether the business has made a 'profit' or a 'loss' on the sale.

For example if a car had been purchased for £20,000 and the accumulated depreciation to date was £8,000, then the estimated current value of the car would be £12,000. If the car was sold for £13,000 a 'profit' of £1,000 has been made. This would be shown on the accounts as follows:

Car Asset disposal account

Date	Details	DR	CR	Balance
200—	Cost price of car	20,000		20,000 DR
	Accumulated depreciation on car		8,000	12,000 DR
	Cash on sale		13,000	1,000 CR

The credit balance is a 'profit', which will be shown as INCOME on the Profit and Loss Account.

If the account came out with a debit balance this would be a loss/EXPENSE for the Profit and Loss account.

5.4.1   Disposing of part of a group of assets

The same principle as above will apply. As before the cost price of the asset being sold and the accumulated depreciation on the asset being sold will be transferred to the asset disposal account, leaving the cost price of the remaining assets, and the accumulated depreciation of the remaining assets behind.

EXAMPLE

Chandra, a solicitor, prepared final accounts on 31 December. The cost price of cars are shown on the Trial Balance as £80,000. Accumulated depreciation on all the cars is shown as £28,000. Depreciation on cars is calculated at 20% per annum. A car is sold during the current year for £13,000. The car cost £20,000, and accumulated depreciation on the car is £8,000, being two years depreciation at 20%. Chandra's accounts to record the above will be as follows:

Cars account

Date	Details	DR	CR	Balance
31 Dec	Balance			80,000 DR
	Asset disposal		20,000	60,000 DR

Asset disposal account (Car)

Date	Details	DR	CR	Balance
31 Dec	Car	20,000		20,000 DR
	Depreciation		8,000	12,000 DR
	Cash		13,000	1,000 CR
	Profit and loss account:			
	Transfer profit on sale	1,000		—

Accumulated depreciation account (motor cars)

Date	Details	DR	CR	Balance
1 Jan	Balance			28,000 CR
	Asset disposal	8,000		20,000 CR
31 Dec	Depreciation this year		12,000	32,000 CR

Profit and Loss account for the year ended 31 December

INCOME		XX
Profit on sale of car	1000	
LESS EXPENDITURE		
Depreciation: on remaining cars	12,000	

Balance Sheet as at 31 December

FIXED ASSETS		
Cars at cost	60,000	
Less: Accumulated depreciation	32,000	
		28,000
CURRENT ASSETS		XX

Note: the current year's depreciation is calculated by taking the cost price of the car which has been sold (£20,000) from the balance on the motor cars account (£80,000), and finding 20% of the remainder (£60,000) = £12,000.

5.5 Summary

Bad debts

Profit and Loss account:

Show as an EXPENSE.

Balance Sheet:

Only reduce the debtors figure by any bad debts written off after the Trial Balance. If Bad debts are shown on the Trial Balance then the debtors figure has already been reduced, it should not be changed.

Provision for doubtful debts

Current year's provision:

Profit and Loss account:

Show as an EXPENSE.

Balance Sheet

REDUCE debtors figure by the provision.

Last year's provision:

> Profit and Loss account:
>
> > REDUCE expense of Bad debts by last year's provision
>
> Balance Sheet:
>
> > NO effect.

Depreciation

Profit and Loss account:

> Show the depreciation for the current year only as an EXPENSE.

Balance Sheet:

> Show the Cost price of the asset
>
> > LESS any accumulated depreciation from previous years
> >
> > AND less the depreciation for the current year.

5.6 Check list

By the end of this chapter you should be able to:

1. understand that bad debts are an expense;

2. understand that a provision for doubtful debts is an adjustment, its effect on the Profit and Loss account and the Balance sheet, and on the next year's accounts;

3. understand that depreciation records the fall in value of assets as an expense, its effect on the Profit and Loss account and the Balance sheet, and on the next year's accounts;

4. note how a firm would deal with the sale of an asset or assets;

5. use information supplied in respect of bad debts and provision and depreciation in drawing up a Profit and Loss account and Balance Sheet;

6. complete all the self test exercises at the end of the chapter.

5.7 Exercises on adjustments and final accounts

1 An extract from the Trial Balance of Lightfoot drawn up on 31 December 200— shows the following:

Name of account	DR	CR
Debtors	4,340	
Bad debts	625	

It is decided to make a provision for doubtful debts of £450 for the year. Show the figures for expenses on the Profit and Loss account for the year and the figures that would be shown on the Balance sheet as at 31 December 200—.

2 An extract from the Trial Balance of Davis drawn up on 31 March 200— shows the following:

Name of account	DR	CR
Cost price of cars	30,000	
Accumulated depreciation on cars		9,000

Depreciation for the year ending 31 March 200— is to be 15% of the cost price. Show the figure for expenses on Profit and Loss account and the details in respect of cars on the Balance Sheet.

3   The Trial Balance for Karsh on 30 September 200— is set out below:

Name of account	DR	CR
Capital		170,000
Profit costs		90,000
Drawings	32,000	
Office furniture	8,500	
Accumulated depreciation on office furniture		2,550
Premises cost price	160,000	
General and administrative expenses	46,000	
Cash at bank office account	13,915	
Petty cash	165	
Creditors		1,980
Debtors	3,544	
Bad debts	406	
Cash at bank client account	249,000	
Due to clients		249,000
	513,530	513,530

Depreciation for the year on office furniture is 10% of the cost price. The provision for doubtful debts for the year is £360 and work in progress at the end of the year is £6,200. Draw up the Profit and Loss account for the year ending 30 September and Balance Sheet as at that date

4   The trial balance of J. Milton, prepared on 31 December 200—, is as follows:

Trial balance as at 31 December 200—

Name of account	DR	CR
Drawings	19,000	
Fixtures and fittings	5,200	
Cars	20,600	
Accumulated depreciation (cars)		4,120
Accumulated depreciation (fixtures and fittings)		1,300
Premises	132,000	
Capital		140,000
Telephone/postage	1,300	
Council tax	2,950	
Light and heat	1,550	
Salaries	25,270	
Cash at bank:		
Office account	14,190	
Client account	315,000	
Petty cash	123	
Debtors	4,422	
Due to creditors		4,763
Due to clients		315,000
Profit costs		76,422
	541,605	541,605

In addition:

(a) Depreciation at 10% and 5% is to be charged against the cost price of cars and fixtures and fittings, respectively.

(b) At 31 December 200— electricity and telephone bills outstanding amount to £551 and £505 respectively.

(c) Included in the amount for debtors is £122 which is to be written off. A provision for doubtful debts of 5% of remaining debtors is to be made.

(d) Work in progress at 31 December 200— is valued at £8,569.

Prepare final accounts for the year ended 31 December 200—.

5 The following balances were taken from the accounts of C. Arnold, solicitor, on 31 December 200—.

Capital	223,059
Work in progress at 1 January 200—	16,582
Petty cash	55
Bank overdraft on office account	4,552
Bank client account	450,000
Debtors	12,009
Creditors	9,235
Car: cost price	20,000
Accumulated depreciation: car	8,000
Drawings	20,459
Fixtures and fittings at cost	8,000
Accumulated depreciation: fixtures and fittings	1,200
Costs	78,021
Rent and rates	2,626
Salaries	30,226
General expenses	12,500
Interest on overdraft	735
Insurance commission received	369
Freehold premises	200,500
Bad debts	2,400
Provision for doubtful debts b/d (last year's)	1,656
Due to clients	450,000

C. Arnold provides the following additional information about the practice:

(a) Work in progress was valued at £14,270 on 31 December 200—.

(b) Salaries outstanding on 31 December 200— were £426.

(c) Council tax paid in advance on 31 December 200— amounted to £500.

(d) This year's provision for doubtful debts is to be increased to £2,600.

(e) Depreciation is to be charged at 20% per annum on cost of cars and 5% per annum on cost of fixtures and fittings.

Prepare a Profit and Loss account and balance sheet for the year ended 31 December 200—.

5.8 Suggested answers to exercises on adjustments and final accounts

1 Lightfoot Profit and Loss account for the year ending 31 December 200—

Expenses	
Bad debts	625
Add this year's provision for doubtful debts	450
	1,075

Lightfoot Balance Sheet as at 31 December 200—	
Current assets	
Debtors	4,340
Less provision for doubtful debts	450
	3,890

2 Davis Profit and Loss account for the year ending 31 March 200—

EXPENSES	
Depreciation on cars	4,500
(15% of £30,000)	

Davis Balance Sheet as at 31 March 200—	
FIXED ASSETS	
Cost price of cars	30,000
Less total accumulated depreciation	
(being 9,000 plus 4,500)	13,500
	16,500

3 Karsh Profit and Loss account for the year ending 30 September 200—

INCOME		
Profit Costs	90,000	
ADD		
Work in Progress at end of year	6,200	
Value of work done	96,200	
ADDITIONAL INCOME	Nil	
TOTAL INCOME		96,200
LESS EXPENSES		
General and administrative expenses	46,000	
Depreciation on office furniture	850	
Bad debts	406	
Provision for doubtful debts	360	
Total expenses		47,616
NET PROFIT		48,584

Karsh Balance Sheet as at 30 September 200—

FIXED ASSETS

Premises cost price		160,000	
Office furniture cost price	8,500		
Less total depreciation			
(2,550 + 850)	3,400		
		5,100	
			165,100

CURRENT ASSETS

Work in progress		6,200	
Debtors (due from clients)	3,544		
Less provision for doubtful			
Debts	360		
		3,184	
Cash at bank office a/c		13,915	
Petty cash		165	
		23,464	

LESS CURRENT LIABILITIES

Creditors		1,980	
NET CURRENT ASSETS			21,484
TOTAL			186,584
LESS LONG TERM LIABILITIES			
TOTAL NET ASSETS			186,584
Capital Employed			
Capital	170,000		
plus Net profit	48,584		
		218,584	
less drawings		32,000	
TOTAL			186,584
CLIENT ACCOUNT			
Cash at bank client account			249,000
Amount due to clients			249,000

4 J Milton: Profit and Loss account for the year ended 31 December 200—

INCOME

Profit costs		76,422	
Add closing work in progress		8,569	84,991

LESS EXPENDITURE

Telephone and postage		1,300	
Add provision		505	1,805
Council tax			2,950
Light and heat		1,550	
Add provision		551	2,101
Salaries			25,270

Depreciation:			
Motor cars		2,060	
Fixtures and fittings		260	2,320
Bad debts and provision			337	34,783
(£122 + £215 provision)				
NET PROFIT				50,208

J Milton: Balance Sheet as at 31 December 200—

FIXED ASSETS			
Premises		132,000	
Fixtures and fittings at cost	5,200		
Less accumulated depreciation	1,560		
		3,640	
Motor cars at cost	20,600		
Less accumulated depreciation	6,180		
		14,420	
			150,060
CURRENT ASSETS			
Closing work in progress		8,569	
Debtors	4,300		
Less provision	215		
		4,085	
Cash at bank, office account		14,190	
Petty cash		123	
		26,967	
LESS CURRENT LIABILITIES			
Creditors		4,763	
Outstanding expenses		1,056	
		5,819	
NET CURRENT ASSETS			
			21,148
TOTAL			171,208
CAPITAL EMPLOYED			
Capital at start		140,000	
Add net profit		50,208	
		190,208	
Less drawings		19,000	
TOTAL			171,208
Client account			
Cash at bank, client account		315,000	
Due to clients		315,000	

5 **C. Arnold: Profit and Loss account for the year ended 31 December 200—**

INCOME

Profit costs	78,021	
Add: closing work in progress	14,270	
	92,291	
Less: opening work in progress	16,582	75,709
Additional income		
Insurance commission received		369
		76,078

LESS EXPENDITURE

Rent and rates	2,626		
Less: paid in advance	500	2,126	
Salaries	30,226		
Plus: outstanding	426	30,652	
General expenses		12,500	
Interest		735	
Bad and doubtful debts		3,344* [see note below]	
Depreciation: cars	4,000		
Fixtures and fittings	400	4,400	53,757
NET PROFIT			22,321

*Note:

Bad debts	2,400
Add this year's provision	2,600
	5,000
Less last year's provision	1,656
	3,344

C. Arnold: Balance Sheet as at 31 December 200—

FIXED ASSETS

Freehold premises		200,500	
Fixtures and fittings at cost	8,000		
Less accumulated depreciation	1,600		
		6,400	
Motor cars at cost	20,000		
Less accumulated depreciation	12,000		
		8,000	
			214,900

CURRENT ASSETS

Closing work in progress		14,270	
Debtors	12,009		
Less provision	2,600	9,409	
Petty cash		55	

Payment in advance			
Rates		500	
		24,234	
LESS CURRENT LIABILITIES			
Creditors	9,235		
Office bank account overdraft	4,552		
Outstanding expenses: salaries	426		
		14,213	
NET CURRENT ASSETS			10,021
TOTAL			224,921
CAPITAL EMPLOYED			
Capital at start	223,059		
Add net profit	22,321		
		245,380	
Less drawings		20,459	
TOTAL			224,921
CLIENT ACCOUNT			
Cash at bank, client account	450,000		
Less: due to clients	450,000		

Partnership accounts

6.1 The accounts kept by a partnership—introduction

6.1.1 General

The accounts kept by a partnership are largely the same as those kept by a sole practitioner. The asset and income and expense accounts are the same and the clients' accounts are the same, as are the accounting procedures up to the preparation of final accounts. The main differences are as follows:

6.1.1.1 Profit and Loss account—Appropriation account

There is an extension to the Profit and Loss account, known as the Appropriation account, which will show how the profit is divided between the partners.

6.1.1.2 The Balance Sheet

In the Capital Employed section, the partners each have a separate capital account and a separate current account, which shows details of all the profit allocated to the partner, less drawings.

6.2 Final accounts

6.2.1 Profit and Loss account—the Appropriation account

Up to the point of calculating the firm's net profit, the profit and loss account of a partnership is the same as that of a sole practitioner. In a partnership the profit and loss account is extended to show the allocation of the net profit amongst the partners in the profit-sharing ratio provided for in the partnership agreement, after such items as salaries and interest on capital, also provided for in the partnership agreement, have been taken into account. The extension of the profit and loss account is called an Appropriation account.

EXAMPLE

The firm has three partners A, B and C. The profit and loss account records a net profit for the year of £120,000. The partnership agreement provides that A is to receive interest on capital of £2,000 and a salary of £8,000, C is to receive interest on capital of £1,000 and a salary of £2,000 and B is to receive a salary of £2,000. Profits are then shared in the ratio A2 : B2 : C1. The Appropriation account for A, B and C will appear as follows:

A, B & C: Appropriation account for the year ending

NET PROFIT			120,000
SALARIES:			
A	8,000		
B	2,000		
C	2,000		
		12,000	
INTEREST ON CAPITAL:			
A	2,000		
C	1,000	3,000	
PROFIT SHARE:			
A: 2/5ths	42,000		
B: 2/5ths	42,000		
C: 1/5th	21,000	105,000	
			120,000

Note the following with regard to the Appropriation account:

(a) Net profit is carried down from the Profit and Loss account.

(b) Partners' entitlements to salary and interest on capital, for example, are deducted first from the net profit.

(c) The resulting balance is shared amongst the partners in the profit-sharing ratio.

6.2.2 The Balance Sheet

The current account for each partner will show any salary, interest on capital and profit share that they are entitled to. This will form part of the Balance Sheet—see **6.3.5**.

To continue the above example, the current account for partner A would appear as follows:

Current account: A

Date	Details	DR	CR	Balance
	Appropriation: salary		8,000	8,000 CR
	Appropriation: interest on capital		2,000	10,000 CR
	Appropriation: profit share		42,000	52,000 CR

EXAMPLE where a net loss is made

D and E are in partnership as solicitors. The partnership agreement provides that D is to receive a salary of £8,000 per annum and 6% per annum interest on capital, which stands at £50,000. E is to receive 6% per annum interest on capital, which stands at £25,000. Profits and losses are shared equally. The Profit and loss account shows a net loss of £2,000.

D & E: Appropriation account for the year ending

NET LOSS b/d		2,000
SALARIES:		
D		8,000
INTEREST ON CAPITAL:		
D 6% on £50,000	3,000	
E 6% on £25,000	1,500	4,500
TOTAL LOSS		14,500
DIVISION OF NET LOSS:		
D:	7,250	
E:	7,250	

Current account: D

Date	Details	DR	CR	Balance
	Appropriation: salary		8,000	8,000 CR
	Appropriation: interest on capital		3,000	11,000 CR
	Appropriation: share of loss	7,250		3,750 CR

Current account: E

Date	Details	DR	CR	Balance
	Appropriation: interest on capital		1,500	1,500 CR
	Appropriation: share of loss	7,250		5,750 DR

6.2.3 Partners' expenses

If genuine business expenses are paid by the partners these will be recorded by means of a debit entry in the appropriate expense account. At the end of the year the balance on the expense account will be transferred to the Profit and Loss account as a business expense.

EXAMPLE

Edwina, a partner in a provincial firm, travels to London on firm's business. She travels first class and pays the return train fare of £150 out of her own money. Edwina submits a claim to recoup the £150.

(a) If the cashier pays Edwina her £150, the entries in the accounts will be:
  (i) DEBIT travelling expenses account.
  (ii) CREDIT cash account.

Travelling expenses account

Date	Details	DR	CR	Balance
	Cash (partner's travel)	150		150 DR

This is a nominal expense account.

Cash account

Date	Details	DR	CR	Balance
	Travelling expenses		150	150 CR

(b) If Edwina is not to be paid in cash, the travelling expenses will be credited to her current account, in which case the entries in the accounts will be:
   (i)   DEBIT the travelling expenses account.
   (ii) CREDIT the current account of Edwina.

Profit and Loss account for the year ended ...

INCOME

LESS EXPENDITURE

Partners' travelling expenses   50

Current account: Edwina

Date	Details	DR	CR	Balance
	Travelling expenses		150	150 CR

6.3 Drawings

A drawings account may be opened for each partner or alternatively drawings may be debited to the partners' current accounts when they are made.

6.3.1 Cash drawings

If a drawings account is used the following entries will be made to record the partners' cash drawings.

(a) DEBIT drawings account.

(b) CREDIT cash account.

EXAMPLE

On 31 March partner A draws £2,000, on 30 April A draws £2,000, on 10 May the firm pays A's home gas bill, £150.

Drawings account: A

Date	Details	DR	CR	Balance
31 Mar	Cash	2,000		2,000 DR
30 Apr	Cash	2,000		4,000 DR
10 May	Cash: home gas bill	150		4,150 DR

If the firm does not use a drawings account for the partners but debits drawings into the partners' current accounts, when the drawings are made, the above entries would have been recorded in A's current account.

6.3.2 End of the financial year

At the end of the financial year the partner's drawings account will be closed and the balance on the account will be transferred to the partner's current account.

6.3.3 Capital accounts

In a partnership the capital is introduced by more than one person and therefore a separate capital account is kept for each partner.

Note, however, that the net profit is not transferred from the Profit and Loss account to the partners' capital account at the end of the financial year as happens with a sole practitioner.

Drawings are not transferred to the partners' capital account at the end of the year as happens with a sole practitioner.

Thus partners' capital accounts will only show capital which they introduced into the practice.

EXAMPLE

A and B enter into partnership introducing £30,000 and £90,000 capital respectively.

Capital account: A

Date	Details	DR	CR	Balance
	Balance			30,000 CR

Capital account: B

Date	Details	DR	CR	Balance
	Balance			90,000 CR

6.3.4 Current accounts

A current account is opened for each partner.

A partner's current account is credited with any sums which the partner is entitled to receive from the practice, for example, the profit share, interest on capital and salary.

A partner's current account is debited with any sums which the partner has taken out of the practice or which are owed to the practice, for example, drawings (transferred at the end of the financial year from the partner's drawings account).

If a partner's current account has a credit balance, the firm owes money to the partner. If the current account has a debit balance, the partner owes money to the firm which is a current asset of the firm.

However by convention, the balances on the partners' current accounts are always shown on the capital employed part of the Balance Sheet.

EXAMPLE

In the example in **6.3.3**, assume that on 30 June 200—, the end of the financial year for A and B's first year of practice, net profit is £86,000. Interest on capital is allowed to both partners at the rate of 5% per annum. A has made drawings of £20,000 and B has made drawings of £30,000. B is paid a salary of £5,000 per annum. A's share of the net profit is £25,000 and B's share is £50,000.

Current account: A

Date	Details	DR	CR	Balance
200—				
30 June	Profit share		25,000	25,000 CR
	Interest on capital		1,500	26,500 CR
	Drawings	20,000		6,500 CR

Thus at the end of the year the firm owes A £6,500.

Current account: B

Date	Details	DR	CR	Balance
200—				
30 June	Profit share		50,000	50,000 CR
	Salary		5,000	55,000 CR
	Interest on capital		4,500	59,500 CR
	Drawings	30,000		29,500 CR

Thus at the end of the year the firm owes B £29,500.

6.3.5 Loan accounts

If partners loan money to the firm over and above their capital contribution, a loan account will be opened in the partners' names and they will be treated as creditors of the firm.

Any loan will be shown on the balance sheet as a long-term liability.

If interest is payable on the loan, a nominal expense account will be opened to record the payment of interest; the interest payable account. At the end of the financial year the debit balance on the interest payable account will be transferred to the Profit and Loss account as a business expense.

The partner may take payment of the loan interest in cash or may have the loan interest credited to the current account.

The bookkeeping entries to record the payment of loan interest in cash will be:

(a) DEBIT interest payable account.

(b) CREDIT cash account.

The bookkeeping entries to record loan interest credited to the partner's current account will be:

(a) DEBIT interest payable account.

(b) CREDIT current account of partner making the loan.

EXAMPLE

Lawrence, Alice and Mark practise together in partnership. It is agreed that Lawrence will make a loan of £5,000 to the practice to be used towards the purchase of a computer. Lawrence is to receive interest of £250 per annum for so long as the loan remains unpaid. Lawrence asks that the interest be dealt with in his current account.

When the loan is negotiated the entries in the accounts will be:

(a) DEBIT office cash account when the loan is paid into firm's bank account.

(b) CREDIT the loan account.

Cash account

Date	Details	DR	CR	Balance
	Loan: Lawrence	5,000		5,000 DR

Loan account: Lawrence

Date	Details	DR	CR	Balance
	Cash		5,000	5,000 CR

When the first year's interest of £250 becomes due:

(a) DEBIT the loan interest payable account.

(b) CREDIT Lawrence's current account. (Had Lawrence asked for payment to be made to him, the cash account and not Lawrence's current account would have been credited.)

Loan interest payable account

Date	Details	DR	CR	Balance
	Current account: Lawrence	250		250 DR

At the end of the financial year the loan interest will be shown as a business expense.

Current account: Lawrence

Date	Details	DR	CR	Balance
	Interest payable: loan		250	250 CR

6.3.6   Balance Sheet

The balance sheet of a partnership is the same as that of a sole practitioner except:

(a) The capital accounts of the partners are shown separately. The capital accounts show capital at the start of the year.

(b) Net profit and drawings are *not* transferred to a partner's capital account and therefore are not shown as additions to and deductions from capital, respectively, as happens with a sole practitioner.

(c) The current accounts of the partners are shown on the liabilities part (capital employed) of the balance sheet. If there is a credit balance on the current accounts, this is added to the capital account balance. If there is a debit balance on the current accounts this is deducted from the capital account balance.

(d) It is not usual to show movements on partners' current accounts on the Balance Sheet itself. At the end of the Balance Sheet is a schedule showing the movement on the current accounts.

6.3.7   Example on partners' final accounts

Ginger, Tom and Arnold are in partnership, sharing profits and losses in the ratio 2 : 2 : 1. Each partner is entitled to interest on capital at 10% per annum and to salaries of £10,000 to Ginger and £7,000 to Arnold.

An abridged trial balance prepared from the partnership books shows the following position at 30 September 200—.

	DR	CR
Total assets	320,000	
Total liabilities		150,000
Profit for the year from the Profit and Loss account		140,000
Drawings		
Ginger	30,000	
Tom	25,000	
Arnold	25,000	
Capital accounts		
Ginger		50,000
Tom		40,000
Arnold		20,000
	400,000	400,000

From the above, prepare the profit and loss appropriation account for the year ended 30 September 200—, together with a balance sheet as at that date.

6.3.8   Answer to example on partners' final accounts

Profit and Loss and appropriation account for the year ended 30 September 200—

NET PROFIT		140,000
INTEREST ON CAPITAL:		
Ginger 10% on £50,000	5,000	
Tom 10% on £40,000	4,000	
Arnold 10% on £20,000	2,000	11,000
		129,000
SALARIES:		
Ginger	10,000	
Arnold	7,000	17,000
		112,000
SHARE OF PROFIT:		
Ginger: 2/5ths	44,800	
Tom: 2/5ths	44,800	
Arnold: 1/5th	22,400	112,000

Ginger, Tom and Arnold: Balance Sheet as at 30 September 200—

ASSETS	320,000		
Less: liabilities	150,000		
Total Net Assets			170,000
CAPITAL EMPLOYED			
Capital accounts:			
Ginger	50,000		
Tom	40,000		
Arnold	20,000		
		110,000	
Current accounts (see movements on current accounts):			
Ginger	29,800		
Tom	23,800		
Arnold	6,400		
		60,000	
TOTAL due to partners			170,000

Movements on partners' Current Accounts

	Ginger	Tom	Arnold
Opening balance			
Salary	10,000	—	7,000
Interest on capital	5,000	4,000	2,000
Profit share	44,800	44,800	22,400
	59,800	48,800	31,400
Less: drawings	30,000	25,000	25,000
	29,800 CR	23,800 CR	6,400 CR

6.4 Partnership changes

The constitution of a partnership may change during the financial year as a result of a partner dying, retiring from the practice, a new partner joining the practice or because the partners decide to vary their profit sharing agreement.

When there is a partnership change during the year, the format of the Balance Sheet and the Profit and Loss account to the net profit stage will not change.

The format of the Appropriation account will change as there will be a split appropriation. This means that there will be one Appropriation account for the period before the change and one for the period after the change to the end of the financial year. Each Appropriation account will reflect the terms of the partnership agreement in force for the period to which the Appropriation account relates. Unless you are told the net profit for the period before and after the change you will have to apportion the net profit for each period on a time basis.

The net profit, interest on drawings, interest on capital and salaries must be apportioned. For example, if there is a partnership change three months into the year, in the first Appropriation account, net profit, etc., for the year will be divided by four to reflect the fact that the Appropriation account relates to only one quarter of the year.

If a sole practitioner takes in a partner part way through the year, the profits for the time as a sole practitioner will belong wholly to the sole practitioner. There will be no salary, interest on capital, etc., in the first part of the Appropriation account as these are relevant only where there is a partnership. It therefore follows that provision for salaries, etc. in the partnership agreement can apply only to the second appropriation period.

EXAMPLE

A and B are in partnership. A's capital is £60,000 and B's is £40,000. They share the profits in the ratio 3:2. Their financial year runs from 1 January to 31 December. C joins the partnership on 1 July 200—. C is to receive a salary of £12,000 per annum and A and B interest on capital of 10% per annum. A, B and C are to share the profits in the ratio of 2:2:1.

Net profit for the year ended 31 December 200— is £140,000.

A, B & C: profit and loss account for the year ended 31 December 200—

NET PROFIT			140,000

Appropriation account 1 January to 30 June 200—

PROFIT SHARE:			
A: 3/5ths	42,000		
B: 2/5ths	28,000		70,000

1 July to 31 December 200—

INTEREST ON CAPITAL:			
A for half year on 60,000 at 10%	3,000		
B for half year on 40,000 at 10%	2,000	5,000	
SALARIES:			
C for half year at 12,000 p.a.		6,000	
PROFIT SHARE:			
A: 2/5ths	23,600		
B: 2/5ths	23,600		
C: 1/5th	11,800	59,000	70,000
			140,000

6.4.1   Revaluation of partnership assets

As a result of a change in the partnership constitution the partners may decide to revalue some or all of the fixed assets. This ensures that the partners in the firm before the change takes place have the benefit of any increase in value and bear the burden of any reduction in value, before the change.

The revaluation of the fixed assets is recorded in a revaluation account, the corresponding double entry being made in the asset account for the asset which is being revalued.

To record an increase in the value of an asset:

(a) DEBIT the asset account with the increase in value.

(b) CREDIT the revaluation account.

To record a reduction in the value of an asset:

(a) CREDIT the asset account with the reduction in value.

(b) DEBIT the revaluation account.

The revaluation account is closed by transferring the net increase or decrease in value to the existing partners' capital accounts in the old profit sharing ratio. If there is an increase in value the entries will be:

(a) DEBIT the revaluation account.

(b) CREDIT the capital accounts of the existing partners.

If the revaluation account shows a decrease in value the entries will be reversed.

If the partners receive interest on capital it is important to remember that the revaluation alters their capital account balances. Interest should therefore be calculated on the old balances for the period before the change, and on the new balances for the period after the change.

EXAMPLE

A and B are in partnership, sharing profits equally. They have Capital account balances of £50,000 and £80,000 respectively. C is to be admitted into the partnership on 1 April. A and B revalue premises and motor cars which have a book value of £100,000 and £18,000 respectively. On revaluation, premises are valued at £125,000 and cars at £14,000.

Revaluation account

Date	Details	DR	CR	Balance
31 Mar	Premises		25,000	25,000 CR
	Motor cars	4,000		21,000 CR
	Capital: A	10,500		
	Capital: B	10,500		—
	(transfer profit on revaluation)			

Premises account

Date	Details	DR	CR	Balance
	Balance b/d			100,000 DR
31 Mar	Revaluation	25,000		125,000 DR

Motor cars account

Date	Details	DR	CR	Balance
	Balance b/d			18,000 DR
	Revaluation		4,000	14,000 DR

Capital account: A

Date	Details	DR	CR	Balance
	Balance			50,000 CR
	Revaluation		10,500	60,500 CR

Capital account: B

Date	Details	DR	CR	Balance
	Balance			80,000 CR
	Revaluation		10,500	90,500 CR

6.5 Check list

By the end of this chapter you should be able to:

1. appreciate that there will be an addition to the Profit and Loss account which will show how the profit is divided between the partners, known as the Appropriation account;

2. note the difference between the Balance Sheet of a partnership and that of a sole owner;

3. appreciate that on the Balance Sheet in the Capital Employed section the partners will have separate accounts, broken down into Capital accounts and Current accounts;

4. understand that the details on the Current accounts may be shown as a schedule to the Balance Sheet;

5. understand that partners may split the profit in different ways, providing for any partners' salaries and interest on capital as a prior allocation of the profit;

6. draw up an Appropriation account;

7. draw up details of movement on partners' Current accounts;

8. draw up a partnership Balance Sheet;

9. complete the self test exercises at the end of the chapter.

6.6 Exercises on partnership final accounts

1 Allan, Black and Clark are in partnership sharing profits as to Allan 50%, Black 25% and Clark 25%.

Each partner is entitled to interest on capital of 5% and Clark is entitled to a partnership salary of £5,000 a year. The net profit at the end of the year is £250,000 and the partners' capital account balances are Allan £60,000, Black £40,000 and Clark £20,000.

Draw up the Appropriation account for the partners.

2 The Trial Balance of Javid and Khan at the end of the year 31 December 200— showed the following Capital and Current account balances.

Capital accounts
Javid	40,000
Khan	20,000

Current accounts
Javid	5,426
Khan	3,040

Net profit for the partnership at the end of the year was £110,000. Interest on capital is 6% a year. Khan has a salary of £2,000 a year and the profit share ratio is Javid 2: Khan 1. Drawings for the year were Javid £50,000 and Khan £35,000.

Draw up the Appropriation account, the movement on Current accounts and the capital employed section of the Balance Sheet at the end of the year.

3 The bookkeeper of the firm Bertram, Crawford and Norris, solicitors, draws up a trial balance in respect of the year ending 31 December 200—.

Trial balance at 31 December 200—

	DR	CR
Profit Costs less work in progress at start of year		544,060
General and administrative expenses	372,900	
Due to clients		943,560
Bad debts	4,900	
Capital accounts		
Bertram		130,000
Crawford		100,000
Norris		80,000
Current Accounts		
Bertram		5,000
Crawford		4,000
Norris		6,000
Sundry creditors		8,100
Interest received		6,420
Freehold premises	320,000	
Library furniture & equipment at cost	42,000	
Accumulated depreciation on library		
Furniture & equipment		12,600
Motor cars	45,000	
Accumulated depreciation on motor cars		18,000
Due from clients	51,820	
Overdraft office account		3,000
Cash at bank client current account	493,560	
Cash at bank client deposit account	450,000	
Petty cash	560	
Drawings		
Bertram	30,000	
Crawford	25,000	
Norris	25,000	
	1,860,740	1,860,740

The partnership agreement provides that Crawford has a partnership salary of £5,000 per annum, interest on capital for the partners is 5% per annum and profits and losses are shared equally.

Work in progress as at 31 December 200— is £50,000. Payments in advance are £1,800 and outstanding expenses are £2,100. Provision for doubtful debts for the year to 31 December 200— is set at £1,200. Depreciation for the year on the library furniture and equipment is 10% of the cost price, and depreciation for the year on motor cars is 20% of the cost price.

Draw up the Profit and Loss and Appropriation account for the partners together with the Balance Sheet. Show full details of the movement on Current accounts.

4 Ash and Rowan are in partnership as solicitors, sharing profits and losses as to Ash two-thirds and Rowan one-third. Each partner is entitled to interest on capital in the firm at the rate of 5% per annum. Rowan is also entitled to a salary of £10,000 per annum.

The following trial balance was prepared from the firm's accounts for the year ended 31 December 200—.

Trial balance at 31 December 200—

	DR	CR
Capital accounts		
Ash		50,000
Rowan		25,000
Current accounts		
Ash		3,450
Rowan		1,620
Lease at cost price	15,000	
Motor cars	30,000	
Furniture, library and equipment	22,000	
Partners' drawings		
Ash	23,500	
Rowan	28,000	
Administration and general expenses	118,520	
Profit costs		190,425
Interest received		2,900
Due to clients		425,380
Provision for doubtful debts b/d		560
Creditors		18,375
Cash at bank: clients' account:		
Deposit account	350,000	
Current account	75,380	
Petty cash	270	
Cash at bank: office account	12,840	
Work in progress (1 January 2002)	34,200	
Due from clients	24,000	
Loan account: bank		10,000
Rent received		6,000
	733,710	733,710

Work in progress at 31 December 200— is valued at £38,000. This year's provision for doubtful debts is £800.

Depreciation on motor cars for the year ending 31 December 200— is £6,000. Depreciation on furniture, library and equipment is £4,800.

From the above information prepare a Profit and Loss and Appropriation account for the year ended 31 December 200— together with a Balance Sheet as at that date.

5 Beth and Amy are in partnership as solicitors sharing profits and losses in the ratio 3 : 2. Each partner is entitled, under the partnership agreement, to interest on capital at the rate of 10% per annum and Amy is entitled, in addition, to a partnership salary of £12,000 per annum.

On 1 July 200—, Jo is admitted into the partnership, contributing £10,000 as her share of the capital in the firm. The new partnership agreement provides that, as from 1 July 200—, profits and losses will be shared between Beth, Amy and Jo in the ratio 2 : 2 : 1 respectively. Furthermore, partnership salaries of £20,000, £15,000 and £10,000 per annum will be allowed to Beth, Amy and Jo respectively. No interest is to be allowed on capital, and no interest is to be charged on partners' drawings.

An abridged trial balance, prepared from the partnership books, shows the following position as at 31 December 200—.

NET PROFIT for the year, before charging interest on capital, and other appropriations		120,000
Partners' drawings:		
Beth	30,700	
Amy	28,400	
Jo	11,000	
Partners' capital accounts:		
Beth		70,000
Amy		50,000
Jo		10,000
Sundry assets	194,700	
Sundry liabilities		14,800
	264,800	264,800
Amounts due to clients		894,568
Cash at bank: clients	894,568	
	1,159,368	1,159,368

From the above information, prepare the Profit and Loss and Appropriation account for the year ended 31 December 200—, together with a Balance Sheet as at that date. The allocation of profits between the partners is to be determined on a time basis. (Calculations to be made in months.) Detailed movements on partners' Current accounts should also be shown.

6 Hale and Hearty are in partnership as solicitors. Hale and Hearty receive interest on capital of 5% per annum and Hearty receives a salary of £2,000 per annum. The remaining profits are shared equally. Their financial year ends on 31 December. On 31 December 200— the Trial Balance is:

	DR	CR
Freehold premises	145,000	
Fixtures and fittings	15,000	
Accumulated depreciation on fixtures and fittings		3,000
Library	2,000	
Accumulated depreciation on library		500
Capital accounts:		
Hale		80,000
Hearty		75,000
Current accounts:		
Hale		2,500
Hearty		2,000
Drawings:		
Hale	24,000	
Hearty	24,500	

Profit		
Profit Costs		78,000
Insurance commission received		600
Salaries	20,000	
Insurance paid	1,500	
Council tax	1,620	
Light and heat	1,400	
Stationery	900	
Travelling	400	
Creditors		820
Debtors	3,000	
Office bank account	3,000	
Petty cash	100	
Client bank account	465,000	
Client ledger account		465,000
	707,420	707,420

At 31 December 200— work in progress amounts to £5,000; there is a stock of stationery valued at £300. Depreciation is charged on fixtures and fittings and library at 10% on the cost price. There is an amount outstanding for electricity of £100.

Prepare final accounts for Hale and Hearty for the year ended 31 December 200—.

6.7 Suggested answers to exercises on partnership final accounts

1 Allan, Black and Clark appropriation account for the year ending ....

NET PROFIT		250,000
Less		
Salary Clark		5,000
		245,000
INTEREST ON CAPITAL		
Allan 5% on 60,000	3,000	
Black 5% on 40,000	2,000	
Clark 5% on 20,000	1,000	
		6,000
		239,000
PROFIT SHARE		
Allan 50%	119,500	
Black 25%	59,750	
Clark 25%	59,750	
		239,000
		—

2 Appropriation account for Javid and Khan for the year ending 31 December 200—

NET PROFIT		110,000
INTEREST ON CAPITAL		
Javid 6% on 40,000	2,400	
Khan 6% on 20,000	1,200	

			3,600
			106,400

SALARY

Khan

			2,000
			104,400

PROFIT SHARE

Javid	69,600
Khan	34,800

			104,400

Movement on Current accounts

	Javid	Khan
Opening balance	5,426	3,040
Interest on capital	2,400	1,200
Salary		2,000
Profit share	69,600	34,800
Total	77,426	41,040
Less: Drawings	50,000	35,000
Balance	27,426	6,040

Javid and Khan Balance sheet as at 31 December 200—

CAPITAL EMPLOYED

Capital accounts

Javid	40,000
Khan	20,000

			60,000

Current accounts (see movement on current accounts)

Javid	27,426
Khan	6,040

			33,466
			93,466

3 Bertram, Crawford and Norris

Profit and Loss and Appropriation account for the year ending 31 December 200—

INCOME

Profit costs		544,060	
Add: work in progress at end of year		50,000	
Value of work done			594,060
ADDITIONAL INCOME			
Add: interest received		6,420	600,480
LESS: EXPENDITURE			
General and admin expenses	372,900		
Bad debts	4,900		
Provision for doubtful debts	1,200		
depreciation on cars	9,000		
depreciation on furniture etc.	4,200		
Add: outstanding expenses	2,100		
	394,300		
Less: payments in advance	1,800		392,500

NET PROFIT			207,980
APPROPRIATION ACCOUNT			
Profit available			207,980
SALARY			
Crawford			5,000
INTEREST ON CAPITAL			
Bertram		6,500	
Crawford		5,000	
Norris		4,000	15,500
PROFIT SHARE			
Bertram		62,494	
Crawford		62,493	
Norris		62,493	187,480

Bertram, Crawford and Norris: Balance Sheet as at 31 December 200—

FIXED ASSETS			
Freehold premises		320,000	
Library etc. cost price	42,000		
Less depreciation	168,000		
		25,200	
Motor cars cost price	45,000		
Less depreciation	27,000		
		18,000	
			363,200
CURRENT ASSETS			
Work in progress		50,000	
Debtors (due from clients)	51,820		
Less provision	1,200		
		50,620	
Petty cash		560	
Payments in advance		1,800	
			102,980
Less CURRENT LIABILITIES			
Sundry creditors		8,100	
Overdraft office account		3,000	
Outstanding expenses		2,100	
			13,200
Net current assets			89,780
TOTAL NET ASSETS			452,980
CAPITAL EMPLOYED			
Capital accounts:			
Bertram	130,000		
Crawford	100,000		
Norris	80,000		

			310,000
Current accounts (see schedule movement on current accounts)			
Bertram	43,994		
Crawford	51,493		
Norris	47,493		
		142,980	

TOTAL DUE TO PARTNERS   452,980

CLIENT ACCOUNT

Due to clients		943,560	
Cash at bank client			
current account	493,560		
Cash at bank client			
deposit account	450,000		
		943,560	

Movements on partners' current accounts

	Bertram	Crawford	Norris
Opening Balance	5,000	4,000	6,000
Salary	—	5,000	—
Interest on capital	6,500	5,000	4,000
Profit share	62,494	62,493	62,493
	73,994	76,493	72,493
Less: Drawings	30,000	25,000	25,000
	43,994	51,493	47,493

4 Ash and Rowan

Profit and Loss and Appropriation account for the year ended 31 December 200—

Profit costs		190,425	
Add: closing work in progress		38,000	
		228,425	
Less: opening work in progress		34,200	
Value of work done		194,225	
ADDITIONAL INCOME			
Interest received	2,900		
Rent received	6,000		
		8,900	
			203,125
LESS: EXPENDITURE			
Administrative and general expenses		118,520	
Provision for doubtful debts			
This year's provision	800		
Less: last year's	560	240	
Depreciation:			
Cars	6,000		
Furniture etc.	4,800	10,800	129,560

NET PROFIT		73,565
APPROPRIATION		73,565
SALARIES:		
Rowan		10,000
INTEREST ON CAPITAL:		
Ash	2,500	
Rowan	1,250	3,750
PROFIT SHARE:		
Ash: 2/3rds		39,877
Rowan: 1/3rd		19,938

(round up or down to nearest pound to balance)

Note that last year's provision for doubtful debts brought down will reduce the expense this year.

Schedule to Balance Sheet

Movement on partners' current accounts

	Ash	Rowan
Balance	3,450 CR	1,620 CR
Salary	—	10,000
Interest on capital	2,500	1,250
Profit share	39,877	19,938
	45,827	32,808
Less: drawings	23,500	28,000
	22,327 CR	4,808 CR

Ash and Rowan: Balance Sheet as at 31 December 200—

FIXED ASSETS			
Leasehold premises		15,000	
Furniture, library and equipment			
at cost	22,000		
Less: depreciation	4,800		
		17,200	
Motor cars		30,000	
Less: depreciation		6,000	
			24,000
			56,200
CURRENT ASSETS			
Closing work in progress		38,000	
Debtors	24,000		
Less: provision	800		
		23,200	
Cash at bank office account		12,840	
Petty cash		270	
		74,310	

Less: CURRENT LIABILITIES			
Creditors		18,375	
NET CURRENT ASSETS			55,935
			112,135
Less: LONG TERM LIABILITIES			
Bank loan			10,000
TOTAL NET ASSETS			102,135
CAPITAL EMPLOYED			
Capital accounts:			
Ash	50,000		
Rowan	25,000		
		75,000	
Current accounts:			
(see schedule to the Balance sheet)			
Ash	22,327		
Rowan	4,808		
		27,135	
TOTAL DUE TO PARTNERS			102,135
CLIENT ACCOUNT			
Bank balance:			
Deposit account	350,000		
Current account	75,380		
		425,380	
Less: Due to clients		425,380	

5 Beth, Amy and Jo

Profit and Loss and Appropriation account for period 1 January 200— to 30 June 200—

NET PROFIT (for 6 months)		60,000
SALARY (for 6 months):		
Amy	6,000	
INTEREST ON CAPITAL (for 6 months):		
Beth	3,500	
Amy	2,500	
		12,000
PROFIT SHARE:		
Beth: 3/5ths	28,800	
Amy: 2/5ths	19,200	48,000

Profit and Loss and Appropriation account for period 1 July to 31 December 200—

NET PROFIT (for 6 months)		60,000
SALARIES (for 6 months):		
Beth	10,000	

Amy	7,500	
Jo	5,000	
		22,500

PROFIT SHARE:

Beth: 2/5ths	15,000	
Amy: 2/5ths	15,000	
Jo: 1/5th	7,500	37,500

Schedule to Balance Sheet

Movement on partners' current accounts

	Beth	Amy	Jo
Salary	10,000	13,500	5,000
Interest on capital	3,500	2,500	—
Profit share	43,800	34,200	7,500
	57,300	50,200	12,500
Less balance	30,700	28,400	11,000
	26,600 CR	21,800 CR	1,500 CR

Beth, Amy and Jo: Balance Sheet as at 31 December 200—

ASSETS	194,700	
Less: liabilities	14,800	
TOTAL NET ASSETS		179,900

CAPITAL EMPLOYED

Capital accounts:

Beth	70,000	
Amy	50,000	
Jo	10,000	
		130,000

Current accounts:

Beth	26,600 CR	
Amy	21,800 CR	
Jo	1,500 CR	
		49,900
TOTAL DUE TO PARTNERS		179,900

CLIENT ACCOUNT

Client bank balance	894,568
Less: due to clients	894,568

6   Hale and Hearty

Profit and Loss and Appropriation account for the year ended 31 December 200—

INCOME

Profit costs	78,000
Add closing work in progress	5,000

Value of work done			83,000
Add insurance commission received		600	
			83,600
LESS EXPENDITURE			
Salaries		20,000	
Insurance paid		1,500	
Council tax		1,620	
Light and heat	1,400		
Plus outstanding expense	100	1,500	
Stationery	900		
Less closing stock	300	600	
Travel expenses		400	
Depreciation:			
Fixtures and fittings	1,500		
Library	200	1,700	27,320
NET PROFIT			56,280

APPROPRIATION ACCOUNT			
Salary:			
Hearty	2,000	2,000	
Interest on capital:			
Hale	4,000		
Hearty	3,750	7,750	
Profit share:			
Hale: $^1/_2$	23,265		
Hearty: $^1/_2$	23,265	46,530	
		56,280	

Hale and Hearty: Balance Sheet as at 31 December 200—

FIXED ASSETS			
Premises		145,000	
Fixtures and fittings	15,000		
Less accumulated depreciation	4,500		
		10,500	
Library	2,000		
Less accumulated depreciation	700		
		1,300	
			156,800
CURRENT ASSETS			
Closing work in progress	5,000		
Debtors	3,000		
Office bank account	3,000		
Petty cash	100		
Stock of stationery	300		
		11,400	

Less CURRENT LIABILITIES		
Creditors	820	
Outstanding expenses	100	
		920
NET CURRENT ASSETS		10,480
TOTAL NET ASSETS		167,280
CAPITAL EMPLOYED		
Capital accounts:		
Hale	80,000	
Hearty	75,000	
		155,000
Current accounts: see movement on current accounts		
Hale	5,765	
Hearty	6,515	
		12,280
TOTAL DUE TO PARTNERS		167,280
CLIENT ACCOUNT		
Client bank balance	465,000	
Less amount due to clients	465,000	

Movement on partners' current accounts

	Hale	Hearty
Opening balance	2,500	2,000
Salary		2,000
Interest on capital	4,000	3,750
Profit share	23,265	23,265
	29,765	31,015
Less drawings	24,000	24,500
	5,765	6,515

6.8 Test on partnership final accounts

Allow 2 to 3 hours to complete this test.

1 The bookkeeper of the firm Gold and Silver solicitors, extracts the following information from the books of account in respect of the year ended 31 December 200—.

Due to clients	440,460
Profit costs	160,500
Interest received	7,450

General and administrative expenses	94,840
Rent received	4,000
Provision for doubtful debts (last year's)	600
Partners' capital accounts	
Gold	30,000
Silver	20,000
Partners' current accounts	
Gold	2,500 DR
Silver	800 CR
Leasehold property at cost	34,000
Library, furniture and equipment at cost	16,500
Accumulated depreciation on library, furniture and equipment to 1 January 200—	3,300
Due from clients	21,790
Work in progress at 1 January 200—	12,100
Cash at the bank: client account	440,460
office account	7,360
Petty cash balance	140
Partners' drawings:	
Gold	24,960
Silver	18,890
Creditors	6,430

The following information is relevant:

(a) Profits and losses are shared between Gold and Silver so that Gold receives three-fifths and Silver two-fifths.

(b) Silver is to receive a partnership salary of £8,000 per year.

(c) Interest is to be allowed on partners' capital, as follows:

Gold	£3,000
Silver	£2,000

(d) Work in progress at 31 December 200— is valued £14,150.

(e) At 31 December 200— prepaid general expenses amount to £350, whilst there are administration expenses outstanding and not yet accounted for amounting to £900.

(f) The provision for doubtful debts is to be increased to £760.

(g) Depreciation of £1,650 is to be charged against library, furniture and equipment.

From the above information prepare a Profit and Loss and Appropriation account for the year ended 31 December 200— together with the Balance Sheet as at that date.

2 From the Trial Balance of Rip, Van and Winkle set out below draw up a Profit and Loss account and Appropriation account for the year ended 31 December 200—, together with a Balance Sheet as at that date.

	DR	CR
Current accounts		
Rip		2,771
Van		3,055
Winkle	760	

Capital accounts		
Rip		160,000
Van		120,000
Winkle		80,000
Drawings		
Rip	25,000	
Van	25,000	
Winkle	25,000	
Creditors		5,923
Premises—cost price	300,000	
Office equipment—cost price	25,000	
Office furniture—cost price	30,000	
Motor cars—cost price	45,000	
Accumulated depreciation on office equipment		5,000
Accumulated depreciation on office furniture		6,000
Accumulated depreciation on motor cars		9,000
General expenses	415,000	
Cash at bank—office account	7,543	
Petty cash	96	
Profit costs		539,700
Interest received		7,150
Work in progress as at 1 January 200—	35,000	
Cash at Bank Client account		
current account	176,000	
deposit account	490,000	
Amount due to clients		666,000
Due from clients	5,200	
	1,604,599	1,604,599

Note the following:

Expenses due and not yet paid during the year amount to £895, those expenses prepaid amount to £625. A bad debt has to be written off in the sum of £600, and provision for bad and doubtful debts amounts to £530. Work in progress as at 31 December 200— amounts to £38,800. Depreciation on office equipment and on office furniture is 10% per annum on the cost price, and depreciation on cars is 20% per annum on the cost price. Rip has a partnership salary of £5,000, and the partners allow interest on capital at 5% per annum. The profits are then shared equally between the partners.

6.9   Suggested answers to test on partnership final accounts

1   Gold and Silver

Profit and loss appropriation account for the year ended 31 December 200—

INCOME

Profit costs	160,500	
Add: closing work in progress	14,150	

		174,650	
Less: opening work in progress		12,100	
Value of work done			162,550
ADD			
Interest received		7,450	
Rent received		4,000	
			11,450
Total income			174,000
LESS EXPENDITURE			
General and administrative expenses	94,840		
Add: outstanding expenses	900		
	95,740		
Less: paid in advance	350		
		95,390	
Bad debts		160	
Depreciation: library, furniture and equipment		1,650	
Total expenses			97,200
NET PROFIT			76,800
APPROPRIATION			
Profit			76,800
SALARY			
Silver			8,000
INTEREST ON CAPITAL			
Gold	3,000		
Silver	2,000		
			5,000
SHARE OF PROFIT			
Gold: 3/5ths		38,280	
Silver: 2/5ths		25,520	
			63,800

Workings

Bad debts account

Date	Details	DR	CR	Balance
200—				
1 Jan	Provision b/d (last year's)		600	600 CR
31 Dec	Provision c/d (this year's)	760		160 DR
	Transfer to Profit and Loss		160	—

Schedule to the Balance Sheet

Movement on partners' current accounts

	Gold	Silver
Balance	2,500 (DR)	800 CR
Interest on capital	3,000	2,000
Salary	—	8,000
Profit share	38,280	25,520
	38,780	36,320
Less: drawings	24,960	18,890
	13,820 CR	17,430 CR

Gold and Silver: Balance Sheet as at 31 December 200—

FIXED ASSETS			
Leasehold property at cost		34,000	
Library, furniture and equipment at cost	16,500		
Less: accumulated depreciation	4,950		
		11,550	
			45,550
CURRENT ASSETS			
Closing work in progress		14,150	
Debtors (due from clients)	21,790		
Less: provision for this year	760		
		21,030	
Cash at bank: office account	7,360		
Petty cash	140		
Payments in advance re general expenses	350		
		43,030	
Less CURRENT LIABILITIES			
Creditors	6,430		
Outstanding expenses	900		
		7,330	
NET CURRENT ASSETS			35,700
TOTAL			81,250
CAPITAL EMPLOYED			
Capital accounts:			
Gold	30,000		
Silver	20,000		
			50,000
Current accounts:			
Gold	13,820		
Silver	17,430		
			31,250
TOTAL			81,250

CLIENT ACCOUNT

Client bank balance	440,460
Amount due to clients	440,460

2 Rip, Van and Winkle

Profit and Loss and Appropriation account for the year ended 31 December 200—

INCOME			
Profit costs	539,700		
Add: Work in progress at the end of			
the year 31 December 200—	38,800		
	578,500		
Less: Work in progress at the start			
of the year 1 January 200—	35,000		
Value of work done	543,500		
ADD ADDITIONAL INCOME			
Interest received	7,150		
		550,650	
Less: EXPENDITURE			
Admin and General Expenses	415,000		
Outstanding expenses	895		
Bad debt written off	600		
Provision for doubtful debts	530		
	417,025		
Less: prepaid	625		
	416,400		
Add: depreciation			
On office equipment	2,500		
On office furniture	3,000		
On motor cars	9,000		
		14,500	
			430,900
NET PROFIT			119,750
APPROPRIATION ACCOUNT			
Profit available for distribution			119,750
SALARY			
Rip			5,000
INTEREST ON CAPITAL			
Rip	8,000		
Van	6,000		
Winkle	4,000		
			18,000

Profit share

Rip	32,250	
Van	32,250	
Winkle	32,250	
		96,750

Rip, Van and Winkle: Balance Sheet as at 31 December 200—

FIXED ASSETS

Premises cost price		300,000	
Office equipment cost price	25,000		
Less: Total depreciation	7,500	17,500	
Office furniture cost price	30,000		
Less: Total depreciation	9,000		
		21,000	
Motor cars cost price	45,000		
Less: Total depreciation	18,000		
		27,000	
			365,500

CURRENT ASSETS

Work in Progress		38,800	
Debtors (5,200 − 600)	4,600		
Less: Provision	530		
		4,070	
Cash at Bank office		7,543	
Petty cash		96	
Prepaid		625	
		51,134	
Less: CURRENT LIABILITIES			
Creditors		5,923	
Outstanding expenses		895	
		6,818	
NET CURRENT ASSETS			44,316
TOTAL			409,816

CAPITAL EMPLOYED
CAPITAL ACCOUNTS

Rip	160,000		
Van	120,000		
Winkle	80,000		
			360,000

CURRENT ACCOUNTS
See schedule movement on current accounts

Rip	23,021		
Van	16,305		
Winkle	10,490		
			49,816
TOTAL			409,816

Schedule movement on current accounts

	Rip	Van	Winkle
Opening Balance	2,771	3,055	760 (DR)
Salary	5,000	—	—
Interest on Capital	8,000	6,000	4,000
Profit share	32,250	32,250	32,250
	48,021	41,305	35,490
Less drawings	25,000	25,000	25,000
	23,021	16,305	10,490

Basic accounting concepts and manufacturing and trading accounts

7.1 Introduction

This chapter includes accounting concepts which underpin accounts, and explains briefly accounting bases and policies. It then deals with basic trading accounts and gives an example of a manufacturing account.

7.2 Financial accounting concepts

Accounting has certain rules, known as accounting concepts, which are applied in drawing up accounts and making adjustments. There are detailed accounting standards set out for accountants, earlier these were known as Statements of Standard Accounting Practice (SSAPs), later standards are known as Financial Reporting Standards (FRSs).

Any accounting methods used are supposed to give a true and fair view of a business, of its profit and loss and its value.

Fundamental accounting concepts are the assumptions on which accounts of businesses are drawn up. They include the following:

7.2.1 The business entity concept

This means that for accounting purposes a business is treated as a separate entity from its owner or owners, even though in law this may not be the case for a sole trader or a partnership. Thus when an owner puts money into the business this is recorded as the business having received the money and that the business owes that money to the owner (see capital accounts at **1.5.2**).

7.2.2 The money measurement concept

Accounts give information about a business, but only in money terms. They do not, for example, give information about the motivation of the workforce or how competent the managing director is.

7.2.3 The cost concept

This means that assets would be valued at cost price rather than by estimating their current value.

7.2.4 The going-concern concept

This is the assumption that the business will continue to operate in the future. Thus the Profit and Loss account and the Balance Sheet will be drawn up on the assumption that the business will continue at the same level and not be sold. For example, if a business ceases to operate, its assets may be worth considerably less on a closing down sale than if the business continues.

7.2.5 The accruals concept

This is the assumption that income and expenses should be matched and actually recorded in the period in which they are earned or incurred, rather than the period in which they are actually received or paid, e.g. adjustments for work in progress, payments in advance, outstanding expenses, etc. that we have seen previously (see **Chapter 2**). Thus if work has been carried out within a particular accounting period, then the amount earned in respect of that work should be shown as income. Or if a payment is made in advance it should not be treated as an expense of the period in which it has been paid, but should be shown as an expense in the next period.

7.2.6 The consistency concept

This means that there should be consistency in the accounting methods used for similar items, in the same accounting period and in later periods. If a firm changes the basis on which it values stock or work in progress then the profit figure may be different from the figure that would be obtained had stock or work in progress been valued in the same way. Thus if businesses wish to change the basis on which they value stock, or value assets, then they must mention the effect on the profit of the change in accounting method.

7.2.7 The concept of prudence

This is the principle that profit should not be overstated. Thus income should not be anticipated and should be recorded in the Profit and Loss account only when received in cash, or as assets (e.g. debtors) which can be converted readily into cash. However, provision should be made for all possible known or expected future losses.

7.2.8 The concept of materiality

This means that there is no need to make detailed accounting records of items which are regarded as not material. For example, small items purchased, e.g. biros used in the office, will be treated as part of the expenses in the period in which they are purchased, and there will be no need to record on the balance sheet at the end of the year that the firm has six biros. Firms will decide individually whether an item is material, e.g. for a large firm items costing less than £500 may be treated as not material, if the firm is smaller then it may treat items costing less than £50 as not material. All such items will be treated as expenses and any remaining items will not be shown on the balance sheet, i.e. there is no need to make adjustments for small amounts.

7.3 Accounting bases and policies

Accounting bases are methods which have been developed for applying the accounting concepts to accounting transactions and items. These will vary according to the type of business and business transaction. They can be used, for example, to decide the accounting periods in which income and expenses should be recognised in the profit and loss account, and to decide the amounts at which items are considered material for inclusion in the balance sheet.

Accounting policies are particular accounting bases which are considered by individual businesses to be most appropriate to their particular circumstances for the purpose of giving a true and fair view. Accounting policies used by a business should be disclosed by way of a note to the accounts, e.g. how depreciation is treated, or how work in progress or stock is valued.

7.4 Manufacturing and trading accounts

7.4.1 Introduction and example

We have previously looked at the accounts of solicitors, who derive their income from services, or work done (see **Chapters 1–3**). With a trader, goods will be purchased for resale, there will be an account to record the value of all purchases, and a separate account to record the value of all sales.

EXAMPLE

Gary starts business with £20,000 cash, being the capital he has introduced.

DEBIT the cash book £20,000

CREDIT the capital account £20,000

Cash book

Date	Details	DR	CR	Balance
	Capital	20,000		20,000 DR

Capital account

Date	Details	DR	CR	Balance
	Cash		20,000	20,000 CR

He then buys goods for £10,000 cash.

DEBIT the purchases account (an expense account) £10,000

CREDIT the cash book £10,000 recording the payment out

Purchases

Date	Details	DR	CR	Balance
	Cash	10,000		10,000 DR

Cash book

Date	Details	DR	CR	Balance
	Balance			20,000 DR
	Purchases		10,000	10,000 DR

Gary then buys further goods from Suppliers Ltd for £5,000 on credit.

DEBIT the Purchases account £5,000

CREDIT Suppliers Ltd's account (the creditor) £5,000

Purchases

Date	Details	DR	CR	Balance
	Balance			10,000 DR
	Suppliers Ltd	5,000		15,000 DR

Suppliers Ltd

Date	Details	DR	CR	Balance
	Purchases		5,000	5,000 CR

Gary then sells all his goods for £40,000 cash.

DEBIT the Cash book £40,000

CREDIT the Sales account (income account) £40,000

Cash book

Date	Details	DR	CR	Balance
	Balance			10,000 DR
	Sales	40,000		50,000 DR

Sales

Date	Details	DR	CR	Balance
	Cash		40,000	40,000 CR

7.4.2 Trading account

When Gary draws up his final accounts, a trading account will be drawn up, showing the sales less purchases, to give the gross profit. This will be followed by the profit and loss account, showing income, the gross profit and other income not derived from trading, e.g. interest receivable, less expenses, administrative expenses, financial expenses, etc.

Trading account

Sales	£40,000
Less purchases	£15,000
Gross profit	£25,000

This is a simple form of trading account. Additional items to be taken into account might include sales returns: e.g. where goods have been returned to the business, the sales returns account would be debited and then the cash book or the customer's personal ledger card would be credited. The debit balance on the sales returns account will be deducted from the sales figure, to give net sales. For example:

Sales	£700,000
Less sales returns	£10,000
	£690,000

The purchases figure will have to be adjusted, to take account of any stock held by the trader at the start of the year, and any stock left at the end of the year, to give the actual cost of the goods sold.

EXAMPLE

A trader starts the year with £60,000 worth of goods (opening stock). During the year a further £300,000 worth of goods is purchased, and at the end of the year there is £40,000 worth of goods remaining.

The cost of goods sold is therefore:

Opening stock	60,000	
Plus purchases	300,000	
		360,000
Less closing stock		40,000
Cost of goods sold		320,000

The adjustment for stock will be shown on the Purchases account.

Purchases account

Date	Details	DR	CR	Balance
	Opening stock brought down from previous period	60,000		60,000 DR
	Purchases during the year	300,000		360,000 DR
	Closing stock		40,000	320,000 DR
	Transfer to profit and loss		320,000	—
	Opening stock b/d	40,000		40,000 DR

The Trading and Profit and Loss account would therefore appear as set out below:

Trading and Profit and Loss account for the year ending 31 December 200—

Sales	700,000	
Less returns	10,000	
		690,000
Less		
Cost of goods sold		
Opening stock	60,000	
Plus purchases	300,000	
	360,000	
Less closing stock	40,000	
Cost of goods sold		320,000
GROSS PROFIT		370,000
Less general expenses		100,000
NET PROFIT		270,000

7.4.3 Manufacturing account

If the trader is manufacturing goods for sale, i.e., processing raw materials, then the trading account will be preceded by a manufacturing account, showing the cost of manufacturing the goods sold. This will show all the costs and expenses directly and indirectly incurred in producing the goods. Total costs will be divided between:

(a) *Direct costs*   The prime cost, which is the total of costs directly associated with the finished products, consisting of:
  (i)   direct materials—the cost of the raw materials;
  (ii) direct labour—wages paid to the employees directly involved in producing the goods;
  (iii) direct expenses—e.g., the cost of sub-contracting any process needed to produce the goods;

(b) *Indirect costs*   Works overheads or factory overheads—these are the indirect expenses of production including:
  (i)   indirect materials, e.g., consumable stores (oil to lubricate) and supplies of materials for repairs and maintenance;
  (ii) indirect labour, e.g., supervisors, inspectors, cleaners;
  (iii) indirect expenses, e.g., heat, light, power, rent, depreciation of factory buildings, plant and machinery.

7.4.3.1 Stock and work in progress

Adjustments will have to be made for the closing stock of raw materials, and partly finished goods (work in progress), as well as finished goods. We saw that the stock of finished goods will appear in the trading account (see **4.3.2**); the stock of raw materials and partly finished goods will appear in the manufacturing account.

7.4.4   Example of a manufacturing account

EXAMPLE

Jenny Wren & Co. Clothing Manufacturers

Manufacturing and Trading account for the year to 1 April 200—

	'000	'000
Opening stock of raw materials (cloth)	10,000	
Plus work in progress (partly finished		
clothes)	20,000	
		30,000
Plus purchase of cloth during the year		100,000
		130,000
Less		
Closing stock of raw material (cloth)	15,000	
Closing work in progress (partly		
finished clothes)	30,000	
		45,000
Cost of materials		85,000
Add direct wages		60,000
Prime cost of production		145,000
Add works overheads inc. heat, light,		
power, depreciation etc.		20,000
Carried to trading account (trading		
account section)		165,000
Trading account		
Net sales		350,000
Less cost of sales		
Opening stock of finished clothes	25,000	
Manufacturing account b/d	165,000	
	190,000	
Less closing stock of finished clothes	22,000	
Production cost of clothes sold		168,000
Gross profit		182,000

This will be followed by a Profit and Loss account, showing the gross profit plus any other income, less expenses, e.g., administrative, financial, selling expenses, with the usual adjustments for any payments in advance and outstanding expenses.

The resulting net profit (or loss) will be transferred to the credit (debit if loss) of a sole manufacturer's capital account, or, if there is a partnership, it will be appropriated between the partners and then credited to their current accounts (see **Chapter 6** on partnership accounts). Company accounts are dealt with in **Chapter 8**.

The Balance Sheet will be drawn up in the way previously shown (see **Chapter 3**).

7. 5   Check list

By the end of this chapter you should be able to:

1. understand the accounting concepts and their application to accounts including adjustments made;

2. note accounting bases and policies;

3. understand and draw up a simple trading account;

4. note the structure of a Manufacturing account;

5. use the self test exercises at the end of the chapter to achieve the above.

7.6   Practice exercises

1 From the following figures extracted from the Trial Balance of Dell on 30 November 2004 draw up a trading account for the period.

	DR	CR
Purchases	250,000	
Sales		600,000
Sales returns	30,500	
Stock on 1 Dec 2003	18,600	

Stock on 30 November 2004 is £10,400.

2 Figures extracted from the Trial balance of Kirk are shown below. From these draw up a Trading and Profit and Loss account for Kirk for the period.

Kirk Trial Balance 31 December 200—

	DR	CR
Purchases	35,000	
Sales		99,850
Salaries	22,000	
Stock at 1 Jan	3,945	
General expenses	5,680	
Sales returns	4,500	
Light and heat	1,900	
Rent paid	10,000	

Stock on 31 December 200— is £5,625.

3 The Trial Balance for Zodiac drawn up on 31 March 2004 is shown below:

	DR	CR
Loan		40,000
Drawings	55,000	
Capital		200,000
Stock on 1 April 2003	20,800	
Purchases	95,000	
General expenses	12,560	
Administrative expenses	5,490	
Sales		215,280
Sales returns	10,450	
Car cost price	24,000	

Freehold premises cost price	190,000	
Fixtures and fittings cost price	12,300	
Cash at bank	3,240	
Petty cash	520	
Salaries	30,000	
Debtors	8,900	
Creditors		12,980
	468,260	468,260

Closing stock on 31 March 2004 is £11,000. Depreciation of cars is 15% and on fixtures and fittings 10%. Draw up the Trading and Profit and Loss account and the Balance Sheet for Zodiac.

4 From the Trial Balance of Bucket drawn up on 31 July 200— show the Manufacturing, Trading and Profit and Loss account and the Balance Sheet.

Trial Balance

	DR	CR
Capital		270,000
Drawings	210,000	
Work in progress at start of year	104,000	
Stock of raw material at start of year	65,000	
Stock of finished goods at start of year	89,000	
Purchases of raw materials	521,000	
Sales		2,140,000
Factory wages	400,000	
Office salaries	300,000	
Factory general expenses	56,000	
Office general expenses	32,000	
Factory light/heat	20,000	
Factory rent	120,000	
Office light/heat	10,000	
Office rent	80,000	
Insurance (factory)	10,000	
Insurance (office)	9,000	
Advertising	40,000	
Bad debts	28,000	
Plant and machinery	150,000	
Motor cars	81,000	
Bank account	49,000	
Petty cash	7,000	
Creditors		81,000
Debtors	110,000	
	2,491,000	2,491,000

At 31 July 200— closing stock of raw materials was £90,000, work in progress was £120,000 and stock of finished goods was £112,000. For the purposes of this example please ignore depreciation.

7.7 Suggested answers to practice exercises

1 Trading account for Dell for the year ending 30 November 2004

Sales		600,000
Less returns		30,500
		569,500
LESS COST OF GOODS SOLD		
Opening stock	18,600	
Plus purchases	250,000	
	268,600	
Less closing stock	10,400	
		258,200
Net profit		311,300

2 Kirk Trading and Profit and Loss account for the year ending 31 December 200—

Sales			99,850
Less returns			4,500
			95,350
Less cost of goods sold			
Opening stock	3,945		
Plus Purchases	35,000		
		38,945	
Less closing stock		5,625	
			33,320
GROSS PROFIT			62,030
LESS EXPENSES			
Salaries		22,000	
General expenses		5,680	
Light and heat		1,900	
Rent paid		10,000	
			39,580
NET PROFIT			22,450

3 Zodiac Trading and Profit and Loss account for the year ending 31 March 2004

Sales			215,280
Less returns			10,450
			204,830
LESS COST OF GOODS SOLD			
Opening stock	20,800		
Plus Purchases	95,000		
		115,800	
Less closing stock		11,000	
			104,800

GROSS PROFIT			100,030
LESS EXPENSES			
General expenses	12,560		
Administrative expenses	5,490		
Salaries	30,000		
Depreciation on car	3,600		
Depreciation on fixtures and fittings	1,230		
		52,880	
NET PROFIT			47,150

Zodiac Balance Sheet as at 31 March 2004

Fixed Assets			
Freehold premises cost price		190,000	
Car cost price	24,000		
Less depreciation	3,600		
		20,400	
Fixtures and fittings	12,300		
Less depreciation	1,230		
		11,070	
			221,470
CURRENT ASSETS			
Closing stock	11,000		
Debtors	8,900		
Cash at Bank	3,240		
Petty cash	520		
		23,660	
LESS CURRENT LIABILITIES			
Creditors		12,980	
NET CURRENT ASSETS			10,680
Total			232,150
LESS			
LONG TERM LOAN			40,000
Total			192,150
CAPITAL EMPLOYED			
Capital	200,000		
Add Net Profit	47,150		
		247,150	
Less Drawings		55,000	
TOTAL			192,150

Bucket Manufacturing, Trading and Profit and Loss account for the year ending 31 July 200—.

Manufacturing account

Opening stock raw materials	65,000	
Add opening work in progress	104,000	
		169,000

Plus purchases	521,000	
		690,000
Less closing stock raw materials	90,000	
Closing stock work in progress	120,000	
		210,000
Cost of materials		480,000
Add direct factory wages		400,000
Prime cost		880,000
Add factory light/heat	20,000	
factory rent	120,000	
factory insurance	10,000	
factory general expenses	56,000	
		206,000
Factory cost of production carried down		1,086,000

Trading account

Sales		2,140,000
Less cost of sales		
Opening stock of finished goods	89,000	
Plus cost of production carried down	1,086,000	
	1,175,000	
Less closing stock of finished goods	112,000	
Production costs of goods sold		1,063,000
Gross profit		1,077,000

Profit and Loss account

Gross profit brought down		1,077,000
Less		
office salaries	300,000	
office general expenses	32,000	
office light and heat	10,000	
office rent	80,000	
office insurance	9,000	
advertising	40,000	
bad debts	28,000	
		499,000
Net profit		578,000

Bucket: Balance Sheet as at 31 July 200—

FIXED ASSET		
Plant and machinery	150,000	
Motor cars	81,000	
		231,000

CURRENT ASSETS

Stock raw materials	90,000		
Work in progress	120,000		
Stock of finished goods	112,000		
Debtors	110,000		
Bank account	49,000		
Petty cash	7,000		
		488,000	
Less CURRENT LIABILITIES			
Creditors		81,000	
NET CURRENT ASSETS			407,000
			638,000
Less long-term liabilities			—
TOTAL			638,000
CAPITAL EMPLOYED			
Capital		270,000	
Add net profit	578,000		
Less drawings	210,000		
		368,000	
TOTAL			638,000

Company accounts

8.1 Introduction

This chapter deals with the accounts of limited companies, in particular:

1. Entries on the accounts in respect of share capital and debentures.
2. Profit and Loss accounts—layout and treatment of taxation and dividends, retained profit and reserves.
3. Reports and records under the Companies Acts, including form of the Balance Sheet.
4. Practice exercises.

You may find the following web sites useful:
www.companieshouse.gov.uk
www.dti.gov.uk

8.2 Accounts of limited companies

Companies may be incorporated under the provisions of the Companies Acts 1985 and 1989. These include:

(a) a company limited by shares—a member's liability is limited to any part of the issued price of the member's shares not yet paid to the company;

(b) a company limited by guarantee—a member's liability is limited to the sum that the member undertook to contribute to the company in the event of its being wound up;

(c) an unlimited company with no limit on a member's liability.

We will look at companies limited by shares.

8.2.1 Share capital

The capital of a limited company is divided into shares which will have a nominal value, e.g., £1 each, or £5 or £10. When the company issues shares for cash, the entries are the same as the entries made when a sole proprietor or a partner introduces capital. The capital account will be known as the Share Capital account.

EXAMPLE

A company issues 60,000 £1 ordinary shares for £60,000 cash.

DEBIT the Cash Book
CREDIT the Share Capital Account

Cash book

Date	Details	DR	CR	Balance
	Share capital	60,000		60,000 DR

Share capital account
£1 ordinary shares

Date	Details	DR	CR	Balance
	Cash		60,000	60,000 CR

A company may issue the shares at par, i.e., sell the shares at their nominal value. Thus if the company above issued 60,000 shares at a nominal value of £1 for £1 each, then the entries would be as above.

The Balance Sheet would show:

FIXED ASSETS		XX
CURRENT ASSETS		
Cash	60,000	
CAPITAL EMPLOYED		
Share capital £1 ordinary shares	60,000	

8.2.2   Issuing shares at a premium

A company may, however, set a price which is higher than the nominal value, when it will issue the shares at a premium. For example, the company issues 60,000 £1 shares at £1.20 each, giving total cash of £72,000. The Cash book will be debited with the total amount received, broken down into the nominal value of £60,000 and the premium of £12,000. The Share Capital account will be credited with the £60,000 and the Share Premium account will be credited with the £12,000.

Cash book

Date	Details	DR	CR	Balance
	Share capital	60,000		60,000 DR
	Share premium	12,000		72,000 DR

Share capital account

Date	Details	DR	CR	Balance
	Cash		60,000	60,000 CR

Share premium account

Date	Details	DR	CR	Balance
	Cash		12,000	12,000 CR

The Balance Sheet would show:

FIXED ASSETS		XX
CURRENT ASSETS		
Cash		72,000
CAPITAL EMPLOYED		
Share capital £1 ordinary shares	60,000	
Share premium	12,000	
		72,000

Note that a company may not issue all the shares which it is authorised to sell. The shares that are sold are called the issued capital.

Different types of shares may be offered, e.g., ordinary, preference or deferred shares. There may also be voting and non-voting shares.

8.2.3 Preference shares

These will get an agreed percentage rate of dividend before the ordinary shareholders, i.e., they have priority. There may be different classes of preference shares, e.g.:

8.2.3.1 Non-cumulative preference shares

These receive the dividend before the ordinary shareholders up to an agreed percentage. However, if the amount paid in a year is less than the maximum agreed percentage, the shareholder cannot claim the shortage in the next year or years.

8.2.3.2 Cumulative preference shares

In this case, if a full dividend is not received in a year, the arrears of dividend can be carried forward and paid together with the dividend due in the next year before the ordinary shareholders are entitled to receive any dividend.

8.2.3.3 Participating preference shares

In this case the shareholders may also have the right to participate in any remaining profits after the ordinary shareholders have received their dividend.

8.2.3.4 Redeemable preference shares

In such a case the shares will be repaid by the company at some time in the future.

This may sound complicated, but the accounting entries for the issue of all types of preference shares will be the same. A separate share capital account for each type of shares will be opened.

EXAMPLE

A company issues 50,000 ordinary shares at £1 each, and 10,000 7% preference shares at £1.

DEBIT the Cash Book for each
CREDIT the relevant share account for each

Cash book

Date	Details	DR	CR	Balance
	Ordinary shares	50,000		50,000 DR
	7% preference shares	10,000		60,000 DR

Ordinary share capital account

Date	Details	DR	CR	Balance
	Cash		50,000	50,000 CR

7% Preference Share Capital account

Date	Details	DR	CR	Balance
	Cash		10,000	10,000 CR

Note: the cash received from the share issue will be used in the business, e.g., to purchase assets.

8.2.4   Debentures

A debenture is a bond which acknowledges a loan to a company and which bears a fixed rate of interest. As this is really a type of loan to the company, the debenture holder is not a member of the company like a shareholder and the interest will be paid whether the company makes a profit or not. A debenture may be redeemable, i.e., repayable at or before a specified date, or irredeemable and thus only repayable when the company is liquidated.

When debentures are issued, then the entries will be similar to those shown on the issue of share capital.

EXAMPLE

A company issues debentures of £60,000 at fixed interest of 10%.

DEBIT the Cash Book
CREDIT the Debenture stock account

Cash book

Date	Details	DR	CR	Balance
	10% debentures	60,000		60,000 DR

10% Debenture stock

Date	Details	DR	CR	Balance
	Cash		60,000	60,000 CR

8.2.5   Issuing debentures at a discount

EXAMPLE

A company issues 12% (interest) debentures at a discount of 10%. The debentures have a nominal value of £40,000. With the discount of 10%, i.e., £4,000, the cash received will be £36,000. The 12% Debenture account will be credited with £40,000, broken down into the cash received and the amount of the discount. The Cash book will be debited with the cash received, and a Debenture discount account will be debited with the discount.

12% Debenture account

Date	Details	DR	CR	Balance
	Cash		36,000	36,000 CR
	Discount		4,000	40,000 CR

Cash book

Date	Details	DR	CR	Balance
	12% debenture	36,000		36,000 DR

Debenture discount account

Date	Details	DR	CR	Balance
	12% debenture	4,000		4,000 DR

When the company redeems the debentures, it will repay them at the full price, i.e., £40,000. This is shown by the credit balance on the Debenture account, i.e., the company owes £40,000. The debit balance on the Debenture Discount account shows the loss in issuing the debenture. If, e.g., the ordinary share capital of the company was £100,000 the Balance Sheet would show:

LONG-TERM LIABILITY	
12% Debenture	40,000
CAPITAL EMPLOYED	
Ordinary share capital	100,000

The debit balance on the Debenture Discount account will be shown as a deduction in the Capital Employed section until it has been written off.

LONG-TERM LIABILITY		
12% debenture		40,000
CAPITAL EMPLOYED		
Ordinary share capital		100,000
Reserves say (see **8.2.6**)	80,000	
Less debenture discount	4,000	
		76,000
		176,000

8.3 Limited companies' Profit and Loss accounts

A company may draw up its own final accounts for internal use in any way it considers most suitable. However, when the accounts are sent to the Registrar of Companies or to a shareholder, the Companies Acts lay down the information that must be shown, and also how it should be shown, in line with European Community requirements.

There is a choice of layout, four forms for Profit and Loss account, and two forms for the Balance Sheet.

The (vertical form) Format 1 Profit and Loss account is set out below:

Profit and Loss account

1. Turnover
2. Cost of sales
3. Gross profit or loss
4. Distribution costs
5. Administrative expenses
6. Other operating income
7. Income from shares in group undertakings
8. Income from participating interests
9. Income from other fixed asset investments
10. Other interest receivable and similar income
11. Amounts written off investments
12. Interest payable and similar charges
13. Tax on profit or loss on ordinary activities
14. Profit or loss on ordinary activities after taxation
15. Exceptional income
16. Exceptional charges
17. Exceptional profit or loss
18. Tax on Exceptional profit or loss
19. Other taxes not shown under the above items
20. Profit or loss for the financial year

A company's Profit and Loss account is similar to that of a sole trader or a partnership. However, there will be some differences.

Salaries paid to directors will be shown as an expense of the company (like wages of employees). Contrast this with a salary paid to a partner, which was shown as an allocation of profit in the Appropriation account. The Appropriation account shows how the net profit will be used. After the net profit has been calculated, tax will have to be considered, and provided for. Once this has been done then dividends should be provided for, and then any surplus profit may be retained or transferred to reserves.

8.3.1   Appropriation of profit—taxation

Corporation tax is NOT an expense of the company but is regarded as an appropriation of profit.

For large companies corporation tax is paid by quarterly equal instalments. The instalments are paid on the basis of anticipated current year liabilities for tax. The quarterly instalments start in month 7 of the accounting year, so that two instalments will be within the accounting year, i.e., month 7 and month 10. Medium and small companies do not have to pay their corporation tax by instalments.

To provide for taxation, the Appropriation account above will be debited (remember this forms part of the double-entry system), and a Taxation account will be credited. The rate of corporation tax at present is 19% for small companies and 30% for large companies. From 2002 there is a new starter rate of corporation tax at zero for companies with profits up to £10,000. There is a sliding scale between £10,000 and £50,000 when the small companies' rate comes into force.

Large companies are those whose taxable profits are at least £1.5 million per annum. Medium size companies are those with taxable profits of between £0.3 million and £1.5 million per annum. Small companies are those with taxable profits of up to £0.3 million per annum. For convenience, in the following examples, rates have been taken that are easy to calculate.

EXAMPLE

The net profit of a company is £200,000. Assuming the rate of corporation tax to be 19% the tax would be £38,000.

DEBIT the Profit and Loss Appropriation account
CREDIT the Taxation Account

Profit and Loss account

Net profit	200,000
Less corporation tax (debit)	38,000
	162,000

Taxation account

Date	Details	DR	CR	Balance
	Profit and loss account		38,000	38,000 CR

These entries do not involve any payment or transfer of cash. The net profit is merely appropriated, and the credit balance on the taxation account shows that £38,000 is due to the Inland Revenue. Until the tax is paid this will be shown as a current liability on the Balance Sheet. When the tax is actually paid, the cash book will be credited, and the taxation account debited. Continuing the above example:

Cash book

Date	Details	DR	CR	Balance
	Balance say			150,000 DR
	Taxation—Inland Revenue		38,000	112,000 DR

Taxation account

Date	Details	DR	CR	Balance
	Balance			38,000 CR
	Cash	38,000		Nil

8.3.2 Deferred taxation

This is to take account of the fact that the figure for profits shown on the company's profit and loss account may not be the same as the figure for profits on which tax is payable. The reasons for this include:

(a) the difference between the figures used for depreciation by the company each year and the figures for capital allowances allowed by the Inland Revenue;

(b) that the Inland Revenue may not allow all the figures that have been shown as expenses on the Profit and Loss account.

Where there is a difference between the figures used for depreciation and the capital allowances, this will lead to timing differences, as the capital allowances allowed by the Inland Revenue may fall into different periods from the depreciation figures used by the company, even though in the end the amount overall may be the same.

So that a true picture can be given to, e.g., shareholders, deferred taxation is used to adjust the tax shown on the Appropriation account. The tax will be adjusted to show the tax on the profit based on depreciation used by the company, rather than based on the capital allowances allowed by the Inland Revenue.

Where the taxation payable for the year is lower than it would be based on the company's own figures then:

DEBIT the Profit and Loss Appropriation account
CREDIT the Deferred Taxation account.

The credit balance will be shown as a separate item on the Balance Sheet under provisions for liabilities and charges.

Where the taxation payable is higher than it would be based on the company's calculation of profit then the entries would be:

CREDIT the Profit and Loss Appropriation account
DEBIT Deferred Taxation account

EXAMPLE

Year 1
Profit based on the company's
   calculations: £200,000
Tax payable based on taxable profit of
£160,000 at 19%   30,400
Deferred taxation   7,600   38,000
                                      _____   _____
Balance retained profit   162,000

Taxation account

	DR	CR	Balance
		30,400	30,400 CR

Deferred Taxation account

	DR	CR	Balance
		7,600	7,600 CR

The Balance Sheet would show:
Creditors due within one year

taxation	30,400	
Provisions for liabilities and charges		
Deferred taxation	7,600	

Year 2

Profit based on company's calculations		£200,000
Less tax based on taxable profit of £240,000 at 19%	− 45,600	
Add deferred tax adjustment	+ 7,600	
		38,000
Balance retained profit		162,000

Taxation account

	DR	CR	Balance
		45,600	45,600 CR

Deferred Taxation account

	DR	CR	Balance
Brought down			7,600 CR
Year 2	7,600		nil

The Balance Sheet would show:

Creditors due within one year taxation	£45,600
Provisions for liabilities and charges	
Deferred taxation	—

8.3.3 Dividends

The directors of a company will propose that part of the net profit be distributed to the shareholders, usually expressed as a percentage of the nominal value of the shares.

8.3.3.1 Appropriation of dividend

DEBIT the Appropriation account
CREDIT the Dividend account

EXAMPLE

A company declares a dividend of 10% in respect of ordinary shares with a nominal value of £100,000, being £10,000. Net profit after tax is £97,200, The directors will not allocate all the profit remaining after taxation, as:

(a) Profit will need to be retained to run the business, or for expansion.

(b) Net profit will not necessarily be represented by cash at the bank.

Profit and Loss account

Net profit	120,000
Less corporation tax (debit)	22,800
	97,200
Less dividend	10,000
	87,200

Dividend account

Date	Details	DR	CR	Balance
	Profit and Loss account		10,000	10,000 CR

The amount shown on the dividend account shows the amount due for the dividend. This will be shown as a current liability on the balance sheet. The size of the dividend will be agreed at the annual general meeting of the company, when the accounts are agreed. The dividend can then be paid. Continuing the above example:

8.3.3.2   Payment of dividend

CREDIT the Cash Book.
DEBIT the Dividend Account.

Cash book

Date	Details	DR	CR	Balance
	Balance say			25,000 DR
	Dividend		10,000	15,000 DR

Dividend account

Date	Details	DR	CR	Balance
	Balance			10,000 CR
	Cash	10,000		Nil

8.3.3.3   Payment of interim dividend

If the company has paid an interim dividend before the end of the year, the entries to record the payment of the interim dividend will be the same as the payment of the dividend above. The interim dividend will be shown in the appropriation section of the profit and loss account, in the same way that the end of year dividend was shown.

EXAMPLE

During the year a company pays an interim dividend of £10,000. At the end of the year the net profit after taxation is £80,000. A final dividend of £15,000 is recommended by the directors.

1. Payment of the interim dividend during the year.

   CREDIT Cash Book

   DEBIT Dividend Account

Cash book

Date	Details	DR	CR	Balance
	Balance say			48,000 DR
	Interim dividend		10,000	38,000 DR

Dividend account

Date	Details	DR	CR	Balance
	Cash—interim dividend	10,000		10,000 DR

2. Final dividend at end of year

   Profit and Loss account

Net profit after taxation		80,000
Less dividend		
interim	10,000	
final	15,000	
		25,000
		55,000

Dividend account

Date	Details	DR	CR	Balance
	Balance			10,000 DR
	(interim dividend)			
	Profit and Loss account			
	Interim dividend		10,000	Nil
	Final dividend		15,000	15,000 CR

The £15,000 credit balance on the dividend account will be shown on the Balance Sheet as a current liability, being the amount due to the shareholders. When the final dividend is paid the entries will be as shown previously.

8.3.4 Appropriation—retained profit and reserves

After providing for taxation and dividends, the balance of the net profit is retained on the Appropriation account, or it may be transferred to a reserve account. Either way it will be shown as a reserve on the Balance Sheet, in the capital employed section (like the net profit due to a sole proprietor).

Net profit is not necessarily represented by cash—it is represented by an increase in recorded net assets. Thus 'retention of profit' or 'reserves' are merely retaining in the business the assets which are attributable to profit.

The balance of net profit will be transferred to a reserve account if it is to be retained for a specific purpose, e.g., replacement of fixed assets, or redemption (repayment) of debentures. The entries to record a transfer to a reserve account are:

DEBIT the Appropriation account
CREDIT the Reserve account

EXAMPLE

Net profit after taxation is £40,000. A dividend of £10,000 is declared. Of the remaining £30,000, £16,000 is transferred to a reserve account.

Net profit after taxation	£40,000
Less dividend	£10,000
	£30,000
Transferred to reserve	£16,000
	£14,000

Note: both the balance of £14,000 and the reserve of £16,000 will be shown on the balance sheet as part of the capital employed.

Capital employed		
Share capital		100,000 (say)
Reserves		
Special reserve	16,000	
Profit and loss	14,000	
		30,000
		130,000

As mentioned in **3.4.1.2**, this is the same principle as in the Balance Sheet of a sole proprietor, where the net profit would be shown added to their capital.

The share capital and reserves shown above are known as the shareholders' equity, or the ordinary shareholders' funds. These will be represented by the assets of the company, shown in the Employment of Capital section of the Balance Sheet.

In the event of the company being wound up the shareholders would be entitled to the return of their capital, plus a share in the surplus assets of the company, represented by the reserves.

8.3.5 Provisions, reserves and liabilities

A provision, as we have seen in **5.1.3**, may be debited to the Profit and Loss account, or it may be debited to the Appropriation account of a company. A provision may be created in respect of a known liability which exists at the date of the Balance Sheet where the amount cannot be determined with substantial accuracy. The provision may, for example, be for (estimated) doubtful debts, or depreciation, which would be debited to the Profit and Loss section. Provision may also be made for estimated taxation, or a dividend, which would be debited to the Appropriation section.

Provisions are in contrast to liabilities, which are amounts owed and which can be determined with substantial accuracy, e.g., rent due. Provisions may also be contrasted with reserves, which can only be debited to the Appropriation section, and which do not relate to any liability or loss which is known to exist at the time of the Balance Sheet.

Definitions of these are contained in the Companies Act 1985, sch. 9, para. 32.

8.3.6 Capital and revenue reserves

8.3.6.1 Revenue reserves

These are reserves transferred from the Profit and Loss appropriation account (i.e., retained profit) which can be general, or for some particular purpose, e.g., a foreign exchange reserve account, to meet any possible losses through devaluation of a foreign currency. General revenue reserve accounts may be used in future years, should profit be insufficient for dividends, when the reserve may be used for the payment of dividends, provided that cash is available. (If this was done then the revenue reserve account would be debited and the Profit and Loss appropriation account would be credited.)

General reserve accounts may also be used to increase the capital required with inflation as the amount of working capital required by the company will increase. When we looked at final accounts in **Chapter 2**, we saw on the Balance Sheet a figure for net current assets, or working capital—this means the portion of capital invested in the business which is left to run the business after providing the fixed assets.

8.3.6.2 Capital reserves

These are not available for distribution by way of dividend under the Companies Acts.

Capital reserves which cannot be used for the declaration of dividends payable in cash are:

(a) capital redemption reserves;

(b) a share premium account;

(c) a revaluation reserve.

Capital redemption reserves include a preference shares redemption reserve, which can be used to redeem redeemable preference shares, or, e.g., a debenture redemption reserve, which can be used to redeem debentures on the date specified. A company may transfer a certain amount of net profit each year to a redemption reserve account.

A share premium account is needed when the company issues shares at a premium—the additional amount over the nominal value of the shares is shown in the share premium account.

A revaluation reserve is used when a company revalues its assets. If the value of the assets is increased, then there must be a corresponding increase in the capital employed section of the balance sheet. The asset account is to be debited and the revaluation reserve account is to be credited. This cannot be used to pay a dividend as it merely represents the increase in value of the assets.

8.3.7 Capitalisation of reserves: bonus issue of shares

Although reserves may not be available for distribution by way of dividend, they may be capitalised by issuing bonus or free shares to shareholders.

EXAMPLE

A company has an issued share capital of £40,000,000 £1 ordinary shares and general reserves of £15,000,000. It makes a bonus issue of one share for every four shares held. The bonus issue will therefore be £10,000,000.

Before the bonus issue the Balance Sheet would show:

	000
Capital employed	
Share capital	40,000
General reserves	15,000
	55,000

After the bonus issue the Balance Sheet will show:

	000
Capital employed	
Share capital	50,000
General reserves	5,000
	55,000

The entries on the accounts would be:

Share capital account

Date	Details	DR	CR	Balance
		000	000	000
	Balance			40,000 CR
	General reserve		10,000	50,000 CR

General reserve account

Date	Details	DR	CR	Balance
		000	000	000
	Balance			15,000 CR
	Share capital	10,000		5,000 CR

Although each shareholder will own more shares, these will be worth less individually, as the shares are still represented by the same amount of assets. Any dividend payable in respect of the shares may be at a lower percentage, as the same net profit will have to be apportioned between the shares.

8.3.8 Sinking funds

As mentioned in **8.2.4**, retained net profit is not equivalent to cash, it merely represents an increase in assets. If cash is required then it will be necessary, at the same time as profit is transferred to a reserve, to transfer the required amount of cash, or easily realisable assets, to a sinking fund (or reserve fund) which can then be used when needed.

EXAMPLE

A company transfers £200,000 to debenture redemption reserve from net profit after taxation and dividends of £500,000. It also transfers £200,000 from the cash at the bank to a deposit account, to be used as a reserve fund for debenture redemption.

Profit and Loss Appropriation account
Net profit after tax and dividend   £500,000
Transfer to debenture redemption reserve   £200,000
                                           £300,000

Debenture redemption reserve account

Date	Details	DR	CR	Balance
	Profit and loss		200,000	200,000 CR

Cash book

Date	Details	DR	CR	Balance
	Balance say			350,000 DR
	Debenture redemption reserve		200,000	150,000 DR
	(sinking) fund			

Debenture redemption reserve (sinking) fund account

Date	Details	DR	CR	Balance
	Cash	200,000		200,000 DR

The Balance Sheet would show:

FIXED ASSETS
Debenture redemption   200,000
reserve (sinking fund)
NET CURRENT ASSETS
CAPITAL EMPLOYED
Share capital   XX
Debenture redemption reserve 200,000

8.4 Reports and records required under the Companies Acts

The Companies Acts 1985 and 1989 set out the requirements: every company must maintain adequate accounting records, and prepare financial statements in respect of each accounting year.

At the annual general meeting of shareholders the following should be presented:

(a) a Profit and Loss account;

(b) a Balance Sheet;

(c) a directors' report;

(d) an auditors' report.

The auditors must confirm the requirement that the Balance Sheet shall give a true and fair view of the state of affairs of the company as at the end of its financial year, and every Profit and Loss account shall give a true and fair view of the profit or loss of the company for the financial year. Accounting standards and practices should be observed.

The accounting concepts previously mentioned in **7.1** must be used:

(a) the going concern concept;

(b) accounting principles must be applied consistently from one year to the next;

(c) the concept of prudence;

(d) the accruals or matching concept.

Historical cost and alternative accounting rules are prescribed, e.g., current cost accounting. This is outside the scope of this book. The publicity and filing requirements of companies will vary according to their size. Although small and medium size companies must present a full set of accounts to their shareholders they can file modified reports with the Registrar of Companies.

Except for small and medium size companies there is a requirement under the Companies Act 1989 that a statement should be given explaining whether the accounts have been prepared in accordance with applicable accounting standards and giving details of, and the reasons for, any material departures.

There are changes to the accounting requirements in the Companies Act 1985. These come into force for accounts for financial years beginning on or after 1 January 2005.

All companies (except charities) will have the option to prepare their individual accounts using International Accounting Standards rather than UK GAAP (Generally Accepted Accounting Principles). Non-publicly traded companies will also have the option to prepare their consolidated accounts using International Accounting Standards.

All companies using UK GAAP have a new accounting option to use fair value accounting for financial instruments, investment property and/or living plants and animals. There are also further changes to the requirements in respect of where proposed dividends are disclosed in the accounts, how certain items must be presented in the balance sheet and profit and loss account and disclosure of information on derivatives.

8.4.1 Small and medium size companies

A company is defined in the Companies Acts as small or medium sized for a financial year if, both for that year and the preceding year, it satisfies any two or more of the following conditions:

Condition	Small company	Medium size company
Turnover not exceeding	£5.6 million	£22.8 million
Balance sheet total not exceeding	£2.8 million	£11.4 million
Employees	50 or fewer	250
Modifications applicable:		
Directors' report	Not required	Required
Profit and loss account	Not required	Abbreviated
Balance sheet	Only main headings and amounts required but aggregate debtors/ creditors due after more than one year must be disclosed	Full required

Particulars of salaries of directors and higher paid employees	Not required	Required

There are also modifications to the notes to the accounts.

8.4.2 The form of the Balance Sheet

There are two formats, the vertical form and the horizontal form. The vertical format is set out below:

Balance Sheet: format 1—the vertical

A CALLED UP SHARE CAPITAL NOT PAID*
B FIXED ASSETS
I Intangible assets
   1 Development costs
   2 Concessions, patents, licences, trademarks and similar rights and assets
   3 Goodwill
   4 Payments on account
II Tangible assets
   1 Land and buildings
   2 Plant and machinery
   3 Fixtures, fittings, tools and equipment
   4 Payments on account and assets in course of construction
III Investments
   1 Shares in group undertakings
   2 Loans to group undertakings
   3 Participating interests
   4 Loans to undertakings in which the company has a participating interest
   5 Other investments other than loans
   6 Other loans
   7 Own shares
C CURRENT ASSETS
I Stocks
   1 Raw materials and consumables
   2 Work in progress
   3 Finished goods and goods for resale
   4 Payments on account
II Debtors
   1 Trade debtors
   2 Amounts owed by group undertakings
   3 Amounts owed by undertakings in which the company has a participating interest
   4 Other debtors
   5 Called up share capital not paid*
   6 Prepayments and accrued income**
III Investments
   1 Shares in group undertakings
   2 Own shares
   3 Other investments
IV Cash at bank and in hand
D PREPAYMENTS AND ACCRUED INCOME**
E CREDITORS: AMOUNTS FALLING DUE WITHIN ONE YEAR
   1 Debenture loans
   2 Bank loans and overdrafts

---

cont.

3   Payments received on account
4   Trade creditors
5   Bills of exchange payable
6   Amounts owed to group undertakings
7   Amounts owed to undertakings in which the company has a participating interest
8   Other creditors including taxation and social security
9   Accruals and deferred income***
F   NET CURRENT ASSETS (LIABILITIES)
G   TOTAL ASSETS LESS CURRENT LIABILITIES
H   CREDITORS: AMOUNTS FALLING DUE AFTER MORE THAN ONE YEAR
1   Debenture loans
2   Bank loans and overdrafts
3   Payments received on account
4   Trade creditors
5   Bills of exchange payable
6   Amounts owed to group undertakings
7   Amounts owed to related undertakings in which the company has a participating interest
8   Other creditors including taxation and social security
9   Accruals and deferred income***
I   PROVISIONS FOR LIABILITIES AND CHARGES
1   Pensions and similar obligations
2   Taxation, including deferred taxation
3   Other provisions
J   ACCRUALS AND DEFERRED INCOME***
K   CAPITAL AND RESERVES
I   Called up share capital
II   Share premium account
III Revaluation reserve
IV   Other reserves
1   Capital redemption reserve
2   Reserve for own shares
3   Reserves provided for by the articles of association
4   Other reserves
V   PROFIT AND LOSS ACCOUNT
* ** *** These items may be shown in either of the two positions indicated.

Items preceded by letters or Roman numerals must be disclosed on the face of the Balance Sheet, e.g., B fixed assets, KI called up share capital, but those with ordinary Arabic numbers, e.g., 1,2,3, may be combined where they are not material or the combination aids assessment of the company's affairs. Where they are combined the details of each item should be shown in the notes to the accounts.

8.4.2.1 Public companies and the Stock Exchange

Shares of most public companies are dealt with on the Stock Exchange. Private companies cannot issue their shares to the public, their shares cannot be bought and sold on the Stock Exchange. Sale and purchase of shares on the Stock Exchange will have no effect on the accounting entries made in the company's books. However, the price of the shares on the Stock Exchange will affect, e.g., the price at which any new shares are to be issued.

8.4.3 Example Balance Sheet

What follows is an example of a balance sheet using the format required by the Companies Acts.

Balance Sheet as at—

	'000	'000	'000
FIXED ASSETS			
Intangible assets			
Goodwill		10,000	
Tangible assets			
Premises	200,000		
Machinery	80,000		
Motor cars	40,000		
		320,000	
			330,000
CURRENT ASSETS			
Stock	30,000		
Debtors	26,000		
Cash at bank	20,000		
		76,000	
LESS CREDITORS			
Amounts falling due within one year			
Proposed dividend	10,000		
Creditors	18,000		
Corporation tax due	9,000		
		37,000	
			39,000
TOTAL ASSETS LESS CURRENT LIABILITIES			369,000
CREDITORS			
Amounts falling due after more than one year			90,000
TOTAL			279,000
CAPITAL AND RESERVES			
Authorised and issued fully paid ordinary £1 shares		240,000	
Share premium account		13,000	
General reserve		15,000	
Profit and Loss account		11,000	
TOTAL			279,000

8.5 Check list

By the end of this chapter you should be able to:

1. appreciate that shares can be issued as the capital of a company;
2. appreciate that a company can also be funded by loans and debentures;

3. appreciate the structure of a company's Profit and Loss account;

4. understand that taxation is not an expense of a company, but will be an appropriation of profit;

5. understand that dividends will be an appropriation of profit and the treatment of interim dividends;

6. note the treatment of retained profit and reserves;

7. note the reports and records required under the Companies Acts and a form of a company's Balance Sheet;

8. complete some of the practice exercises at the end of the chapter.

8.6 Practice exercises

1 Explain what would be shown on a company's Balance Sheet after it has issued for cash 100,000 £1 ordinary shares at a price of £3.00 per share.

2 A company estimates its taxation liability at the end of the year to be £40,000. Explain where this would be recorded on the company's final accounts.

3 Look at the following abbreviated company's Balance Sheet. Would the directors be able to authorise payment of a cash dividend to shareholders totalling £30,000?

Fixed Assets			800,000
Current Assets			
Stock	45,000		
Debtors	32,000		
Cash at Bank	15,000		
		92,000	
Current liabilities			
Taxation	12,000		
Creditors	26,000		
		38,000	
Net Current Assets			54,000
			854,000
Capital Employed			
Share Capital	700,000		
Reserves	154,000		
			£854,000

4 From the following trial balance of Randall Limited drawn up on 31 March 200—, draw up the Trading and Profit and Loss account and the Balance Sheet for the year ending 31 March 200—.

Trial Balance	DR	CR
Ordinary share capital		120,000
10% preference share capital		25,000
Debentures		20,000
Buildings	150,000	
Equipment	45,000	

Motor cars	20,000	
Accumulated depreciation: equipment		5,000
Accumulated depreciation: motor cars		10,000
Stock at start of year	19,000	
Sales		375,000
Purchases	149,000	
Wages	40,000	
Directors' remuneration	70,000	
Motor expenses	6,000	
Rates insurance	3,000	
General expenses	19,000	
Debenture interest payable	2,000	
Debtors	29,000	
Creditors		18,000
Cash at bank	26,000	
Interim ordinary dividend paid	10,000	
General reserve		15,000
	588,000	588,000

Additional information required to complete the accounts:

    stock at the end of the year is £21,000;

    depreciation on equipment is £2,000, and on motor cars is £5,000;

    taxation is estimated at £20,000;

    the preference share dividend is £2,500; and

    the final dividend for the ordinary shareholders is £2,000.

5 The Trial Balance of Campion Limited as at 31 December 200— was as follows:

	DR	CR
	'000	'000
Share capital ordinary £1 shares		350,000
Reserves		32,000
Profit and loss account 1 January 200—		10,560
Freehold premises at cost	320,000	
Machinery at cost	70,000	
Accumulated depreciation on machinery		14,000
Purchases	310,000	
Sales		483,000
General expenses	40,000	
Wages	40,000	
Directors' fees	50,000	
Light and heat	1,500	
Bad debts	2,000	
Debtors	30,060	
Creditors		25,000
Stock as at 1 January 200—	41,000	
Cash at bank	10,000	
	914,560	914,560

Additional information is as follows:

stock as at 31 December 200— is	38,000
expenses due amount to	2,400
tax due is	9,090
prepayments amount to	4,200
a dividend is proposed	17,500
a provision for doubtful debts is suggested for this year	1,000
depreciation for this year on machinery at cost is 10%.	

Draw up a Trading and Profit and Loss account for the year ending 31 December 200— and a Balance Sheet as at 31 December 200—.

6 From the Trial Balance of Down and Out Limited shown below, draw up a Trading and Profit and Loss account and a Balance Sheet, in the format required under the Companies Acts.

Trial Balance as at 31 December 200—

	DR	CR
	'000	'000
Ordinary share capital £1 shares fully paid		160,000
12% debentures repayable in 2006		40,000
Goodwill at cost	20,000	
Buildings	150,000	
Fixtures and fittings	40,000	
Motor cars	25,000	
Accumulated depreciation: fixtures and fittings		8,000
Accumulated depreciation: motor cars		10,000
Stock as at 1 January 200—	23,000	
Sales		179,000
Purchases	70,000	
Salaries/wages	33,000	
Directors' fees	39,000	
Motor expenses	2,500	
Council tax	2,300	
General expenses	11,400	
Debenture interest	6,000	
Debtors	26,500	
Creditors		19,900
Cash at bank	13,200	
General reserve		15,000
Share premium account		16,000
Interim ordinary dividend paid	3,000	
Profit and Loss account 1 Jan 200—		17,000
	464,900	464,900

The following should be taken into account:

	'000
Stock at the end of the year	26,000
depreciation on cars for the year	5,000
depreciation on fixtures was	4,000
proposed final dividend is	2,000
provision for corporation tax due is	2,640

7 From the Trial Balance of Rosa Limited following, draw up a Trading and Profit and Loss account and a Balance Sheet.

Trial Balance as at 31 December 200—

	DR	CR
Premises	310,000	
Fixtures at cost	50,000	
Accumulated depreciation on fixtures		5,000
Stock at the start of the year	21,000	
Debtors	18,000	
Cash at bank	17,000	
Creditors		19,000
Share capital		320,000
Reserves		6,500
Purchases	110,000	
Sales		310,000
Salaries	35,000	
Council tax	3,000	
Office expenses	6,000	
Sundry expenses	500	
Directors' fees	90,000	
	660,500	660,500

Note the following:

Stock at the end of the year was	23,000
outstanding expenses were	1,000
depreciation on fixtures and fittings was	5,000
taxation is estimated at	11,700
the proposed dividend totals	16,000
transfer to reserves	10,000

8.7 Suggested answers to practice exercises

1 The Balance Sheet would show a current asset of cash of £300,000 and in the Capital Employed section share capital £1 ordinary shares at £100,000 and share premium at £200,000.

2 The taxation would be shown as a deduction from net profit in the Appropriation section. It would also be shown as a liability in current liabilities on the Balance Sheet.

3 Although the company has net current assets of £54,000 it only has £15,000 cash, it is likely this will be needed to pay creditors etc. If stock could be sold and debtors paid then the company may be able to consider a cash distribution. Note that reserves in the Capital Employed section are not cash, nor are they necessarily represented by cash. Reserves show the total due to shareholders, and only reflect any increase in assets.

4 **Randall Limited: Trading and Profit and Loss account for the year ending 31 March 200—**

Sales			375,000
Less cost of goods sold			
Opening stock	19,000		
Add purchases	149,000		
	168,000		
Less closing stock	21,000		
			147,000
Gross profit			228,000
Less expenses			
Wages	40,000		
Motor expenses	6,000		
Directors' remuneration	70,000		
Rates and insurance	3,000		
General expenses	19,000		
Debenture interest payable	2,000		
Depreciation on equipment	2,000		
Depreciation on cars	5,000		
			147,000
Profit before taxation			81,000
Taxation			20,000
Profit after taxation			61,000
Less appropriation			
Preference share dividend		2,500	
Ordinary share dividend			
Interim paid	10,000		
Final dividend	2,000		
		12,000	
			14,500
Reserves (retained profit)			46,500

Randall Limited: Balance Sheet as at 31 March 200—

FIXED ASSETS			
Buildings		150,000	
Equipment	45,000		
Less depreciation	7,000		
		38,000	
Motor cars	20,000		
Less depreciation	15,000		
		5,000	
			193,000
CURRENT ASSETS			
Stock	21,000		

Debtors	29,000		
Cash at bank	26,000		
		76,000	
Less			
CURRENT LIABILITIES			
Creditors	18,000		
Preference share dividend	2,500		
Final dividend	2,000		
Taxation	20,000		
		42,500	
NET CURRENT ASSETS			33,500
TOTAL ASSETS LESS CURRENT LIABILITIES			226,500
Less			
Debentures			20,000
			206,500
CAPITAL AND RESERVES			
Ordinary share capital		120,000	
Preference shares		25,000	
		145,000	
Reserves	15,000		
This year	46,500		
		61,500	
			206,500

5 **Campion Limited: Trading and Profit and Loss account for the year ending 31 December 200—**

	'000	'000	'000
Sales			483,000
Less cost of goods sold			
Opening stock	41,000		
Add purchases	310,000		
	351,000		
Less closing stock	38,000		
			313,000
Gross profit			170,000
Less expenses			
General expenses	40,000		
Wages	40,000		
Directors' fees	50,000		
Light and heat	1,500		
Bad debts	2,000		
Provision for doubtful debts	1,000		
Depreciation: machinery	7,000		
Add outstanding expenses	2,400		

		143,900
Less prepaid		4,200
		139,700
Net profit		30,300
Less provision for taxation		9,090
Profit after taxation		21,210
Add retained profit from last year		10,560
		31,770
Less proposed dividend		17,500
Retained profit carried forward to next year		14,270

Campion Limited: Balance Sheet as at 31 December 200—

FIXED ASSETS	'000	'000	'000
Premises at cost		320,000	
Machinery at cost	70,000		
Less accumulated depreciation	21,000		
		49,000	
			369,000
CURRENT ASSETS			
Stock		38,000	
Debtors	30,060		
Less provision	1,000		
		29,060	
Cash at bank		10,000	
Prepayment		4,200	
		81,260	
LESS CURRENT LIABILITIES			
Creditors	25,000		
Oustanding expenses	2,400		
Proposed dividend	17,500		
Corporation tax due	9,090		
		53,990	
NET CURRENT ASSETS			27,270
			396,270
LESS LONG-TERM LIABILITIES			—
TOTAL			396,270
CAPITAL EMPLOYED			
Share capital ordinary £1 shares fully paid			350,000
Reserves			32,000
From Profit and Loss account			14,270
TOTAL			396,270

6 **Down and Out Limited: Trading and Profit and Loss account for the year ending 31 December 200—**

	'000	'000	'000
Sales			179,000
Less cost of goods sold			
opening stock	23,000		
plus purchases	70,000		
	93,000		
Less closing stock	26,000		
			67,000
Gross profit			112,000
Less expenses			
Salaries	33,000		
Directors' fees	39,000		
Motor expenses	2,500		
Council tax	2,300		
General expenses	11,400		
Debenture interest	6,000		
Depreciation on fixtures	4,000		
Depreciation on cars	5,000		
			103,200
Profit for the year			8,800
Less provision for corporation tax			2,640
Profit after tax			6,160
Add retained profit from last year			17,000
			23,160
Less dividends			
Interim dividend paid	3,000		
Final dividend proposed	2,000		
			5,000
Retained profit carried forward to next year			18,160

Down and Out Limited: Balance Sheet as at 31 December 200—

	'000	'000	'000
FIXED ASSETS			
Intangible assets			
Goodwill			20,000
Tangible assets			
Premises		150,000	
Fixtures costs	40,000		
Less depreciation	12,000		
		28,000	
Cars cost	25,000		
Less depreciation	15,000		
		10,000	
			188,000
			208,000

CURRENT ASSETS:

Stock	26,000	
Debtors	26,500	
Cash at bank	13,200	
	65,700	

Creditors: amounts falling due within one year

Creditors	19,900	
Proposed dividend	2,000	
Taxation due	2,640	
	24,540	

NET CURRENT ASSETS		41,160
Total assets less current liabilities		249,160
Less longterm liabilities		
Debentures		40,000
TOTAL		209,160
CAPITAL AND RESERVES		
Share capital £1 ordinary shares	160,000	
Share premium	16,000	
General reserve	15,000	
Profit and Loss account	18,160	
TOTAL		209,160

7 **Rosa Limited: Trading and Profit and Loss account for the year ending 31 December 200—**

Sales		310,000
Less cost of goods sold		
opening stock	21,000	
add purchases	110,000	
	131,000	
Less closing stock	23,000	
		108,000
Gross profit		202,000
Less expenses		
Salaries	35,000	
Council tax	3,000	
Office expenses	6,000	
Sundry expenses	500	
Depreciation on fixtures and fittings	5,000	
Directors' fees	90,000	
Outstanding expenses	1,000	
		140,500
Net profit		61,500
Less taxation		11,700
Profit after taxation		49,800

Less appropriations

Proposed dividened	16,000		
To general reserve	10,000		
			26,000
			23,800

Rosa Limited: Balance Sheet as at 31 December 200—

FIXED ASSETS

Premises		310,000	
Fixtures costs	50,000		
Less depreciation	10,000		
		40,000	
			350,000

CURRENT ASSETS

Stock at end on year	23,000		
Debtors	18,000		
Cash at bank	17,000		
		58,000	

LESS CURRENT LIABILITIES

Creditors	19,000		
Outstanding expenses	1,000		
Proposed dividend	16,000		
Tax due	11,700		
		47,700	

NET CURRENT ASSETS		10,300
		360,300
LESS LONG-TERM LIABILITIES		—
TOTAL		360,300

CAPITAL EMPLOYED

Share capital authorised and issued

Ordinary £1 shares	320,000
Reserves £6,500 plus £10,000	16,500
Profit and loss account	23,800
TOTAL	360,300

Group companies and consolidated accounts

9.1 Introduction

This chapter deals with companies and their subsidiaries and the requirements for consolidated accounts, which aggregate the Profit and Loss accounts and Balance Sheets of the companies and their subsidiaries.

Separate companies operating independently will have separate accounting records and financial statements. Where one company controls another then this is regarded as a group, with a controlling, or parent, company which is called the parent undertaking, and the subsidiary company, called the subsidiary undertaking. Although the companies are still separate legal entities with separate financial records, the idea is that the shareholders of the parent company should be given some information about the subsidiary company. This information is provided by consolidated accounts for the group, being a consolidated Profit and Loss account and a consolidated Balance Sheet. These are created by aggregating the separate Profit and Loss accounts and Balance Sheets of the parent and subsidiary undertaking and are produced *in addition* to the separate final accounts for each company.

An undertaking is a parent undertaking in relation to another undertaking, a subsidiary, if:

(a) it holds a majority of the voting rights in the undertaking; or

(b) it is a member of the undertaking and has the right to appoint or remove a majority of its board of directors; or

(c) it has the right to exercise a dominant influence over the undertaking;
   (i) by virtue of provisions contained in the undertaking's memorandum or articles; or
   (ii) by virtue of a control contract; or

(d) it is a member of the undertaking and controls alone, pursuant to an agreement with other shareholders or members, a majority of the voting rights in the undertaking.

An undertaking is also a parent undertaking in relation to another undertaking, a subsidiary undertaking, if it has a participating interest in the undertaking, and:

(a) it actually exercises a dominant influence over it; or

(b) it and the subsidiary undertaking are managed on a unified basis.

The above is really based on a company's ability to exercise control over another company. A group will thus exist whenever legal entities which are independent of each other are under central management, regardless of the share ownership. This legislation implements the EC Seventh Directive. It should be noted that certain partnerships and joint ventures can also come within the consolidation requirement.

9.2 The consolidated Balance Sheet

9.2.1 Merging the Balance Sheets

The Balance Sheets of each company will be merged. The issued capital shown will be that of the parent company only, represented by the assets of the two companies. Merging does not mean that the two Balance Sheets are added together: the inter company shares should be cancelled out first, and then the assets of the two companies will be added together. Inter company shares mean those shares in the subsidiary undertaking owned by the parent undertaking shown in its Balance Sheet, and the subsidiary company's capital and reserves which represent those shares shown in the subsidiary undertaking's Balance Sheet.

EXAMPLE

Company P Ltd owns the whole share capital of company S Ltd and the two separate Balance Sheets show:

	P Ltd	(parent company)
	'000	
Fixed assets	25,000	
Shares in B Ltd		
(at cost)	15,000	inter company shares (investment in subsidiary)
Net current assets	10,000	
	50,000	
Share capital	50,000	
	50,000	

	S Ltd	(subsidiary company)
	'000	
Fixed assets	10,000	
Net current assets	5,000	
	15,000	
Share capital	15,000	(representing the above)
	15,000	

The inter company shares are to be cancelled out, i.e., the shares held in S Ltd by P Ltd are to be taken out from P Ltd's Balance Sheet and the share capital representing this must be taken out from S Ltd's Balance Sheet.

	P Ltd	(parent company)
	'000	
Fixed assets	25,000	
Net current assets	10,000	
	35,000	
Share capital	50,000	
	50,000	

	S Ltd	(subsidiary company)
	'000	
Fixed assets	10,000	
Net current assets	5,000	
	15,000	

Next, the assets of S Ltd must be added into P Ltd's Balance Sheet to make the consolidated account for P Ltd and S Ltd.

P Ltd and S Ltd: Consolidated Group Balance Sheet

	'000	'000
Fixed assets: P Ltd		25,000
S Ltd		10,000
		35,000
Net current assets: P Ltd	10,000	
S Ltd	5,000	
		15,000
Total		50,000
Share capital		50,000

If the subsidiary undertaking has reserves, then the share capital and the reserves (shareholder's funds) in the subsidiary undertaking must be excluded.

EXAMPLE

P Ltd has purchased all the shares in S Ltd. The two Balance Sheets are as follows:

	P Ltd	(parent company)
	'000	
Fixed assets	40,000	
Shares in S Ltd	30,000	investment in subsidiary
(at cost)		
Net current assets	10,000	
	80,000	
Share capital	60,000	
Reserves	20,000	
	80,000	

	S Ltd	(subsidiary company)
	'000	
Fixed assets	25,000	
Net current assets	5,000	
		30,000
Share capital	20,000	
Reserves	10,000	(representing the above)
		30,000

The inter company shares and reserves (in S) must be cancelled out and then the assets of both companies added together.

P Ltd and S Ltd: Consolidated Balance Sheet

	'000	'000
Fixed assets: P Ltd	40,000	
S Ltd	25,000	
		65,000
Net current assets: P Ltd	10,000	
S Ltd	5,000	
		15,000
		80,000
Share capital	60,000	
Reserves	20,000	
		80,000

In the above two examples, P Ltd, the acquiring company, paid the book value of the assets owned by S Ltd. However, the acquiring company may pay more, or less, than the book value of the assets of the subsidiary undertaking.

9.2.2 Acquiring shares for more than the book value of the assets

EXAMPLE

P Ltd purchases the shares and reserves of S Ltd for £100,000,000. The balance sheet value of these are £90,000,000. The excess paid of £10,000,000 is known as goodwill, which will be included in the consolidated Balance Sheet.

The Balance Sheets before consolidation will look like this:

	P Ltd	(parent company)
	'000	
Fixed assets	200,000	
Shares in S Ltd		
(at cost)	100,000*	less £90,000,000 (book value of investment
Net current assets	30,000	in S Ltd)
	330,000	
Share capital	250,000	
Reserves	80,000	
	330,000	

	S Ltd	(subsidiary company)
	'000	
Fixed assets	80,000	
Net current assets	10,000	
	90,000	
Share capital	75,000	
Reserves	15,000	
	90,000*	(representing the above inter company shares)

The book value of the investment in S Ltd and the share capital and reserves of S Ltd totalling £90,000,000 must be cancelled out from the shares in S Ltd shown on P Ltd's Balance Sheet.

This will leave £10,000,000 on P Ltd's Balance Sheet in respect of the shares in S Ltd, which will be called goodwill, being the additional payment in respect of the shares.

The assets of the two companies are then to be added together as before.

P Ltd and S Ltd: Consolidated Balance Sheet

	'000	'000
Goodwill re S Ltd shares		10,000
Fixed assets: P Ltd		200,000
S Ltd		80,000
		280,000
Net current assets: P Ltd	30,000	
S Ltd	10,000	
		40,000
		330,000
Share capital		250,000
Reserves		80,000
		330,000

9.2.3 Acquiring shares for less than the book value of the assets

EXAMPLE

Company P Ltd acquires all the share capital and reserves of S Ltd for £100,000,000 when the balance sheet value of these is £120,000,000. P Ltd has therefore made a 'profit' in respect of the purchase. This is due to the shareholders of P Ltd, but it cannot be distributed to them. A capital reserve account will be opened in respect of the profit of £20,000,000.

The Balance Sheets before consolidation will look like this:

	P Ltd	(parent company)
	'000	'000
Fixed assets	200,000	
Shares in S Ltd		
(at cost)	100,000	(less value of S Ltd £120,000,000)*
Net current assets	150,000	
		450,000
Share capital	400,000	
Reserves	50,000	
		450,000
	S Ltd	(subsidiary company)
Fixed assets	85,000	
Net current assets	35,000	
		120,000
Share capital	110,000	
Reserves	10,000	
		120,000* (representing the above)

When the total value of S Ltd, i.e., £120,000,000, is removed from P Ltd's Balance Sheet, this would result in a minus figure of £20,000,000 in the assets. This is a credit balance which should be shown as a capital reserve in the share capital and reserves section.

	P Ltd	(parent company)
	'000	'000
Fixed assets	200,000	

(Shares in S Ltd—£20,000,000 now a credit—move to the share capital and reserves section)

Net current assets	150,000	

The consolidated balance sheet will appear as follows:

P Ltd and S Ltd: Consolidated Balance Sheet

	'000	'000
Fixed assets: P Ltd	200,000	
S Ltd	85,000	
		285,000
Net current assets: P Ltd	150,000	
S Ltd	35,000	
		185,000
		470,000
Share capital	400,000	
Capital reserve (re shares in S Ltd)	20,000	
Other reserves	50,000	
		470,000

9.3 The consolidated Profit and Loss account

9.3.1 Merging the Profit and Loss accounts

These can be fairly complicated. The sales, cost of sales and expenses will be merged and the net profits, taxation, and transfers to reserves will be merged, but the dividend payable to the parent undertaking (inter company dividend) will be excluded. In order to keep things simple, the following example will just show the net profit onwards.

EXAMPLE

The Profit and Loss accounts of P Ltd and S Ltd are as follows:

P Ltd (parent)

	'000	'000
Net profit		50,000
Add dividend from S Ltd		10,000
		60,000
Taxation, say		15,000
Profit after tax		45,000
Dividend (to P Ltd's shareholders)		15,000
Retained profit (reserves)		30,000

S Ltd (subsidiary)

	'000	'000
Net profit		40,000
Taxation		12,000
Profit after tax		28,000
Dividend to P Ltd		10,000
Retained profit (reserves)		18,000

P Ltd and S Ltd: consolidated Profit and Loss account

	'000	'000
Net profit: P Ltd	50,000	
S Ltd	40,000	
		90,000
Taxation: P Ltd	15,000	
S Ltd	12,000	
		27,000
		63,000
Dividend		15,000
Reserves: P Ltd	30,000	
S Ltd	18,000	
		48,000

9.3.1.1   Effect on the consolidated Balance Sheet

The share capital of P Ltd will be shown, together with the increased reserves of P Ltd and the increase in reserves of S Ltd. This will be represented by the increased assets of P Ltd and S Ltd.

EXAMPLE

Consolidated Balance Sheet before the Profit and Loss accounts

	'000	'000
Fixed assets: P Ltd	100,000	
S Ltd	60,000	
		160,000
Net current assets: P Ltd	65,000	
S Ltd	25,000	
		90,000
		250,000
Share capital	200,000	
Reserves	50,000	
		250,000

Consolidated Balance Sheet after the Profit and Loss accounts

	'000	'000
Fixed assets: P Ltd	100,000	
S Ltd	60,000	
		160,000

Net current assets: P Ltd	95,000	
S Ltd	43,000	
		138,000
TOTAL		298,000
Share capital		200,000
Reserves: P Ltd	80,000	
S Ltd	18,000	
		98,000
TOTAL		298,000

9.4 Where a company holds a majority interest in the subsidiary

In these circumstances consolidated final accounts will still be required.

9.4.1 The Balance Sheet

This will show the whole of the subsidiary's assets and liabilities. The minority shareholders' interest will be shown as liabilities.

EXAMPLE

Company P Ltd has acquired 80% of the issued share capital of S Ltd: the Balance Sheets show:

P Ltd (parent company)

	'000	'000
Fixed assets	200,000	
80% of shares (reserves) in S Ltd at cost	80,000	
Net current assets	70,000	
		350,000
Share capital	300,000	
Reserves	50,000	
		350,000

S Ltd (subsidiary company)

	'000	'000
Fixed assets	60,000	
Net current assets	40,000	
		100,000
Share capital	80,000	
Reserves	20,000	
		100,000

To consolidate the accounts the inter company shares figure must be excluded, i.e., £80,000,000. This is attributable to the share capital and reserves of S Ltd, i.e., it is made up of:

	'000
80% of £80,000,000 share capital of S Ltd	64,000
80% of reserves of £20,000,000 of S Ltd	16,000
	80,000

Thus the amount of share capital and reserves attributable to the minority shareholders will be:

	'000
Share capital	80,000
Less 80%	64,000
20%	16,000
Reserves	20,000
Less 80%	16,000
20%	4,000

The consolidated Balance Sheet will show:

	'000	'000
Fixed assets: P Ltd	200,000	
S Ltd	60,000	
		260,000
Net current assets: P Ltd	70,000	
S Ltd	40,000	
		110,000
Total assets less current liabilities		370,000
Less		
Interest of minority shareholders		
in S Ltd capital	16,000	
reserves	4,000	20,000
		350,000
Share capital	300,000	
Reserves	50,000	
		350,000

9.4.2 The Profit and Loss account where a company holds a majority of shares

That part of the subsidiary's net profit after tax which belongs to the minority shareholders in respect of dividend and reserves will be deducted first, before appropriations are made for dividend and reserves.

EXAMPLE

Company P Ltd holds 80% of the share capital of S Ltd.
The Profit and Loss accounts for P Ltd and S Ltd are as follows:

P Ltd (parent company)

	'000	'000
Net profit		90,000
Dividend from S Ltd		8,000
		98,000
Taxation, say		27,000
		71,000
Dividend		20,000
Reserves		51,000

S Ltd (subsidiary company)

	'000	'000
Net profit		40,000
Taxation		12,000
		28,000
Dividend: P Ltd	8,000	
Others	2,000	
		10,000
Reserves: P Ltd	14,400	
Others	3,600	
		18,000

Consolidated Profit and Loss account for P Ltd and S Ltd

	'000	'000
Net profit: P Ltd	90,000	
S Ltd	40,000	
		130,000
Taxation: P Ltd	27,000	
S Ltd	12,000	
		39,000
		91,000
Less minority interest		
Dividend	2,000	
Reserve	3,600	
		5,600
		85,400
Dividend		20,000
Reserves: P Ltd	51,000	
S Ltd	14,400	
		65,400

9.5 Check list

By the end of this chapter you should be able to:

1. understand how the Balance Sheets of each company are merged;

2. understand how the Profit and Loss accounts of each company are merged;

3. understand the structure of a consolidated Profit and Loss account and a consolidated Balance Sheet;

4. complete some of the exercises at the end of the chapter.

9.6 Practice exercises

1 Ball Limited owns all the shares in Chain Limited. The summarised Profit and Loss accounts and Balance Sheets for Ball and Chain drawn up on 30 September 200— are

shown below. The Balance Sheets take into account retained profit (reserves) shown on the Profit and Loss account. Draw up the consolidated Profit and Loss account and the consolidated Balance Sheet for Ball Limited and Chain Limited.

Ball Limited: Profit and Loss account for the year ending 30 September 200—

	'000	'000
Net profit	100,000	
Add dividend from Chain Limited	12,000	
	112,000	
Less taxation, say	30,000	
Profit after tax	82,000	
Dividend to Ball Limited's shareholders	20,000	
Reserves	62,000	

Chain Limited: Profit and Loss account for the year ending 30 September 200—

	'000	'000
Net profit	44,000	
Less taxation	13,200	
Profit after tax	30,800	
Dividend to Ball Limited	12,000	
Reserves	18,800	

Ball Limited: Balance Sheet as at 30 September 200—

	'000	'000
Fixed assets		300,000
Shares in Chain Limited at cost		89,000
Net current assets		192,000
TOTAL		581,000
Share capital		500,000
Reserves	19,000	
	62,000	
		81,000
TOTAL		581,000

Chain Limited: Balance Sheet as at 30 September 200—

	'000	'000
Fixed assets		65,000
Net current assets		42,800
TOTAL		107,800
Share capital		80,000
Reserves	9,000	
This year's	18,800	
		27,800
TOTAL		107,800

2 Ash Limited has 80% of the share capital of Willow Limited. The summary balance sheets of the two companies are as follows:

Ash Limited: Balance Sheet as at 30 November 200—

	'000	'000
Fixed assets		320,000
Shares in Willow Limited at cost		160,000
Net current assets		120,000
		600,000
Share capital		500,000
Reserves		100,000
		600,000

Willow Limited: Balance Sheet as at 30 November 200—

	'000	'000
Fixed assets		150,000
Net current assets		50,000
		200,000
Share capital		180,000
Reserves		20,000
		200,000

Draw up the consolidated balance sheet for the two companies.

9.7 Suggested answers to practice exercises

1 Ball Limited

**Consolidated Profit and Loss account for Ball Limited
and Chain Limited for the year ending 30 September 200—**

	'000	'000
Net profit: Ball Limited	100,000	
Chain Limited	44,000	
		144,000
Less taxation: Ball Limited	30,000	
Chain Limited	13,200	
		43,200
		100,800
Dividend to Ball Limited shareholders		20,000
Reserves: Ball Limited	62,000	
Chain Limited	18,800	
		80,800

Consolidated Balance Sheet for Ball Limited and Chain Limited as at 30 September 200—

	'000	'000
Fixed assets: Ball Limited	300,000	
Chain Limited	65,000	
		365,000
Net current assets: Ball Limited	192,000	
Chain Limited	42,800	
		234,800
		599,800
Share capital		500,000
Reserves: Ball Limited	19,000	
plus this year's	62,000	
	81,000	
Chain: increase in reserve	18,800	
		99,800
TOTAL		599,800

2 **Ash Limited**

Consolidated Balance Sheet for Ash Limited and Willow Limited as at 30 November 200—

	'000	'000
Fixed assets: Ash Limited	320,000	
Willow Limited	150,000	
		470,000
Net current assets: Ash Limited	120,000	
Willow Limited	50,000	
		170,000
Total assets less current liabilities		640,000
Less interest of minority shareholders		
(being 20% of share capital	36,000	
20% of reserves)	4,000	
		40,000
TOTAL		600,000
Share capital	500,000	
Reserves	100,000	
TOTAL		600,000

Interpretation of accounts and accounting ratios

10.1 Introduction

This chapter deals with the following:

1. Use of accounts by different people.
2. Limitations of accounts and other factors to take into account.
3. Trends in accounts.
4. Accounting ratios with examples.
5. An exercise using ratios.

10.2 Use of accounts

Accounts may be used by many different people, e.g., by the management of a business, by employees, by investors in the business, by shareholders, by long-term lenders or trade creditors or by the Government for taxation and statistics. Each of these may be looking for different things in the accounts. A creditor, for example, would want to make sure that the debt could be repaid, whereas a shareholder in the business may be looking for increasing profit, so that dividends will be higher, or may be looking for capital appreciation.

The interpretation of accounts can help to assess how a business is performing at present and can also enable inferences to be made about its future performance. The current level of profit may be compared with other similar businesses to see if it is satisfactory, and whether it can be improved. By looking at the accounts of a business over a number of years trends may be seen. A business may have sufficient assets to cover liabilities, but if these are tied up in fixed assets, or stock which is not selling, or work in progress, or debtors who are unlikely to pay, it may not be able to pay its current liabilities.

You may wonder whether you need to know about interpretation of accounts at all. Why not leave it to the accountants? One good reason is that, as a sole practitioner or as a partner, the accounts will explain the profit due to you. It is not a good idea to leave the understanding of accounts to your accountants or to one or two of the other partners. You will not be able to make informed decisions about the business where necessary, for example, whether to retain staff, or take on more staff, or change the type of work done by the firm. Understanding accounts will also be necessary where you are dealing with commercial work; even where accountants are involved, you should have at least some idea of the advice given. You may be asked to give advice on proposed investments suggested by a stockbroker for a client or, for example, a trust in which you are a trustee.

Note that there may be financial services implications here. There are few areas of work today where an understanding of accounts will not be needed.

10.3 Check factors outside the accounts

To interpret accounts, ratio analysis may be used, as ratios can be used to compare performances from year to year and to compare different companies. Take care, however, as reading the accounts and looking at ratios on their own will not provide sufficient information about a company; other information should be sought as well. A company may have been doing very well, but may have just lost its managing director, or industrial action may be threatened by its workforce. The business may possibly have been involved in an area which has now expanded to saturation point, and the market may no longer be there. A business should be compared with others of a similar type, i.e., dealing with the same services or products and of a similar size. If profits are disappointing there may be a recession generally. Are the markets for the business still there? Is there increased competition, e.g., from abroad?

10.4 General areas to look at

When accounts are looked at, absolute changes may be found, e.g., is this year's profit more than last year's, have the expenses of the business gone up? Relative changes should also be found, e.g., what are the expenses of the business as a percentage of the turnover or sales? What is the profit as a percentage of the sales? How much profit has been generated from the capital employed (i.e., total assets less current liabilities)? The business may have invested heavily in fixed assets, but profit may have gone up by only a modest amount.

10.4.1 Accounts for past years

In interpreting accounts, the accounts for the last few years should be looked at, as these should establish general trends. Note that the figures shown on the accounts may not always be accurate. The business may be overstating the value of its assets. Examples may include stock or work in progress. If stock is valued at cost price, rather than its sale price, this may sound reasonable, but the stock may not have been sold for some time, and it may be necessary to sell the stock at a lower price than that shown on the Balance Sheet. How work in progress is valued should be checked—is this based on an accurate time recording system, or does it involve some guesswork? Other assets shown may be falling in value, e.g., office furniture, office equipment, and it is important that sufficient provision for depreciation has been made. On the other hand, if the business has freehold premises shown at cost price then the present value should be checked, as it may be much higher.

The figure for debtors (an asset) may be high, but if this is in respect of one or two debtors who are in trouble themselves, the debts may not be paid. Check that sufficient provision has been made for bad debts and doubtful debts.

There may also be changes in circumstances. A company may have just employed a new managing director who has a reputation as a troubleshooter, able to improve companies with poor performance. Thus in future years profit may go up dramatically.

It is also always worth reading the information supplied by a company and the notes attached to the accounts.

There are two main areas that will be looked at in any analysis:

(a) the solvency or liquidity of the business;

(b) the profitability of the business.

10.5 Trends

Figures over the years may be compared, e.g., the profit over the last five years may show a general trend up, even though there may be the odd year when profit has fallen. Has the turnover increased? Have expenses increased?

10.6 Ratios

These will be calculated from a set of accounts for a year, but can then be compared with other years.

10.6.1 Liquidity ratios

Liquidity means the ability of a business to pay its short-term debts. This is not the same as solvency, which means the ability of the business to pay all its liabilities. A firm may have sufficient assets to pay all its liabilities, but will still not be able to pay off short-term liabilities because it has insufficient cash or easily realisable assets.

10.6.1.1 The current assets ratio

$$\frac{\text{Current assets}}{\text{Current liabilities}}$$

This compares current assets with current liabilities. There should normally be enough current assets to cover current liabilities. The comparison is between assets which should be converted into cash in approximately 12 months; with liabilities which will be due for payment within the same 12 months. What is a satisfactory figure will vary with the type of business or with the reputation of the business. For example:

$$\frac{\text{Current assets}}{\text{Current liabilities}} \quad \frac{40{,}000}{20{,}000} = 2:1 \quad \text{'000}$$

This would be a satisfactory ratio.

For example:

$$\frac{\text{Current assets}}{\text{Current liabilities}} \quad \frac{30{,}000}{20{,}000} = 1.5:1$$

Again this may be an acceptable ratio.

A very high figure may not mean that the business is safe and it is essential to look behind the figures. The company may have overvalued its current assets, e.g., the stock (or work in progress). Generally, if the ratio is less than 1:1, there may be a problem.

Where, however, the company has a bank overdraft and the bank is prepared to allow the overdraft to continue long term, this may then be treated as a long-term liability instead of a short-term liability and thus can be left out of the ratio. This will clearly improve the ratio.

10.6.1.2 The acid test

This ratio uses only cash or assets which can be converted quickly into cash, thus stock or work in progress will be excluded from the figure for current assets.

$$\frac{\text{Current assets less stock (or work in progress)}}{\text{Current liabilities}}$$

If this is 1 : 1 or better then the company will have sufficient liquid assets to meet its current liabilities: this is provided that the creditors are paid and debtors pay at approximately the same time. Sometimes an even stricter test is used, that of measuring cash as against current liabilities. If debtors have been included in the ratio then, to check how fast debts will be paid, another ratio can be used; see **10.5.2**.

10.6.2 The average collection period—trade debtors to sales ratio

To find the length of time in days that debtors will pay debts, the following formula is used:

$$\frac{\text{Trade debtors}}{\text{Sales}} \times 365 \qquad \text{or for solicitors' use} \qquad \frac{\text{Debtors}}{\text{Profit costs}} \times 365$$

EXAMPLE

Sales are £200,000 for the year and trade debtors are £10,000.

$$\frac{£10,000}{£200,000} \times 365 = 18.25 \text{ days}$$

If, e.g., sales are £200,000 for the year and trade debtors are £40,000:

$$\frac{£40,000}{£200,000} \times 365 = 73 \text{ days}$$

The ratio may not accurately reflect the length of time allowed to debtors. If, for example, sales had been strong just before the balance sheet was drawn up, this may give a high debtors figure, which would distort the ratio, making it appear that the length of credit given was much longer, as in the second example.

If the length of time allowed for debtors to pay is too long, then steps should be taken to tighten up debt collection. It is usual for a business to allow a specified length of time for debtors to pay the amount due before action is taken by the business. This time should be compared with the actual time which the debtors are taking. Whether the time has increased from previous years will need to be checked, as will the times for other similar businesses. It may also be advisable to check the individual debts to see how long each one has been outstanding. Some of them may be irrecoverable.

To check how quickly the business pays its creditors, a similar ratio is used; see **10.5.3**.

10.6.3 The average payment period—trade creditors to purchases ratio

$$\frac{\text{Trade creditors}}{\text{Purchases}} \times 365$$

If purchases for the year are £90,000 and trade creditors are £20,000:

$$\frac{£20,000}{£90,000} \times 365 = 81.1 \text{ days}$$

Again this should be compared with previous years, with similar businesses, and the length of time that creditors allow for payment. Note that a business may deliberately delay payment of creditors for as long as reasonably possible. Large companies in particular may do this as they have stronger bargaining power than their smaller creditors. If the period has dramatically increased, it may be that the business is having difficulty in paying its bills. However, a large figure for creditors may just be due to an increase in purchases just before the date of the balance sheet, and this may have been in anticipation of increased sales, or to buy in before prices are increased.

10.6.4 Shortage of working capital

Working capital or net current assets is that portion of capital left to run the business after providing for fixed assets. A business needs to pay out money to run the business, e.g., paying salaries and other expenses, or buying goods or services, before receiving payment itself for the goods or services it provides. How much will be needed will vary. It may be that credit is given on purchases: if this is a longer period than the time in which the business collects its own debts, then not as much working capital will be required. The amount of working capital will need to increase if there is inflation, as expenses will increase. If the business wishes to expand then again more working capital will be required. Reserve funds based on retained profit (sec 5.2.8) can be used to finance the increased requirement. If this is not possible then the business will have to raise funds by issuing more shares, or borrowing.

If a business runs short of working capital then it will have insufficient funds to meet its short-term liabilities, and may not be able to take advantage of, e.g., discounts for prompt payment. It may also have to offer discounts itself to customers for prompt payment.

Indications of a shortage of working capital may be found from using the following ratios:

10.6.4.1 The working capital ratio

$$\frac{\text{Net current assets (working capital)}}{\text{Sales (or use profit costs for solicitors)}}$$

EXAMPLE

A company has net current assets of £20,000 and sales are £200,000. The working capital ratio is:

$$\frac{20,000}{200,000} = 0.1 : 1$$

If net current assets were still £20,000 and sales were £400,000 then the ratio would be 0.05 : 1, clearly a lower ratio.

10.6.4.2   The ratio between debtors and creditors

$$\frac{\text{Debtors}}{\text{Creditors}}$$

If this ratio falls then again it may be a sign of overtrading. There may also be a shortage of cash. If the company is unable to find more capital to finance working capital, through borrowing or from the shareholders, then it may have to sell fixed assets, and lease instead, although there may be disadvantages in doing this.

Alternatively the business may be able to reduce the requirement for working capital, by ensuring that stock or work in progress is kept to a minimum and that debtors pay quickly, thereby releasing cash to use in the business.

If the company has over-expanded, i.e., sales have increased too fast, it may be necessary to halt the expansion.

10.6.5   Profitability ratios

10.6.5.1   Return on capital employed

This is the most important ratio in relation to profitability, for those who invest in the business it shows the rate of return on the capital used in the business. If net assets of the business are £2,000,000 and the profit is £20,000 then the return is only 1%, which is too low; as an investment the money would be better used elsewhere.

The ratio is:

$$\frac{\text{Operating profit (before interest and tax)}}{\text{Capital employed (total assets less current liabilities)}} \times 100\%$$

$$\frac{\pounds 20,000}{\pounds 2,000,000} \times 100\% = 1\%$$

The figure taken for profit is before tax and interest. If the figure was taken after interest on debentures, loans and overdrafts, the return on assets would be understated. Any interest received should also be excluded from the calculation, to ensure that the profit shown is that made by operations.

A problem with this particular ratio is that the capital employed is measured at the date of the balance sheet. This may be misleading if, for example, the company has recently increased its capital to fund expansion, by purchasing fixed assets, which have not yet created any increased profit. The figure for capital employed could be taken from the balance sheet at the end of the year, or at the start of the year, or an average of the figure at the start of the year and the figure at the end of the year.

Even if the return is satisfactory, it should be looked at with caution. The true value of the assets on the balance sheet should be checked. They may have been undervalued, e.g., premises may have been shown at cost price.

The ratio may also be adjusted in respect of a bank overdraft. If this is effectively long-term lending, it should be included in the figure for capital employed, i.e., added back.

$$\frac{\text{Operating profit (before taxation and interest)}}{\text{Total assets less current liabilities + overdraft}} \times 100\%$$

10.6.5.2   The gross profit percentage

$$\frac{\text{Gross profit}}{\text{Sales}} \times 100\%$$

This shows the profitability of the sales. Even if sales have increased, this does not necessarily mean that the gross profit has increased.

EXAMPLE

Year 1

$$\frac{30,000}{125,000} \times 100\% = 24\%$$

EXAMPLE

Year 2

$$\frac{40,000}{200,000} \times 100\% = 20\%$$

Although the sales and the gross profit have increased in year 2, it should be noted that the gross profit percentage is lower. If the gross profit percentage has fallen this may be because:

(a) the cost of goods sold has increased, but that selling prices have not been increased by an equivalent amount;

(b) sale prices have been reduced in order to sell more goods;

(c) if different types of goods have been sold, profit margins on some goods may be greater than on other goods.

10.6.5.3 Net profit percentage

$$\frac{\text{Operating or trading profit before interest and tax}}{\text{Sales}} \times 100\%$$

or for solicitors' use $\dfrac{\text{Net profit}}{\text{Profit costs}} \times 100\%$

Both this ratio and the ratio in **10.5.5.2** will vary, depending on the type of business being carried out. As with all ratios they should be compared with similar businesses. Some businesses operate with a very low profit margin, relying on a large turnover.

If the gross profit ratio has remained the same, but the net profit ratio has fallen, then the expenses must have increased.

Each type of expense can be compared with the sales figure, for the current year and previous years, to find whether the increase is general or limited to a particular area.

EXAMPLE

$$\frac{\text{Marketing costs}}{\text{Sales}} \times 100\%$$

$$\frac{\text{Administrative expenses}}{\text{Sales}} \times 100\%$$

10.6.6   Efficiency ratio—rate of stock turnover

The faster stock is turned over, or sold, the more profit will be made, provided the gross profit percentage stays the same. There are two ratios which may be used to find stock turnover:

(a) either divide stocks by sales:

$$\frac{\text{Stocks}}{\text{Sales}} \text{ (based on the selling price)}$$

EXAMPLE

If stock was £80,000 and sales were £700,000 the ratio would be:

$$\frac{80,000}{700,000} = 0.114 \text{ or every 41.7 days}$$

(b) or probably the better ratio, divide cost of goods sold by average stock:

$$\frac{\text{Cost of goods sold (sales at cost price)}}{\text{Average stock (at cost)}}$$

As you will not have the detailed accounts of the business to find average stock, use the average of the opening and closing stock:

EXAMPLE

If opening stock was £50,000 and closing stock was £80,000 then the average would be:

$$\frac{50,000 + 80,000}{2} = 65,000$$

If the cost of goods sold was £450,000 then the stock turnover would be:

$$\frac{450,000}{65,000} = 6.92 \text{ times per year, i.e., stock is turned over 6.92 times per year, or every 52.75 days}$$

The rate of stock turnover will vary, depending on the type of stock being carried. Although a fast rate of stock turnover should lead to increased profit, the business must be careful to have enough stock at any given time to meet demand.

If the rate of stock turnover has fallen then the business should check whether it is carrying too much stock, or whether sales have decreased generally.

After analysing the profitability of the business, it may be that profitability is satisfactory, or it may be considered that there is room for improvement. The business may attempt to reduce expenses, or increase prices or sales, to improve profitability. Increasing prices may not be the best solution, as customers may decide to go somewhere cheaper.

If sales are to be increased the business will have to work more efficiently, or expect its workforce to work harder. It may be that the business decides to reduce its workforce but expects them to retain the same level of sales. Increased sales will be possible only if the market for those goods is there.

10.6.7   Capital gearing ratios

Gearing relates to the capital structure of the company, the relationship between the capital provided by shareholders and the capital provided by borrowing. A high-geared company is one which has a high proportion of borrowing. A company with low gearing has most of its funds provided by the ordinary shareholder. The ratios used may be calculated in different ways.

10.6.7.1   A commonly used ratio

$$\frac{\text{Preference shares} + \text{long-term loans}}{\text{All shareholders funds} + \text{long-term loans}} \times 100\%$$

EXAMPLE 1

A company has share capital and long-term borrowings as follows:

Ordinary share capital	100
Reserves	50
7% preference shares	10
12% debentures	30
	190

$$\frac{10 + 30}{190} \times 100 = 21.05\%$$

EXAMPLE 2

A company has share capital and long-term borrowings as follows:

Ordinary share capital	80
Reserves	20
Preference shares	10
Debentures	40
	150

$$\frac{10 + 40}{150} \times 100 = 33.33\%$$

The second company is a higher geared company than the first company.

If a company is highly geared, then any change in the profits will affect the shareholders more than in a low-geared company, as the interest on the borrowing will have to be paid before any dividend is available to the ordinary shareholders. The company will be susceptible to changes in interest rates, e.g., if these increase substantially. The borrowing will also have to be repaid at some stage. If the company requires additional capital to expand the business it may be better to do this through increasing the share capital.

10.6.7.2   An alternative ratio

Another ratio is the ratio of borrowings to shareholders' funds.

EXAMPLE

If borrowing is £200,000 and shareholders' funds are £500,000 then the ratio will be:

Borrowing:	200,000
Shareholders' funds	500,000
Gearing	2 : 5

10.6.8   Investment ratios

An investor will be concerned with the profitability of a business, and whether the investment will give a good return.

10.6.8.1   The return on capital employed ratio

This ratio, shown previously, can be used.

$$\frac{\text{Net profit (before interest and tax)}}{\text{Capital employed}} \times 100\%$$

10.6.8.2   Return on ordinary shareholders' interest

The return on capital employed shows only the return before tax and interest. An ordinary shareholder will want to know what the return is after payment of interest and tax, and after payment of any preference shares dividends.

$$\frac{\text{Net profit after interest, tax and preference share dividend}}{\text{Ordinary shareholders' interest (ordinary share capital plus any reserves attributable to them)}} \times 100\%$$

10.6.8.3   Earnings per share

This will show the return per single share, in money.

$$\frac{\text{Net profit after interest, tax and preference share dividend}}{\text{Number of ordinary shares}}$$

This is an important ratio and FRS14 requires limited companies to show the earnings per share in the published accounts.

However, this figure will not be the amount that the shareholder receives per share—the amount received will be the dividend declared by the directors. As we have seen in **8.2.6**, part of the profit will often be transferred to reserves and, although these belong to the shareholders, they may not be available for distribution.

10.6.8.4   Dividend yield

This is the annual return by way of dividend based on an investment of £100 in the shares at the current price. If, e.g., the shares cost £2.00 each, then 50 shares could be purchased for £100. If the dividend was 10p per share, then the total would be £5.00, giving a dividend yield of 5%.

10.6.8.5   Dividend cover

$$\frac{\text{Earnings per share}}{\text{Dividend per share}}$$

This shows the proportion of earnings distributed against the proportion retained by way of reserves.

EXAMPLE

If net profit after tax and any preference share dividend was £8,000,000 and the number of ordinary shares was 4,000,000, then the earnings per share would be £2.00. If the dividend was £2,000,000, then the dividend per share would be 50p.

$$\frac{2.00}{.50} = 4 \text{ times}$$

An alternative way of showing this would be:

$$\frac{\text{Net profit after tax and preference share dividend}}{\text{Dividend to ordinary shareholders}}$$

Continuing the above example:

$$\frac{8,000,000}{2,000,000} = 4 \text{ times}$$

This shows that the dividend is covered four times by the profit earned, after tax and the preference share dividend. The higher this is, the more the company is reinvesting its profits in the business.

The amount retained will not only increase the underlying value of the shares but ensure that dividends can be paid if in any future year there is insufficient net profit available.

10.6.8.6   Price earnings ratio (PE ratio)

Once the earnings per share has been calculated, the actual earnings based on the present market price of the share (where applicable), rather than the value at which the share was issued, can be calculated.

$$\frac{\text{Market price per share}}{\text{Earnings per share}}$$

E.g. $\dfrac{£2.00}{.20} = 10$

This means that the investor has to pay £2.00 to get the benefit of earnings of 20p per annum—10 times the year's earnings have been paid, or 10 years' purchase of earnings.

When the market is convinced that the future earnings of a company are going to increase, the market price of the shares may go up. The price earnings ratio will therefore be higher. If the market is convinced that future earnings are not going to be as good, then the price of the shares may go down, and the PE ratio will be lower. However, PE ratios will vary depending on the type of business being carried out.

If a takeover bid is rumoured in respect of the company then the value of the shares may well go up, which will lead to a high PE ratio.

If a PE ratio for a company is higher than other companies in a similar business, it may be that the company is highly regarded, or possibly that the shares are overvalued. A lower PE ratio may mean that the company is not highly regarded, or possibly that the shares are undervalued.

10.7 Example

Dilley Tante Limited: Profit and Loss accounts for the year ending

	31 Dec 2002	31 Dec 2003
	'000	'000
Sales	800,000	1,200,000
Less cost of sales	500,000	700,000
Gross profit	300,000	500,000
Less expenses	132,000	240,000
Loan interest	8,000	40,000
Profit before tax	160,000	220,000
Taxation say	40,000	55,000
Profit after tax	120,000	165,000
Dividends	30,000	40,000
Retained profit	90,000	125,000

Dilley Tante Limited: Balance Sheet as at 31 December

	2002	2003
Fixed assets		
	'000	'000
Tangible assets	810,000	960,000
Current assets		
Stock	80,000	175,000
Debtors	50,000	110,000
Cash	10,000	5,000
	140,000	290,000
Creditors:		
Amounts falling due within one year	80,000	80,000
Net current assets	60,000	210,000
Total assets less current liabilities	870,000	1,170,000
Creditors:		
Amounts falling due after more than one year		
Loans and other borrowings	50,000	225,000
	820,000	945,000

	2002	2003
Capital and reserves		
Called up share capital		
Ordinary £1 shares	600,000	600,000
Profit and loss account		
Retained profit	220,000	345,000
	820,000	945,000

Ratios	2002	2003
Liquidity		

Current ratio

$$\frac{\text{Current assets}}{\text{Current liabilities}}$$

	'000	'000
Current assets	140,000	290,000
Current liabilities	80,000	80,000
	= 1.75 to 1	= 3.625 to 1

The liquidity ratio or the acid test

Current assets less stock	60,000	115,000
Current liabilities	80,000	80,000
	= 0.75 to 1	= 1.438 to 1

The average collection period—debtors to sales ratio

$$\frac{\text{Debtors}}{\text{Sales}} \times 365$$

	$\frac{50,000}{800,000} \times 365$	$\frac{110,000}{1,200,000} \times 365$
	= 22.8 days	= 33.46 days

The average payment period—creditors to purchases ratio

$$\frac{\text{Creditors}}{\text{Purchases}} \times 365$$

	$\frac{80,000}{500,000} \times 365$	$\frac{80,000}{700,000} \times 365$

Note: No purchases figure shown
Cost of sales taken as an approximation = 58.4 days   = 41.7 days

The working capital ratio

Net current assets (working capital)	60,000	210,000
Sales	800,000	1,200,000
	= 0.075 to 1	= 0.175 to 1

The ratio between debtors and creditors

Debtors	50,000	110,000
Creditors	80,000	80,000
	= 0.625 to 1	= 1.375 to 1

Return on capital employed

$$\frac{\text{Operating profit (before tax and interest)}}{\text{Capital employed (total assets less current liabilities)}} \times 100\%$$

$$\frac{168,000}{870,000} \times 100\% \qquad \frac{260,000}{1,170,000} \times 100\%$$

$$= 19.31\% \qquad\qquad = 22.22\%$$

The gross profit percentage

$$\frac{\text{Gross profit}}{\text{Sales}} \qquad \frac{300,000}{800,000} \times 100\% \qquad \frac{500,000}{1,200,000} \times 100\%$$

$$= 37.5\% \qquad\qquad = 41.67\%$$

The net profit percentage

$$\frac{\text{Operating or trading profit before interest and tax}}{\text{Sales}} \times 100\%$$

$$\frac{168,000}{800,000} \times 100\% \qquad \frac{260,000}{1,200,000} \times 100\%$$

$$= 21\% \qquad\qquad = 21.67\%$$

Rate of stock turnover

$$\frac{\text{Stocks}}{\text{Sales}} \qquad \frac{80,000}{800,000} \qquad \frac{175,000}{1,200,000}$$

$$0.1 \quad 36.5\,\text{days} \qquad 0.146 \quad 53.29\,\text{days}$$

Capital gearing

$$\frac{\text{Preference shares + lone-term liabilities}}{\text{Capital employed}} \times 100\%$$

$$\frac{50,000 \times 100\%}{870,000} \qquad \frac{225,000 \times 100\%}{1,170,000}$$

$$= 0.057\,\text{to}\,1 \qquad = 0.192\,\text{to}\,1$$

or $\qquad\qquad 5.7\% \qquad\qquad 19.2\%$

Return on ordinary shareholders' interest

$$\frac{\text{Net profit after interest, tax and preference share dividend}}{\text{Ordinary shareholders' interest}} \times 100\%$$

$$\frac{120,000}{820,000} \times 100\% \qquad \frac{165,000}{945,000} \times 100\%$$

$$= 14.63\% \qquad\qquad = 17.46\%$$

Earnings per share

$$\frac{\text{Net profit after interest, tax and preference share dividend}}{\text{Number of ordinary shares}}$$

$$\frac{120,000}{600,000} \qquad \frac{165,000}{600,000}$$

$$= 20\text{p} \qquad\qquad = 27.5\text{p}$$

Dividend cover

Net profit after tax, etc.	120,000	165,000
Dividend to ordinary shareholders	30,000	40,000
	= 4 times	= 4.125 times

Comment

Liquidity: the current ratio was acceptable in 2002 at 1.75 to 1. In 2003 it increased to 3.625 to 1 as current assets, particularly stock and debtors, have increased dramatically, but creditors have remained the same. Clearly sales have increased, but the rate of stock turnover has reduced from 36.5 days to 53.29 days. This should be checked; also debtors should be checked to make sure that these will pay. Funding has come from increased long-term borrowing, now £225,000,000 instead of £50,000,000. Presumably the company has decided to increase turnover. The liquidity or acid test again shows an improvement from a rather weak 0.75 to 1 to an acceptable 1.438 to 1.

Given the high debtors figure, the average collection period has increased from 22.8 days to 33.46 days. This should be looked at with care and possibly steps taken to ensure that debtors pay within a set time.

The average payment period shown is an approximation; seemingly this has improved from 58.4 days to 41.7 days.

The working capital ratio has again improved, showing more working capital as mentioned above. The ratio of debtors to creditors has increased.

Return on capital employed has improved from 19.31% to 22.22%. There is also an improvement in the gross profit percentage. However, the net profit percentage has not improved much, i.e., from 21% to 21.67%. Expenses have increased, in particular the loan interest on the increased borrowing.

As mentioned previously, the rate of stock turnover has slowed and this should be looked at.

Given the increased long-term borrowing the gearing is now higher at 19.2% instead of the very low 5.7%. However, this is still not a high-geared company.

The return on ordinary shareholders' interest has improved as have earnings per share. Dividend cover remains approximately the same.

Clearly a decision was made to increase borrowing to invest in the company. Perhaps a further year is needed to consolidate.

10.8 Check list

By the end of this chapter you should to be able to:

1. appreciate that accounts can be looked at for different purposes;
2. appreciate the limitations in looking at accounts without checking other factors;
3. understand the types of ratios that can be used and their uses;
4. complete a short exercise using some accounting ratios.

10.9 Exercise

Below are shown the accounts of Perry and Mason for the year ending 30 November 200—

Perry and Mason: Profit and Loss account for the year ending 30 November 200—

Income				
Profit costs			300,000	
Add work in progress at 30 Nov 200—			50,000	
			350,000	
Less work in progress at start of year			40,000	
Work done				310,000
Interest received				4,000
				314,000
Less expenses				
General and administrative expenses				
including staff wages			210,000	
Add outstanding expenses			920	
			210,920	
Less payments in advance			1,040	
			209,880	
Travelling expenses			1,000	
Depreciation: library, furniture				
and equipment			7,000	
				217,880
Net profit				96,120
Appropriation account				
Interest on capital at 5%	Perry	8,500		
	Mason	6,000		
			14,500	
Profit share	Perry	40,810		
	Mason	40,810		
			81,620	
				96,120

Perry and Mason: Balance Sheet as at 30 November 200—

FIXED ASSETS			
Freehold premises			240,000
Library furniture and equipment		35,000	
Less depreciation		14,000	
			21,000
			261,000

CURRENT ASSETS

Work in progress	50,000	
Debtors	60,000	
Petty cash	360	
Payments in advance	1,040	
		111,400

LESS CURRENT LIABILITIES

Creditors	10,000	
Outstanding expenses	920	
Bank overdraft	35,000	
		45,920

NET CURRENT ASSETS		65,480
		326,480
LESS LONG-TERM LIABILITIES		—
		326,480

CAPITAL EMPLOYED

Capital accounts:

Perry	170,000	
Mason	120,000	
		290,000

Current accounts: see movement on current accounts:

Perry	22,310	
Mason	14,170	
		36,480
		326,480

Client account

Cash at the bank client account

Current account	190,510	
Deposit account	266,380	
		456,890
Amount due to clients		456,890

Movement on current accounts

	Perry	Mason
Interest on capital	8,500	6,000
Profit share	40,810	40,810
	49,310	46,810
Less drawings	27,000	32,640
	22,310	14,170

From these calculate:

(a) the current ratio;

(b) the acid test;

    (c) the net profit percentage;

    (d) the average collection period;

    (e) the return on capital employed.

Comment on these ratios and on the accounts themselves. How relevant is the return on capital employed ratio? What suggestions would you have for the partners, who are concerned at the overdraft and would like to draw out more cash if possible. What further information would you ask for?

10.10 Suggested answer to exercise

The current ratio

$$\frac{\text{Current assets}}{\text{Current liabilities}} \qquad \frac{111{,}400}{45{,}920} = 2.43 \text{ to } 1$$

The acid test

$$\frac{\text{Current assets less work in progress}}{\text{Current liabilities}} \qquad \frac{61{,}400}{45{,}920} = 1.34 \text{ to } 1$$

The net profit percentage

$$\frac{\text{Net profit}}{\text{Profit costs}} \qquad \frac{96{,}120}{300{,}000} \times 100 = 32.04\%$$

The average collection period

$$\frac{\text{Debtors}}{\text{Profit costs}} \qquad \frac{60{,}000}{300{,}000} \times 365 = 73 \text{ days}$$

The return on capital employed

$$\frac{\text{Net profit}}{\text{Capital employed}} \times 100 \qquad \frac{96{,}120}{326{,}480} \times 100 = 29.44\%$$

The current ratio measures the short-term financial position of the firm. Here clearly there are sufficient current assets to cover current liabilities, a ratio of 2.43 to 1 is good. The acid test is also satisfactory at 1.34 to 1. However, the figures for work in progress and debtors are high; there is no cash at the bank. The value of work in progress should be checked, and bills should be sent out. Debtors should also be checked. There may be some debtors that have been outstanding for a long time, some of these may be irrecoverable, and provision for doubtful debts should be checked. Debtors should be chased, and much tighter control exerted over the length of time that they are taking to pay—see the average collection period of 73 days. However, if a large number of bills were sent out just before the balance sheet was drawn up this would distort the period calculated.

    The net profit percentage at 32.04% may be reasonable, but previous years should be checked, and comparison made, if possible, with similar firms.

The return on capital employed is not very useful in a partnership, as account must be taken of the partners' work—notional salaries could be taken to give a more accurate ratio. The partners have provided for interest on capital as part of the appropriation of profit.

Note that the profit is not cash, and the partners must solve the cash flow problem. Provided that the work in progress figure is realistic, and that the bulk of the debtors are able to pay, this should be possible—see above. It is also possible that the bank is happy to continue financing the firm by way of an overdraft, when the overdraft could be treated as long-term lending. However, given the work in progress and debtors, this would not seem to be necessary, and the firm will save interest charges, etc. if they manage to convert these assets into cash.

As mentioned above, previous years' accounts would be helpful to establish any trends. Is the firm checking bad debts, provision, etc.? What are other similar firms doing? The value of the premises should be checked—is this the correct value, or has it increased or decreased? Should the partners consider sale/leaseback or do they regard this as investment for the future? Any new partner coming in would have to fund this, if, e.g., one of the existing partners left. How old are the partners? Possibly check expenses; can these be reduced?

Basic solicitors' accounts

11.1 Introduction

This chapter deals with the following:

1. The basic principles of the Solicitors' Accounts Rules 1998 (SAR).
2. The need to keep client and office money separate.
3. A form of account showing office and client account.
4. The definition of client money and the rules relating to receipt and payment out.
5. The definition of controlled trust money and the rules applicable.
6. The definition of office money.
7. Basic accounting entries in respect of office and client money.
8. Accounting entries in respect of delivery of a bill to the client.
9. Treatment of agreed fees as defined under the SAR.
10. Record keeping and powers of the Law Society to ensure compliance.
11. Practice exercises.

You should use the Solicitors' Accounts Rules 1998 and become familiar with them.
You may also find the Law Society's web site www.lawsociety.org.uk useful.

11.2 The Solicitors' Accounts Rules 1998 (SAR)

11.2.1 Basic principles, Rule 1

This rule gives the principles which underpin the SAR.
Solicitors must:

(a) comply with the requirements of practice rule 1 re the solicitor's integrity, the duty to act in the client's best interests, and the good repute of the solicitor and the profession;

(b) keep other people's money separate from money belonging to the solicitor or the practice;

(c) keep other people's money safely in a bank or building society account identifiable as a client account (except where the rules specifically provide otherwise);

(d) use each client's money for that client's matters only;

(e) use controlled trust money for the purposes of that trust only;

(f) establish and maintain proper accounting systems, and proper internal controls over those systems, to ensure compliance with the rules;

(g) keep proper accounting records to show accurately the position with regard to the money held for each client and each controlled trust;

(h) account for interest on other people's money in accordance with the rules;

(i) cooperate with the Law Society in checking compliance with the rules; and

(j) deliver annual accountant's reports as required by the rules.

11.2.2   Keeping clients' and office money separate

Solicitors must keep money belonging to clients (clients' money) separate from their own money (office money). This means having at least two separate accounts at the bank or building society, the Client bank account and the Office bank account.

A Client account must be in the name of the solicitor, the solicitors' firm, or solicitors' company, and must contain the word 'Client'. SAR Rule 14.

The solicitor must therefore have two cash accounts in the ledger system: the Office cash account and the Client cash account. For convenience these two are shown side by side, as follows:

Cash account

Date	Details	Office account			Client account		
		DR	CR	Balance	DR	CR	Balance

Each client ledger card will also show that there are two accounts:

Smith: re conveyancing

Date	Details	Office account			Client account		
		DR	CR	Balance	DR	CR	Balance

Although the money for all clients will, as a general rule, be kept in one bank account, the solicitor must record separately in respect of each client the money which is being held for that client. This means that the solicitor must not use money belonging to one client for the purposes of another client, nor may the solicitor transfer the money of one client from that client's ledger account to the ledger account of another client except as provided for in the rules (see **12.1.3**).

11.2.3   The definition of clients' money, Rule 13

Whenever a solicitor receives or pays money on behalf of a client, the solicitor must decide whether it is clients' or office money. The rules define clients' money as money held or received by a solicitor for a client. This includes money held as agent, bailee, stakeholder or as the donee of a power of attorney, or as a liquidator, trustee in bankruptcy or Court of Protection receiver.

11.2.3.1 Solicitors not to operate banking facilities

Note that the Solicitors' Disciplinary Tribunal stated in the case of Wood and Burdett that it is not a proper part of a solicitor's everyday business or practice to operate a banking facility for third parties, whether they are clients of the firm or not.

Solicitors should also bear in mind that there are criminal sanctions against assisting money launderers. See Rule 15 note (ix).

11.2.4 Payments into client account

Where a solicitor receives clients' money, the solicitor must normally pay it into a client bank account without delay. This means on the day the money is received or, if that is not possible, on the next working day, Rule 15.

11.2.4.1 Money received from client on account of costs and disbursements rules 13 and 19

Money paid generally on account of costs and disbursements is clients' money and must be paid into client account.

11.2.4.2 Money which may be paid into client account, Rule 15

The following 'non-client' money may be paid into a client account:

(a) Controlled trust money (see **11.2.8**);

(b) the solicitor's own money required to open or maintain the account;

(c) an advance from the solicitor to fund a payment on behalf of a client or controlled trust in excess of funds held for that client or controlled trust, the sum becomes client money or controlled trust money on payment into the account;

(d) money to replace that withdrawn in contravention of the rules;

(e) a sum in lieu of interest paid into client account;

(f) cheques which the solicitor would be entitled to 'split' but does not (i.e., mixed office/client money).

11.2.4.3 Receipt of mixed office/client money, Rules 19 and 20

Where mixed money is received this can be:

(1) split, part paid into office account, and part into client account;

(2) all paid into client account and then the office money transferred to office account within 14 days;

(3) if the mixed money consists of office money and unpaid professional disbursements only (for example unpaid counsel's fees) then the money can be paid into office account, and within 2 working days the unpaid disbursement must either be paid or the unpaid amount transferred to client account.

There are also special rules relating to the treatment of monies received from the Legal Aid Board and payments from a third party in respect of legal aid work (see **11.2.5** and **11.2.6**).

11.2.4.4 Money which must be withheld from client account

(a) Money should not be paid into a client account if the client has asked for it not to be paid into a client account. Such a request from the client should be in writing, or confirmed in writing by the solicitor, Rule 16.

(b) Where a solicitor agrees to hold a cheque 'to the order' of a third party, the cheque should not be paid into a client account until it is released by the third party, as until that point it does not become the client's money.

11.2.4.5   Money which may be withheld from client account, Rule 17

A solicitor is not obliged to pay into a client account, clients' money held or received:

(a) in cash, which is, without delay, paid in cash, in the ordinary course of business, to the client or on the client's behalf to a third party; or

(b) in the form of a cheque or banker's draft received which is endorsed over in the ordinary course of business to the client or on the client's behalf to a third party; or

(c) which is paid into a separate bank account or building society account opened in the name of the client or a third party designated in writing by the client or acknowledged in writing by the solicitor.

Note: if a solicitor negotiates cash or endorses a cheque made out to him, then the solicitor has handled clients' money and must make entries in the account to show the receipt and payment of clients' money. Note also that many cheques are now non-endorsable (see **11.3.5**).

If a solicitor receives a cheque made payable to a third party which the solicitor passes on to that third party then the solicitor has not handled clients' money and should not record a receipt and payment of clients' money in the accounts. It is, however, advisable to record the fact that the cheque has been received and passed on. This can be done by a file note and/or an entry on the client's ledger account by way of memorandum.

11.2.4.6   Record keeping for accounts held jointly with outsiders

Where two firms of solicitors place stakeholder money in an account in their joint names, this is subject to limited compliance with the rules, records must be kept, statements and passbooks retained and it is subject to monitoring and inspection by reporting accountants and the Law Society. If the stakeholder money is in the sole control of one firm it is clients' money and must be paid into client account.

11.2.5   Payments from the Legal Services Commission, Rule 21

An advance payment in anticipation of work to be carried out, although client money, may be placed in office account provided the Commission instructs in writing that this may be done. A payment for costs, interim or final, may be paid into office account, although it may include client money re advance payments for fees of disbursements or money for unpaid professional disbursements provided all money for payment of disbursements is transferred to client account or the disbursements paid within 14 days of receipt.

Regular payments from the Commission are office money and must be paid into office account. Within 28 days of submitting a report to the Commission notifying completion a solicitor must either:

pay any unpaid professional disbursements; or

transfer to a client account a sum equivalent to the amount of the unpaid professional disbursements.

11.2.6   Legal aid—payments from a third party, Rule 21(2)

If the Legal Services Commission has paid any costs to a solicitor or paid professional disbursements direct and costs are later settled by a third party, the entire third party settlement must be paid into client account (either the individual's client account or a separate account in the Commission's name). Any balance belonging to the solicitor must be transferred to office account within 14 days of the solicitor sending a report of the details of the payment to the Commission. A sum representing the payments made by the Commission must be retained in client account until the Commission notifies the solicitor that it has recouped an equivalent sum from subsequent payments due to the solicitor, when the retained sum should be transferred to office account within 14 days.

11.2.7 Withdrawals from a client account, Rule 22

The following, in particular, should be noted with regard to the withdrawal of money from a client account:

(a) Clients' money can be used to make payments only if enough money is held in client account for the particular client on whose behalf it is desired to make the payment, Rule 22(5).

(b) If insufficient money is held in client account for the particular client the solicitor may either:

    (i)   pay the disbursement out of office account (the solicitor may then transfer the balance held on client account, to office account); or

    (ii)   draw two cheques, one on client account for the balance held and one on office account for the remainder.

Note also that the solicitor may advance money to fund a payment on behalf of a client in excess of funds held for that client.

(c) **client money** can be withdrawn if:

    (i)   properly required for a payment to or on behalf of the client;

    (ii)   properly required for payment of a disbursement on behalf of the client;

    (iii)   properly required in full or partial reimbursement of money spent by the solicitor on behalf of the client. Money is spent by the solicitor at the time when the solicitor dispatches a cheque unless the cheque is to be held to the solicitor's order. Money is also spent by the use of a credit account, for example, search fees or taxi fares.

    (iv)   transferred to another client account;

    (v)   withdrawn on the client's instructions provided the instructions are for the client's convenience and are given in writing or confirmed by the solicitor in writing;

    (vi)   a refund to the solicitor of an advance no longer required to fund a payment on behalf of a client;

    (vii)   money which has been paid into the account in breach of the rules (e.g., money paid into the wrong separate designated client account or interest wrongly credited to a general client account);

    (viii) money withdrawn from the account on the written authorisation of the Law Society.

Office money can be withdrawn from client account if it is:

    (i)   money which had properly been paid in to open or maintain the account;

    (ii)   money properly required for payment of the solicitors' costs, where a bill of costs or other written notification of the costs incurred has been given to the client. Once the solicitor has done this the money must be transferred out of client account within 14 days.

(iii) the whole or part of payment re legal aid payment paid in;

(iv) part of a mixed office/client payment previously paid in.

Note that similar rules apply to controlled trust money.

Note it is possible to draw against an uncleared cheque under the rules.

However, a solicitor should use discretion in drawing against an uncleared cheque. If the cheque is not met then other client's money will have been used to make the payment in breach of the rules and the breach must be remedied. A solicitor may be able to avoid a breach of the rules by instructing the bank or building society to charge all unpaid credits to the solicitor's office or personal account.

11.2.8   Controlled trusts

11.2.8.1   Definition

A solicitor may hold money as a 'controlled trustee'. A solicitor will be a controlled trustee if a sole trustee or the only other trustees are his or her partners or employees. If a solicitor is a trustee with an outside third party then the solicitor is not a controlled trustee.

11.2.8.2   Rules

Normally controlled trust money should be paid without delay into a client account under Rule 15. This is subject to the same exceptions as client money, for example, cash received and without delay paid in cash in the execution of the trust to a beneficiary or third party (see para **11.2.4.2** previously) and, in accordance with the trustee's powers, it may be paid into or retained in an account of the trustee which is not a client account (e.g., a building society share account or an account outside England and Wales) or properly retained in cash in the performance of the trustee's duties.

11.2.8.3   Interest on controlled trust money

The general law requires a solicitor to act in the best interests of a controlled trust and not to benefit personally from it. Note that the rules as to interest on client money do not apply to controlled trust money. A solicitor must obtain the best reasonably obtainable rate of interest for the controlled trust money and must account to the relevant controlled trust for all the interest earned, whether the controlled trust money is held in a separate designated client account or in a general client account.

To ensure that all interest is accounted for, solicitors may set up a general client account just for controlled trust money or can set up a designated account for each controlled trust.

When controlled trust money is held in a general client account, interest will be credited to the office account in the normal way, but all interest must be promptly allocated to each controlled trust—either by transfer to the general client account or to separate designated client accounts for the particular trust or by payment to each trust in some other way.

11.2.8.4   Indirect benefit

Solicitors must also consider whether they have received any indirect benefit from controlled trust money at the expense of the controlled trust. For example, the bank might charge a reduced overdraft rate on office account by reference to the total funds (including controlled trust money) held by the solicitors on client account in return for paying a lower rate of interest on those funds. The solicitor may have to do more for the trust than merely account for such interest earned in these circumstances.

Note that if controlled trust money is invested in the purchase of assets other than money, e.g., stocks and shares, it is no longer controlled trust money, but it will become controlled trust money again when the investments are later sold.

11.2.8.5 Delegation to outside manager

There is a special provision that controlled trustees may delegate to an outside manager the day-to-day keeping of accounts of the business or property portfolio of an estate or trust, provided the manager keeps and retains appropriate accounting records which are available for inspection by the Law Society.

11.2.8.6 Solicitor co-trustee with outsiders

Contrast the above with the position where the solicitor is trustee with others outside the firm and is not a controlled trustee. In such circumstances monies held will be normal client account money and the normal rules will apply, including the rules as to interest payable.

11.2.9 Note also the following under the SAR 1998

Liquidators, trustees in bankruptcy and Court of Protection receivers are now included in the rules, limited to record keeping requirements, and subject to monitoring and inspection by the Law Society and reporting accountants, to protect the clients and the profession from claims on the Solicitors' Indemnity and Compensation Funds.

Solicitors operating a client's account, e.g., under a power of attorney, should receive all statements and passbooks and retain these, as they will be subject to monitoring and inspection by the Law Society and reporting accountants.

11.2.10 The definition of office money, Rule 13

This is money that belongs to the solicitor or to the practice. It includes:

(a) money held or received in connection with running the practice, e.g. PAYE or VAT on the firm's fees;

(b) interest on general client accounts (but see the rules related to interest on controlled trust money);

(c) payments received in respect of:
   (i)   fees due to the practice against a bill or written notification of costs incurred;
   (ii)   disbursements already paid by the practice;
   (iii) disbursements incurred but not yet paid by the practice but excluding unpaid professional disbursements;
   (iv)   money paid for or towards an agreed fee;

(d) money held in a client account and earmarked for costs (transfer costs from client account to office account).

11.2.10.1 Partners' money is office money

Money belonging to a principal solicitor or one of his partners cannot be treated as clients' money and must always be paid into office account. For example, if the firm acts for one of the partners in the purchase of a house in his sole name, free of mortgage, and the partner hands a cheque for the deposit to the firm's cashier, the cheque must be paid into office account. Note the following, however:

(a) If the firm is acting for a partner and that partner's spouse (who is not a partner), any moneys received will be held on behalf of both as trustees and must be treated as clients' money.

(b) If the firm is acting for a partner in the purchase of a property with the aid of a mortgage, the mortgage advance is clients' money.

(c) If the firm is acting for an assistant solicitor, a consultant or a non-solicitor employee, or in the case of a recognised body, a director, they will be regarded as clients even if dealing with the matter personally.

11.3 Basic entries

Note that office and client columns are separate. An entry in the client column of one account must have its corresponding double entry in the client column of another account. The same obviously applies also to office account entries.

11.3.1 Receipt of office moneys

The firm must pay money owed to it into office account. The entries to record this are:

(a) CREDIT client's ledger account—office column.

(b) DEBIT Cash account—office column.

EXAMPLE

On 1 February the solicitor receives £100 in respect of disbursements already paid out of office account for his client, Black.

Black

Date	Details	Office account			Client account		
		DR	CR	Balance	DR	CR	Balance
	Balance			100 DR			
1 Feb	Cash		100	—			

Cash account

Date	Details	Office account			Client account		
		DR	CR	Balance	DR	CR	Balance
1 Feb	Black	100		100 DR			

11.3.2 Payments of office money

The firm must pay disbursements out of office account if there is insufficient money in client account for that particular client, unless the solicitor decides to transfer office money to client account (see **11.2.4.2**). The entries to record a payment of office monies are:

(a) DEBIT client's ledger account—office column.

(b) CREDIT Cash account—office column.

EXAMPLE

Brown's solicitors are acting on his behalf with regard to a personal injury claim. They are not holding any money on Brown's behalf and pay £400 to counsel for an opinion on liability on 1 March.

Brown: re personal injury action

Date	Details	Office account			Client account		
		DR	CR	Balance	DR	CR	Balance
1 Mar	Cash: counsel	400		400 DR			

Cash account

Date	Details	Office account			Client account		
		DR	CR	Balance	DR	CR	Balance
1 Mar	Brown—counsel		400	400 CR			

The client's ledger account should generally show a debit balance or a nil balance on office account. A credit balance may indicate a breach of the Solicitors' Accounts Rules. Exceptions to this include agreed fees (see **7.5.2**) mixed monies, including unpaid professional disbursements, and interest (see **15.1.3**)

If there is money held in client account but not enough to pay the particular disbursements, so that the whole payment is made out of office account, the solicitor may transfer the money held in client account to office account once the disbursement has been paid. As an alternative, two cheques could be drawn to pay the disbursement, one on client account for the amount held and the remainder on office account. In practice this is rarely done.

11.3.3 Receipt of clients' money

Once it has been decided that money received is clients' money it must be paid into client account promptly. The entries are:

(a) CREDIT client's ledger account—client column.

(b) DEBIT Cash account—client column.

EXAMPLE

On 1 April the firm receives a cheque for £2,000 from the Bramchester Building Society to be used as a deposit on the purchase of Blackacre by the firm's client, White.

White: re purchase of Blackacre

Date	Details	Office account			Client account		
		DR	CR	Balance	DR	CR	Balance
1 Apr	Cash: Bramchester Building Society					2,000	2,000 CR

Cash account

Date	Details	Office account			Client account		
		DR	CR	Balance	DR	CR	Balance
1 Apr	White: Bramchester Building Society				2,000		2,000 DR

If money is received from a third party on behalf of a client, as in the preceding example, the receipt is recorded in the ledger account of the client on whose behalf the money is received. An account is not opened for the third party.

Remember the solicitor must not pay the following into client account:

(a) the solicitor's own or a partner's money (except as allowed by the rules);

(b) money received to pay costs after a bill has been delivered;

(c) money the client asks him or her not to pay into client account.

Solicitors may receive cash on behalf of a client and are permitted to pay this over to the client. However they must still record the receipt and payment out of client money on the accounts.

11.3.4 Payment out of clients' money

Before making a payment out of client account, the solicitor should check:

(a) that sufficient money is held in client account for the client on whose behalf the payment is being made;

(b) that the payment is permissible within the Solicitors' Accounts Rules 1998.

The bookkeeping entries are:

(a) DEBIT the client's ledger account—client column.

(b) CREDIT the Cash account—client column.

EXAMPLE

On 7 April the firm pays the £2,000 deposit received from the Bramchester Building Society for White, to Fleets the seller's solicitors.

White: re purchase of Blackacre

Date	Details	Office account			Client account		
		DR	CR	Balance	DR	CR	Balance
1 Apr	Cash: Bramchester Building Society					2,000	2,000 CR
7 Apr	Cash: Fleets re deposit				2,000		—

Cash account

Date	Details	Office account			Client account		
		DR	CR	Balance	DR	CR	Balance
1 Apr	White: Bramchester Building Society				2,000		2,000 DR
7 Apr	White: Fleets re deposit					2,000	—

11.3.5 Cheques made payable to third parties

You may be required to show that you appreciate that when you hand over to a third party a cheque made payable to the third party, you have not handled clients' money. You can do this by making no entry at all in the accounts. Alternatively, you can make what is known as a memorandum entry. If you do this, remember; no entry is made in the cash account at all, no balance column entry is made in the client's ledger account and the details column should show clearly that the entry is by way of memorandum only.

EXAMPLE

You act for Charles to recover a debt owed to him by Janis. On 1 February Janis sends you a cheque for £250 made payable to Charles.

Charles: re debt collection

Date	Details	Office account			Client account		
		DR	CR	Balance	DR	CR	Balance
1 Feb	Cheque received from Janis payable to Charles memorandum entry only				[250	250]	

11.4 Payments out of petty cash—office account

Small disbursements paid on behalf of clients, for example, commissioner's fees, may be paid in cash rather than by cheque.

The solicitor maintains a petty cash float by drawing money out of office account at the bank. Any petty cash payments must therefore be made from the office account.

To record dealings with petty cash, a petty cash account is used, or a petty cash book if the ledger system is operated.

To record the transfer of money from the office bank account to the petty cash account the following entries are made:

(a) CREDIT the Cash account in the office column.

(b) DEBIT the Petty Cash account (office account).

EXAMPLE

On 10 January a solicitor draws £500 out of office account for petty cash.

Cash account

Date	Details	Office account			Client account		
		DR	CR	Balance	DR	CR	Balance
	Balance say			2,000 DR			
10 Jan	Petty cash		500	1,500 DR			

Only office money can be held in petty cash, therefore only office account columns are necessary.

Petty cash account (office account only)

Date	Details	DR	CR	Balance
10 Jan	Cash float	500		500 DR

As payments made out of petty cash are always office account payments, even if there is money in client account, a petty cash payment must always be recorded as coming out of office account.

To record the payment of a petty cash disbursement on a client's behalf the following entries are made in the accounts:

(a) DEBIT the client's ledger account in the office column.

(b) CREDIT the Petty Cash account (office).

EXAMPLE

On 15 January the firm pays £40 out of petty cash for local advertisements in the administration of Kate's estate.

Kate deceased: administration of estate

Date	Details	Office account			Client account		
		DR	CR	Balance	DR	CR	Balance
15 Jan	Petty cash: local advertisements	40		40 DR			

Petty cash account (office account)

Date	Details	DR	CR	Balance
10 Jan	Cash float	500		500 DR
15 Jan	Kate deceased		40	460 DR

11.5 Profit costs

11.5.1 Delivery of bills of costs

When a solicitor delivers a bill of costs to the client, a central record or file of copies of bills must be kept. This is in addition to the entries shown below.

When a bill of costs is delivered to a client the following entries are made in the accounts:

(a) DEBIT client ledger account office column with profit costs and VAT (on separate lines).

(b) CREDIT the Profit Costs account with profit costs.

(c) CREDIT the Customs and Excise account with VAT.

The Profit Costs account and Customs and Excise accounts only record dealings with office money and therefore only have office columns.

EXAMPLE

On 15 June 2002 the firm delivers a bill of costs to Beryl, for whom it has acted in divorce proceedings, for £100 plus £17.50 VAT.

Beryl: re divorce

Date	Details	Office account			Client account		
		DR	CR	Balance	DR	CR	Balance
15 June	Profit costs	100					
	VAT	17.50		117.50 DR			

Profit costs account

Date	Details	Office accounts		
		DR	CR	Balance
15 June	Beryl		100	100 CR

Customs and excise account

Date	Details	Office accounts		
		DR	CR	Balance
15 June	Beryl		17.50	17.50 CR

Entries are made to record the delivery of the bill of costs on the date of delivery regardless of the date of payment. When payment of the bill is made entries are made in the accounts to record a receipt of office moneys.

EXAMPLE

Beryl pays her bill on 1 July

Date	Details	Office account			Client account		
		DR	CR	Balance	DR	CR	Balance
15 June	Profit costs	100		100 DR			
	VAT	17.50		117.50 DR			
1 July	Cash you		117.50	—			

Note: DEBIT the Cash account—office column, £117.50.

11.5.2   Agreed fees

A solicitor and client may agree a fee for work which the solicitor has done or is to do on the client's behalf. When the solicitor receives the agreed fee it must be paid into office account even though a bill of costs is not delivered until a later date. The agreed fee must be evidenced in writing. It is not necessary to draw a bill when a fee is agreed.

EXAMPLE

On 10 July the firm receives £94 from Jill in respect of a fee agreed at the beginning of the month for work done by the firm on Jill's behalf in connection with a tenancy dispute. A bill is delivered on receipt of the fee.

Jill: re housing

Date	Details	Office account			Client account		
		DR	CR	Balance	DR	CR	Balance
10 July	Cash you		94	94 CR			
	Profit costs (agreed fee)	80		14 CR			
	VAT	14		—			

Note:

(a) It would be a breach of the Solicitors' Accounts Rules to pay money, expressly paid in respect of an agreed fee, into client account.

(b) The tax point for VAT arises when the fee is received, not when a bill is subsequently delivered.

11.6   Record keeping and compliance

11.6.1   Solicitors' duty to keep accounts

A solicitor has a duty to keep accounts to record transactions involving clients' money. The accounts and all bank statements must be preserved for a minimum period of six years

(r. 32(9) of the Solicitors' Accounts Rules 1998). Where a computerised system is used the solicitor must ensure that a hard copy can be produced reasonably quickly and that it remains capable of reproduction for at least six years.

In addition, all paid cheques and copies of authorities for withdrawal of money from a client account must be retained for at least two years. To avoid the practical problems associated with storage, there is provision in the rules for the solicitor to obtain written confirmation from the bank that it will retain cheques for the required two-year period.

Under Rule 35, solicitors who hold client money or controlled trust money during an accounting period must have their client accounts inspected by an accountant 'qualified' within the meaning of the rules, and must submit an accountant's report to the Law Society for that accounting period within six months of the end of the accounting period.

The Law Society has the power to appoint an accountant to investigate a solicitor's practice.

11.6.2 Powers of the Law Society to secure compliance

Section 34 of the Solicitors Act 1974 requires solicitors to deliver an annual accountant's report to the Law Society. If solicitors fail to deliver such a report or fail to comply with the Solicitors' Accounts Rules 1998, a complaint may be made to the Solicitors' Disciplinary Tribunal by the Law Society.

Under Rule 34 of the Solicitors' Accounts Rules 1998, solicitors must produce to any person appointed by the Law Society records necessary to enable preparation of a report on compliance with the Rules. Any report made by the person appointed may be sent to the Crown Prosecution Service or the Serious Fraud Office and/or used in proceedings before the Solicitors' Disciplinary Tribunal.

11. 7 Check list

By the end of this chapter you should be able to:

1. identify office and client money;
2. understand when client money may be withdrawn from client account;
3. identify controlled trust money and appreciate the position in respect of interest and possible indirect benefit;
4. understand and be able to draw up basic entries in respect of the receipt and payment of office and client money;
5. appreciate that petty cash must be office money;
6. understand and be able to draw up entries on the relevant accounts in respect of the delivery of a bill of costs to the client;
7. understand that agreed fees as defined under the SAR should be paid into office account;
8. know the accounts record keeping requirements for solicitors and the powers of the Law Society to secure compliance;
9. complete the self test exercises at the end of the chapter.

11.8   Practice exercises

Treat each of the first six questions separately, and assume in each example the cash account starts with nil balances on office and client account.

1   On 1 January the firm receives an agreed fee of £470 from their client Abraham. Show the entries that would be made on the client ledger account for Abraham and on the firm's cash book.

2   On 2 February the firm receives a cheque for £270,000 in respect of the sale of a property on behalf of a partner, Quasim. Show the entries required on the relevant accounts for the receipt.

3   On 3 March the firm pays out £40 being a court fee, on behalf of their client Silver. Silver has not yet made any payment on account of costs and disbursements. Show the relevant entries.

4   On 4 April the firm receives a cheque for £300 on general account of costs and disbursements from their client Manikai in respect of property transactions. The firm then pays a search fee of £120 on behalf of the client. Show the relevant entries on the accounts.

5   On 5 May the firm pays an expert £500 from office account on behalf of their client Humbert. On 10 May Humbert pays the firm £500 in respect of the disbursement paid. Show the relevant entries on the accounts.

6   On 6 June the firm pays out an expert's fee of £200 on behalf of their client Campbell from office account. On 9 June the firm sends a bill to Campbell for £160 plus VAT. On 15 June Campbell pays the total due to the firm. Show the relevant entries on the accounts.

11.9   Answers to practice exercises

1   Abraham—general matters

Date	Details	Office account			Client account		
		DR	CR	Bal	DR	CR	Bal
1 Jan	Cash—you—agreed fee		470	470 CR			

Cash account

Date	Details	Office account			Client account		
		DR	CR	Bal	DR	CR	Bal
1 Jan	Abraham agreed fee	470		470 DR			

Note that as the date of receipt of the agreed fee is the tax point for VAT purposes then it would be advisable to send out a VAT invoice and record the fee and VAT on the account (see Chapter 13 on VAT).

2 Quasim—sale of property

Date	Details	Office account			Client account		
		DR	CR	Bal	DR	CR	Bal
2 Feb	Cash—sale proceeds		270,000	270,000 CR			

Cash account

Date	Details	Office account			Client account		
		DR	CR	Bal	DR	CR	Bal
2 Feb	Quasim—sale proceeds	270,000		270,000 DR			

Note that this money must be paid into office account as the partner is solely entitled to the money. See SAR rule 13 note (xii).

3 Silver—litigation

Date	Details	Office account			Client account		
		DR	CR	Bal	Dr	CR	Bal
3 Mar	Cash—court fee	40		40 DR			

Cash Account

Date	Details	Office account			Client account		
		DR	CR	Bal	DR	CR	Bal
3 Mar	Silver—court fee		40	40 CR			

4 Manikai—property sale and purchase

Date	Details	Office account			Client account		
		DR	CR	Bal	DR	CR	Bal
4 Apr	Cash—you on account of costs & disbursements					300	300 CR
	Cash—search fee				120		180 CR

Cash account

Date	Details	Office account			Client account		
		DR	CR	Bal	DR	CR	Bal
4 Apr	Manikai—on account of costs				300		300 DR
	Manikai—search fee					120	180 DR

5 Humbert—general matters

Date	Details	Office account			Client account		
		DR	CR	Bal	DR	CR	Bal
5 May	Cash—expert	500		500 DR			
10 May	Cash—you payment of disbursement		500	—			

Cash account

Date	Details	Office account			Client account		
		DR	CR	Bal	DR	CR	Bal
5 May	Humbert—expert		500	500 CR			
10 May	Humbert—payment of disbursement	500		—			

6 Campbell—general matters

Date	Details	Office account			Client account		
		DR	CR	Bal	DR	CR	Bal
6 June	Cash—expert	200		200 DR			
9 June	Profit Costs—bill	160		360 DR			
	Customs & Excise VAT	28		388 DR			
15 June	Cash—you—balance due		388	—			

Cash account

Date	Details	Office account			Client account		
		DR	CR	Bal	DR	CR	Bal
6 June	Campbell—expert		200	200 CR			
9 June	Campbell—balance due	388		188 DR			

Profit costs account

Date	Details	Office account		
		DR	CR	Bal
9 June	Campbell—bill		160	160 CR

Customs and excise (VAT) account

Date	Details	Office account		
		DR	CR	Bal
9 June	Campbell—bill		28	28CR

Note the balances at the end of each account at the end of the transaction. Campbell's account is clear; he no longer owes the firm any money. The firm is holding £188 on the Cash book, which represents £160 for the firm's profit costs and £28 for Customs and Excise. It has been repaid the £200 it paid out.

Transfers and mixed money

12.1 Introduction

This chapter deals with the following:

1. Transfers from client to office account.
2. Transfers from office to client account.
3. Transfers between client accounts.
4. Methods of dealing with the receipt of mixed office and client money.

12.2 Transfers

12.2.1 Transfers from client to office account

A transfer may be made from client to office account if it is permissible, within the Solicitors' Accounts Rules 1998, to withdraw money from client account.

A solicitor may wish to transfer money from client to office account if:

(a) disbursements have been paid out of office account on the client's behalf;

(b) a bill of costs has been delivered to the client and the solicitor needs to obtain payment of costs by transferring money held in client account;

(c) a cheque for mixed office/client money has been paid into client account.

The bookkeeping entries to record a transfer from client to office account are:

(1) the entries to record a payment out of clients' money (see **12.5.4**);

(2) the entries to record a receipt of office money (see **12.5.1**).

EXAMPLE

On 2 December 2002 the firm delivered a bill of costs to its client Green, showing profit costs of £200 and VAT £35. The firm is holding £500 in client account for Green. On 5 December the firm transfers £235 from client to office account.

Green

Date	Details	Office account			Client account		
		DR	CR	Balance	DR	CR	Balance
200—							
	Balance						500 CR
2 Dec	Profit costs	200					
	VAT	35		235 DR			
5 Dec	Cash: transfer		235[2] IN	—	235[1] OUT		265 CR

Cash account

Date	Details	Office account			Client account		
		DR	CR	Balance	DR	CR	Balance
200—							
	Green				500		500 DR
5 Dec	Cash: transfer	235[2] IN		235 DR		235[1] OUT	265 DR

Note:
(1) Payment of client's money.
(2) Receipt of office money.

12.2.2 Transfer from office account to client account

A solicitor must make an immediate transfer from office account to client account if he or she has breached the Solicitors' Accounts Rules 1998 by overdrawing on client account, for example, by drawing against an uncleared cheque which is later dishonoured.

The bookkeeping entries to record a transfer of money from office account to client account are as follows:

(1) entries to record a payment of office money (see **12.5.2**);

(2) entries to record a receipt of clients' money (see **12.5.3**).

EXAMPLE

Brown has a credit balance on client account of £50. On 20 October her solicitor inadvertently pays counsel's fee of £70 out of client account. She makes an immediate transfer from office to client account to correct the breach.

Brown

Date	Details	Office account			Client account		
		DR	CR	Balance	DR	CR	Balance
	Balance						50 CR
20 Oct	Cash: counsel				70		20 DR
	Cash: transfer	20[1] OUT		20 DR		20[2] IN	—

Cash account

Date	Details	Office account			Client account		
		DR	CR	Balance	DR	CR	Balance
20 Oct	Balance				50		50 DR
	Cash: counsel: Brown					70	20 CR
	Cash: transfer: Brown OUT		20[1]	20 CR	20[2] IN		—

Note:
(1) Entries to record payment of office money.
(2) Entries to record receipt of clients' money.

12.2.3 Transfers between client accounts

Money is not moved from one bank account to another and therefore no entries are made in the Cash account.

A transfer can be made from one client ledger account to another client ledger account if:

(a) it is permissible within the rules to withdraw money from the account of client A;

(b) it is permissible within the rules to pay money into the account of client B.

When a transfer is made from one client ledger account to another, a separate record must be made. This may be, for example, in a journal if the ledger system is used, or on a transfer sheet if a card system is used. Rule 32(2) SAR.

The bookkeeping entries to record transfers between client accounts are as follows:

(a) DEBIT the ledger account of the client from whose account the transfer is being made. (Make a separate record.)

(b) CREDIT the ledger account of the client to whose account the transfer is being made. (Make a separate record.)

EXAMPLE

The firm is holding £10,000 in client account for its client Blue. The firm also acts for Blue's son-in-law, Red, with regard to his house purchase. Blue is making a gift to Red of the deposit of £8,000 and asks the firm to pay Red's deposit on 7 April out of the money held for him.

Blue

Date	Details	Office account			Client account		
		DR	CR	Balance	DR	CR	Balance
	Balance						10,000 CR
7 Apr	Red: transfer sheet				8,000		2,000 CR

Red

Date	Details	Office account			Client account		
		DR	CR	Balance	DR	CR	Balance
7 Apr	Blue: transfer sheet					8,000	8,000 CR
	Cash: deposit paid				8,000		—

Note: a transfer may be made from the client account of one client to the office account of another or vice versa. For example, if one client has agreed to moneys being taken from his or her client account to discharge another client's liability for costs. If this is done the four entries used to make a transfer from client to office account or vice versa must be shown (see **12.2.1** and **12.2.2**).

EXAMPLE

The firm acts for the executors of Alexander. It also acts for Olivia, Alexander's daughter and the sole beneficiary. There is a balance of £12,000 on Alexander's account. The firm has acted for Olivia in her divorce proceedings and a bill has been delivered to Olivia for £1,000 plus VAT. The executors agree to this being paid out of the estate.

Executors of Alexander deceased

Date	Details	Office account			Client account		
		DR	CR	Balance	DR	CR	Balance
	Balance						12,000 CR
	Cash transfer—Olivia				1,175 OUT(1)		10,825 CR

Olivia: re divorce

Date	Details	Office account			Client account		
		DR	CR	Balance	DR	CR	Balance
	Profit costs	1,000					
	VAT	175		1,175 DR			
	Cash—Alexander		1,175 IN(2)	—			

Cash account

Date	Details	Office account			Client account		
		DR	CR	Balance	DR	CR	Balance
	Balance						12,000 DR
	Alexander—						
	transfer to Olivia	1,175 IN(2)		1,175 DR		1,175 OUT(1)	10,825 DR

The Solicitors' Accounts Rules 1998 restrict inter-client transfers in respect of private loans. Rule 30(2) states that no sum in respect of a private loan shall be paid out of funds held on account of the lender, either:

(a) directly to the borrower; or

(b) by means of a payment from one client account to another or by a paper transfer from the ledger of the lender to that of the borrower

without the prior written authority of **both** clients.

A private loan on standard terms is defined as meaning a loan other than one provided by an institution which provides loans in the normal course of its activities. The solicitor should keep a register of authorities for transactions of this type.

12.2.4 Mixed office/client money

When a solicitor receives mixed office/client money the alternatives are Rule 20 SAR:

(a) pay the cheque into client account and then make a transfer from client to office account of the office money within 14 days of receipt; or

(b) split the cheque by paying the client's money into client account and the office money into office account.

(c) If the payment consists of office money and client money in the form of unpaid professional disbursements the entire sum may be paid into office account and by the end of the second working day following receipt either the unpaid professional disbursement should be paid or the relevant sum transferred to client account. Rule 19(1)(b) SAR.

There are also special rules relating to the treatment of monies received from the Legal Services Commission and payment from a third party in respect of legal aid work (see **11.2.5** and **11.2.6**).

EXAMPLE

Pink sends a cheque for £250 to his solicitor on 1 March. The cheque represents £200 owed by Pink to a creditor and £50 costs owed to the solicitor in respect of which a bill was delivered to Pink on 1 February.

(a) If the cheque is split the entries in Pink's account will be:

Pink account

Date	Details	Office account			Client account		
		DR	CR	Balance	DR	CR	Balance
	Balance			50 DR			
1 Mar	Cash: you—split cheque		50	—		200	200 CR

(b) If the cheque is not split, the entries in Pink's account will be:

Pink account

Date	Details	Office account			Client account		
		DR	CR	Balance	DR	CR	Balance
	Balance			50 DR			
	Cash: you—mixed money					250	250 CR

When the £50 in respect of costs is transferred to office account, entries will be made in Pink's account and the cash account to record a transfer from client to office account (see **12.2.1**).

12.3 Check list

By the end of this chapter you should be able to:

1. understand when transfers from client to office account are permitted under the SAR and draw up the entries to record a transfer from client to office account on the relevant accounts;

2. understand the limited circumstances when a transfer from office account to client account will be made and draw up the entries to record a transfer from office account to client account on the relevant accounts;

3. understand when transfers can be made between client accounts and that these will not be recorded on the cash account but on the relevant client ledger accounts with a separate record of the transfer and draw up the entries required on the accounts in respect of a transfer between client accounts;

4. understand the options available in respect of the receipt of mixed office and client money and draw up the entries required;

5. complete the self test exercises at the end of the chapter.

12.4 Exercises on basic ledger entries

In the following questions draw up the clients' ledger accounts to record the transactions.

1 Pay counsel's fee £188 on behalf of Nigel. Deliver a bill for £120 plus £21 VAT and disbursement. Receive payment.

2 You act for Mary. Pay search fee £10 by cash. Pay for office copy entries by cheque £15. Receive £100 from Mary on account of disbursements.

3 Lynn pays you £75 on account. Pay £5 out of petty cash on Lynn's behalf for inspection of deeds. Deliver a bill of costs for £100 plus VAT. Receive payment of balance from Lynn and close her account.

4 Receive £235 from John in respect of an agreed fee for conveyancing work, which includes VAT.

5 Margaret's account shows a balance in hand of £500. Margaret asks you to transfer £300 to Daphne, another client of the firm.

6 Keith asks you to pay a premium of £75 on his behalf to the Star Insurance Co. for whom you act. He pays £75 to you one week later, by agreement.

7 You act for Alan, pay counsel's fee £94 including VAT £14. Deliver a bill of costs to Alan for £120 plus VAT. Receive moneys due from Alan.

8 You act for Carol: 1 September pay counsel's fee £235 including VAT £35, 19 September receive £450 from Carol; 23 September pay disbursement £47 and deliver a bill of costs £120 plus VAT £21. Transfer sum due from client to office account. Pay balance due to Carol.

9 The firm's client, Smith, asks the firm to carry out a number of transactions whilst he is abroad. Smith promises to send a cheque for £800 to cover expenditure. The following events take place with regard to Smith's account.

1 June	Pay £30 to enquiry agent.
4 June	Pay counsel's fee £115.
8 June	Receive Smith's cheque for £600. The cheque is to be split between office and client account.
9 June	Send a bill of costs to Smith for £360 plus £63 VAT. Transfer costs and pay Smith the balance due to him.

Prepare Smith's account to record the above transactions.

10 Your firm is acting for John Brown who is purchasing a house for £90,000. The following events occur:

4 September	Pay search fee £80.
20 September	Receive cheque for £9,000 from client for deposit.
21 September	Contracts exchanged—pay deposit of £9,000 to seller's solicitor.
29 September	Pay search fee £4.
9 October	Deliver a bill for £200 plus VAT.
13 October	Receive a cheque from client for £81,319, the balance of the purchase money and costs.
14 October	Complete purchase—pay £81,000 to vendor's solicitors. Transfer profit costs.

Prepare the client ledger card for John Brown and the Cash account to record the above transactions.

11 Your firm is acting for the executors of Olive White in the administration of her estate. The following events occur:

5 October	Pay probate fees of £80.
31 October	Receive £1,000 from the Longlife Insurance Company in respect of a policy which the deceased held with them.
	Pay £535 to the executors' bank to repay the loan.
5 November	Receive £2,000 from the deceased's building society account.
6 November	Receive £400 from sale of household contents.
	Pay legacy of £1,500.
10 November	Deliver a bill of costs £240 plus VAT.
11 November	Pay residuary beneficiary £1,003.
	Transfer £362 from client to office account.

Prepare the ledger account for the executors of Olive White and the cash account to record the above.

12.5 Suggested answers to exercises on basic ledger entries

1 Nigel

Date	Details	Office account			Client account		
		DR	CR	Balance	DR	CR	Balance
	Cash: counsel's fee	188		188 DR			
	Profit costs	120					
	VAT	21		329 DR			
	Cash: you		329	—			

2 Mary

Date	Details	Office account			Client account		
		DR	CR	Balance	DR	CR	Balance
	Petty cash: search fee	10		10 DR			
	Cash: office copies	15		25 DR			
	Cash: you—split cheque		25	—		75	75 CR

3 Lynn

Date	Details	Office account			Client account		
		DR	CR	Balance	DR	CR	Balance
	Cash: you					75	75 CR
	Petty cash: inspection fee	5		5 DR			
	Profit costs	100					
	VAT	17.50		122.50 DR			
	Cash: you		47.50	75 DR			
	Cash: transfer: profit costs		75	—	75		—

4 John

Date	Details	Office account			Client account		
		DR	CR	Balance	DR	CR	Balance
	Profit costs (agreed fee)	200					
	VAT	35		235 DR			
	Cash: you		235	—			

Note: a bill will be drawn up as the receipt of the agreed fee is the tax point for VAT.

5 Margaret

Date	Details	Office account			Client account		
		DR	CR	Balance	DR	CR	Balance
	Balance						500 CR
	Daphne: transfer (transfer sheet)				300		200 CR

Daphne

Date	Details	Office account			Client account		
		DR	CR	Balance	DR	CR	Balance
	Margaret: transfer (transfer sheet)					300	300 CR

6 Keith

Date	Details	Office account			Client account		
		DR	CR	Balance	DR	CR	Balance
	Cash: transfer premium to Star Insurance Co.	75		75 DR			
	Cash—you		75				

Star Insurance Co.

Date	Details	Office account			Client account		
		DR	CR	Balance	DR	CR	Balance
	Cash—Keith: transfer premium					75	75 CR

7 Alan

Date	Details	Office account			Client account		
		DR	CR	Balance	DR	CR	Balance
	Cash: counsel's fee	94		94 DR			
	Profit costs	120					
	VAT	21		235 DR			
	Cash—you		235	—			

8 Carol

Date	Details	Office account			Client account		
		DR	CR	Balance	DR	CR	Balance
1 Sept	Cash: counsel's fee	235		235 DR			
19 Sept	Cash—you					450	450 CR
23 Sept	Cash: disbursement				47		403 CR
23 Sept	Profit costs	120					
	VAT	21		376 DR			
	Cash: transfer: profit costs		376	—	376		27 CR
	Cash—you				27		—

9 Smith

Date	Details	Office account			Client account		
		DR	CR	Balance	DR	CR	Balance
1 June	Cash—enquiry agent	30		30 DR			
4 June	Cash—counsel	115		145 DR			
8 June	Cash—you		145	—		455	455 CR
9 June	Profit costs	360		360 DR			
	VAT	63		423 DR			
	Cash: transfer: profit costs		423	—	423		32 CR
	Cash—you				32		—

10 John Brown: matter—conveyancing

Date	Details	Office account			Client account		
		DR	CR	Balance	DR	CR	Balance
4 Sept	Cash: search fee	80		80 DR			
20 Sept	Cash—you					9,000	9,000 CR
21 Sept	Cash: deposit				9,000		—
29 Sept	Cash: search fee	4		84 DR			
9 Oct	Profit costs	200		284 DR			
	VAT	35		319 DR			
13 Oct	Cash—you					81,319	81,319
14 Oct	Cash: completion				81,000		319 CR
	Cash: transfer profit costs		319	—	319		—

Cash account

Date	Details	Office account			Client account		
		DR	CR	Balance	DR	CR	Balance
4 Sept	Brown: search fee		80	80 CR			
20 Sept	Brown				9,000		9,000 DR
21 Sept	Brown: deposit					9,000	—
29 Sept	Brown: search fee		4	84 CR			
13 Oct	Brown				81,319		81,319 DR
14 Oct	Brown: completion					81,000	319 DR
	Brown: transfer profit costs	319		235 DR		319	—

11 Executors of Olive White deceased

Date	Details	Office account			Client account		
		DR	CR	Balance	DR	CR	Balance
5 Oct	Cash: probate fees	80		80 DR			
31 Oct	Cash: Longlife Insurance Co.					1,000	1,000 CR
	Cash: bank loan				535		465 CR
5 Nov	Cash: Building Society					2,000	2,465 CR
6 Nov	Cash: sale of household contents					400	2,865 CR
	Cash: legacy				1,500		1,365 CR
10 Nov	Profit costs	240		320 DR			
	VAT	42		362 DR			
	Cash: residuary Beneficiary				1,003		362 CR
	Cash: transfer profit costs		362	—	362		—

Cash account

Date	Details	Office account			Client account		
		DR	CR	Balance	DR	CR	Balance
5 Oct	Olive White: probate fee		80	80 CR			
31 Oct	Olive White: Longlife Insurance Co.				1,000		1,000 DR
	Olive White: Bank loan					535	465 DR
5 Nov	Olive White: Building Society				2,000		2,465 DR
	Olive White: re household contents				400		2,865 DR
	Olive White: legacy					1,500	1,365 DR
11 Nov	Olive White: legacy					1,003	362 DR
	Olive White: transfer profit costs	362		282 DR		362	—

Value added tax

13.1 Introduction

This chapter contains the following:

1. Registering for VAT.
2. Accounting to Customs and Excise for VAT including input tax and output tax.
3. How to deal with disbursements paid on behalf of clients, the agency and principal methods.
4. VAT relief for bad debts.
5. Self test exercises.

13.2 Registering for VAT

Solicitors whose taxable supplies exceed the VAT threshold set under the Valued Added Tax Act 1994 (currently £60,000) must register for VAT purposes. This threshold is changed from time to time to take account of inflation. In practice most solicitors will register for VAT.

The current standard rate of VAT is 17.5%.

13.3 Accounting to Customs and Excise for VAT

Solicitors will account to Customs and Excise for the balance on the Customs and Excise (VAT) account, which will be:

	Tax charged on services or goods going out of the firm	OUTPUT TAX
Less	Tax paid on goods or services coming in to the firm	INPUT TAX
	Gives	TAX PAYABLE

Tax is normally paid to Customs and Excise quarterly. Within one month of the end of the quarter, a firm must send a completed return form and payment to Customs and Excise. However there are provisions for small- and medium-sized firms to account yearly.

13.3.1 Tax points

The tax point determines the date on which the solicitor's firm must account to Customs and Excise. Normally VAT becomes payable when a bill of costs is sent to the client, whether the client pays the bill or not. Note that if the firm receives payment in respect of an agreed fee before a bill has been sent, then this becomes the tax point for VAT.

13.3.2   Tax invoices

Solicitors must provide a tax invoice to clients who are themselves registered for VAT. In practice solicitors will usually supply invoices to all their clients. For an example of a tax invoice see the end of the example at **13.3.5.2**.

13.3.3   Account used

A VAT (Customs and Excise) account will be required. This will be on OFFICE account, and is a personal account with Customs and Excise, showing the amount due to, or from, Customs and Excise. The debit column will record all tax paid, the credit column will record all tax charged.

Normally at the end of each quarter the firm will account to Customs and Excise for the tax charged less the tax paid. Note that this is NOT an expense account.

EXAMPLE

VAT (Customs and Excise) account	Office account		
	DR	CR	Balance
	Tax paid	Tax charged	

When VAT due is paid to Customs and Excise then:

DEBIT Customs and Excise account OFFICE account
CREDIT Cash Book OFFICE account

13.3.4   Paying input tax

When solicitors pay VAT on supplies made to the firm the following entries will be made in the accounts
CREDIT the Cash account OFFICE account with the net (tax exclusive) amount and the VAT separately
DEBIT the relevant real or expense account with the net (tax exclusive) amount
DEBIT the Customs and Excise (VAT) account with the VAT paid

EXAMPLE

The firm buys a computer on 1 March and pays £800 plus VAT £140.

Cash account

Date	Details	Office account		
		DR	CR	Balance
	Balance say			2,000 DR
1 Mar	Office computer		800	1,200 DR
	Customs & Excise			
	VAT		140	1,060 DR

Office computer account

Date	Details	Office account		
		DR	CR	Bal
1 Mar	Cash	800		800 DR

Customs and Excise (VAT) account

Date	Details	Office account		
		DR Tax paid	CR tax charged	Bal
1 Mar	Cash	140		140 DR

Note that the debit balance on Customs and Excise will offset any tax charged later.

13.3.5   Making payments out on behalf of a client (disbursements)

If a solicitor makes a payment on behalf of a client which includes VAT then how this is treated on the accounts will depend on who the invoice is made out to.

13.3.5.1   Invoice made out to the client (Agency method)

If the invoice is made out to the client, then the solicitor is not involved with the VAT and will merely make a payment of the TOTAL amount, including the VAT, in the normal way. The VAT (Customs and Excise) account is not used. The solicitor may use office account or client account if funds are available. This is known as the agency method for VAT. Thus:

DEBIT the client ledger account in the normal way with the total including VAT.
CREDIT the cash account in the normal way with the total including VAT.

EXAMPLE

The firm receives an invoice from estate agents addressed to their client Breen, for their fees £6,000 plus VAT £1,050. The firm is holding £10,000 on client account for Breen and pays the amount due from client account.

Client ledger account for Breen

Date	Details	Office account			Client account		
		DR	CR	Bal	DR	CR	Bal
	Balance on account Cash paid estate agents inc VAT				7,050		10,000 CR 2,950 CR

Cash account

Date	Details	Office account			Client account		
		DR	CR	Bal	DR	CR	Bal
	Breen—balance						10,000 DR
	Breen paid estate						
	agents					7,050	2,950 DR

Note that there is an agreement with Customs and Excise that Counsels' fee notes addressed to the firm can be amended and treated as addressed to the client.

13.3.5.2   Invoice made out to the firm (Principal method)

Stage 1

Payment of disbursement

If the invoice is made out to the firm, then the firm's VAT (Customs and Excise) account will be used to record the VAT paid. See paying input tax above. Because of this the payment must always be made out of OFFICE account. The payment out will be broken down on the Cash Book into two credit entries, showing the net amount and the VAT separately. The corresponding debit entries will show the net amount only on the client ledger account, and the VAT will be shown on the VAT (Customs and Excise) account.

On the Cash Book:

CREDIT Net amount paid   Office account

CREDIT VAT separately   Office account

On the Client ledger account:

DEBIT Net amount   Office account

On the Customs and Excise VAT account:

DEBIT the VAT   Office account

Note from the above that at the time of payment only the net amount will be debited to the client ledger account, Office account.

EXAMPLE

1   The firm pays an expert a fee of £800 plus VAT £140 on behalf of their client Leith. The invoice from the expert was made out to the firm. The firm are holding £1,000 on general account of costs on client account.

Note that the firm MUST use office account here, as the VAT account is being used.

Cash Account

Date	Details	Office account			Client account		
		DR	CR	Bal	DR	CR	Bal
	Leith balance						1,000 DR
	Leith expert		800	800 CR			
	Customs and						
	Excise (VAT)		140	940 CR			

Client ledger account for Leith

Date	Details	Office account			Client account		
		DR	CR	Bal	DR	CR	Bal
	Balance on a/c					1,000	1,000 CR
	Cash expert	800		800 DR			
	Note VAT 140						

Customs & Excise (VAT) account

Date	Details	Office account		
		DR	CR	Bal
		Tax paid	Tax charged	
	Cash VAT paid	140		140 DR

Billing the client and charging VAT Stage 2

The firm will then charge the client in respect of the VAT on the disbursement when the client is billed. The client ledger account will record the Profit Costs and then the VAT on BOTH the Profit Costs and the disbursement previously paid.

On the Client ledger account

DEBIT the Profit Costs/bill OFFICE account.

DEBIT the VAT on the Profit Costs and the disbursement OFFICE account.

On the Profit Costs account

CREDIT the Profit costs OFFICE account.

On the VAT account

CREDIT the TOTAL VAT charged on both the Profit Costs/bill and the disbursement OFFICE account.

Thus on the Customs and Excise account the VAT paid on the disbursement will have been shown in the debit column, and the VAT charged to the client in the credit column. The firm will account to Customs and Excise for the balance. Ultimately it is the client who will bear all the VAT.

Continuing the example

Stage 2 The firm sends a bill to Leith for £400 plus VAT.

Client ledger account for Leith

Date	Details	Office account			Client account		
		DR	CR	Bal	DR	CR	Bal
	Balance on a/c					1,000	1,000 CR
(1)	Cash expert	800		800 DR			
(1)	Note VAT 140						
(2)	Profit Costs	400		1,200 DR			
	Customs & Excise						
	VAT (140 + 70)	210		1,410 DR			

Customs & Excise (VAT) account

Date	Details	Office account		
		DR	CR	Bal
(1)	Cash VAT paid	140		140 DR
(2)	Leith tax charged		210	70 CR

Profit Costs account

Date	Details	Office account		
		DR	CR	Bal
(2)	Leith bill		400	400 CR

Note from the Customs and Excise account that the solicitors have already paid the £140 VAT which is offset against the amount of VAT charged, leaving a balance due to Customs and Excise of £70.

Below is set out an example of the tax invoice to the client in respect of the above transaction.

TAX INVOICE

	Supply	VAT
Name of client Leith		
Address of client		
VAT number		
(the solicitor's VAT registration number)		
To supply of legal services (Profit costs)	400	
VAT at 17.5%		70
Taxable disbursement paid by us		
Expert fee	800	
VAT at 17.5% on fee		140
Total due	1,200	210

13.4 Agency method—summary

(a) The invoice is made out to the client.

(b) Office or client account may be used.

(c) On payments show the total figure paid, including the VAT. Do not show the VAT separately, as the Customs and Excise (VAT) account is not used.

13.5 Principal method—summary

(a) The invoice is made out to the firm of solicitors.

(b) OFFICE account must be used.

(c) On the client ledger account show the net amount paid only. (The VAT paid will be shown on the Customs and Excise (VAT) account.)

(d) Charge the VAT on the disbursement paid together with VAT on Profit Costs when the bill is sent to the client.

13.6 VAT relief for bad debts

As the Customs and Excise account is credited when the bill is sent to the client, then this sum will have to be accounted for to Customs and Excise. If the client is unable to pay, then the firm may write off the total bad debt including the VAT. This is hard on a business and so VAT relief is available where the debt has not been paid for at least 6 months.

The entries to write off a bad debt where VAT is recoverable are:

CREDIT the client ledger account with the Profit Costs and the VAT written off (shown as separate entries) Office account.

DEBIT the Bad Debts accounts with the profit costs written off Office account.

DEBIT the Customs and Excise (VAT) account with the VAT Office account.

EXAMPLE VAT RELIEF

The firm delivered a bill to their client Hardy for £200 plus VAT £35. Hardy was then adjudicated bankrupt and the debt was written off.

Hardy

Date	Details	Office account			Client account		
		DR	CR	Bal	DR	CR	Bal
(1)	Profit Costs	200		200 DR			
(1)	Customs and Excise VAT	35		235 DR			
(2)	Bad debt written off		200	35 DR			
	Customs and Excise VAT		35	–			

Customs and Excise (VAT) account

Date	Details	Office account		
		DR	CR	Bal
(1)	Hardy VAT on profit costs		35	35 CR
(2)	Hardy VAT written off	35		–

Profit Costs account

Date	Details	Office account		
		DR	CR	Bal
(1)	Hardy bill		200	200 CR

Bad Debts account

Date	Details	Office account		
		DR	CR	Bal
(2)	Hardy written off	200		200 DR

The above example shows that when the Bad Debt is written off with VAT relief, the firm will only lose the profit costs element, and not the VAT.

13.7 Check list

By the end of this chapter you should be able to:

1. know when a solicitor should register for VAT;

2. understand that a registered firm will account to Customs and Excise for the VAT charged by the firm less the VAT paid by the firm;

3. make the entries required on the accounts in respect of the payment of VAT;

4. understand how a solicitor should deal with disbursements paid on behalf of clients and the difference between the principal method and the agency method in dealing with disbursements;

5. make the entries required on the accounts in respect of the agency method and the principal method in dealing with disbursements;

6. understand when VAT relief is available in respect of bad debts written off;

7. complete the self test exercises at the end of the chapter.

13.8 Exercises on ledger accounts including VAT

1 You are acting for Lucy Blue. A surveyor has been instructed to prepare a report. The surveyor sends a bill addressed to Lucy Blue for £120 plus VAT £21. You are holding £200 on account of costs and disbursements in client account. On 7 November you pay the surveyor's bill. On 1 December you deliver a bill of costs to Lucy for £200 plus VAT.
  Show Lucy Blue's ledger account.

2 You are acting in litigation for your client Jenny Green. You instruct a consulting engineer to prepare a report. The engineer sends you a bill for £200 plus VAT £35 addressed to your firm. You are holding £300 in client account for Jenny Green. On 23 September you pay the engineer's bill. In November the case is concluded and on 21 November you send a bill of costs to Jenny Green of £120 plus VAT.
  Show Jenny Green's ledger account and the cash account to record the above.

3 You are acting for Lyndon Tree. In the month of October the following events occur:

1 October	Pay enquiry agent's fee £75. The enquiry agent is not registered for VAT.
3 October	Pay surveyor's fee £160 plus £28 VAT. The bill is made out to Lyndon Tree.
4 October	Pay expert's fee £200 plus £35 VAT. The fee note is made out to you.
8 October	Receive a payment on account of costs and disbursements of £600 from Lyndon Tree.
9 October	Deliver a bill of costs to Lyndon Tree of £80 plus VAT. Transfer moneys due to you from client to office account and account to Lyndon Tree for the balance.

Show Lyndon Tree's ledger account to record the above transactions.

13.9 Suggested answers to exercises on ledger accounts including VAT

1 Lucy Blue account

Date	Details	Office account			Client account		
		DR	CR	Balance	DR	CR	Balance
	Balance					200	200 CR
7 Nov	Cash: surveyor				141		59 CR
1 Dec	Profit costs	200					
	VAT	35		235 DR			

2 Jenny Green account

Date	Details	Office account			Client account		
		DR	CR	Balance	DR	CR	Balance
	Balance					300	300 CR
23 Sept	Cash: engineer (VAT £35)	200		200 DR			
21 Nov	Profit costs	120		320 DR			
	VAT (£21 + £35)	56		376 DR			

Cash account

Date	Details	Office account			Client account		
		DR	CR	Balance	DR	CR	Balance
23 Sept	Jenny Green: engineer's fee		200	200 CR			
	Customs and Excise (J.G.)		35	235 CR			

3 Lyndon Tree account

Date	Details	Office account			Client account		
		DR	CR	Balance	DR	CR	Balance
1 Oct	Cash: enquiry agent	75		75 DR			
3 Oct	Cash: surveyor's fee	188		263 DR			
4 Oct	Cash: counsel (VAT £35)	200		463 DR			
8 Oct	Cash: you					600	600 CR
9 Oct	Profit costs	80					
	VAT (£14 + £35)	49		592 DR			
	Cash: transfer costs		592	—	592		8 CR
	Cash: you				8		—

Financial statements and property transactions

14.1 Introduction

This chapter deals with the following:

1. Financial statements to clients.
2. A summary of the basic financial transactions in respect of a client's sale and purchase of property.
3. Receipt of deposit on exchange of contracts, as agent for the seller or as stakeholder and the entries required on the accounts.
4. Treatment of mortgage advances and mortgage repayment.
5. Completion of a sale and purchase and the financial statement sent to the client.
6. Entries required on completion of a sale and purchase.

14.2 Financial statements to clients

Solicitors dealing with receipts of money and payments out on behalf of clients will have to account to the client for such receipts and payments. These will be shown on a financial statement, or statement of account, which will often be sent to the client at the same time as the bill of costs. This is common in, e.g., property transactions, or probate or trust matters. Other examples would be in respect of debt collection for a client, or any matter where funds have been received and held for a client.

Although there is no set form for such statements of account, they must be clear, contain a record of all receipts and payments, be relatively easy for the client to understand and show at the end the amount due to or from the client.

In property transactions it is a good idea to show a clear distinction between receipts and payments regarding the purchase of property, and receipts and payments regarding the sale of property. In probate and trust matters, a clear distinction between capital and interest should be made.

Later in this chapter some examples are given of financial statements in respect of property transactions.

14.3 Property transactions

Note that where a client is selling one property and buying another, rather than have two ledger cards for the client, one for the sale and one for the purchase, it is usually more convenient to deal with both purchase and sale on one client ledger card, as the proceeds of sale will be used towards the purchase of the new property. A summary of the most common financial transactions found in respect of a client's sale and purchase is set out below. This is a guide only, as obviously these will vary.

(a) Discuss finance with the client, giving details of solicitor's own charges, disbursements, e.g., search fees, stamp duty, land registry fees, estate agent's commission. If there is a mortgage on the property to be sold, obtain details of the amount required to pay off the mortgage. If there is a mortgage on the purchase, discover how much will be available, less any costs.

(b) Money may be received from the client on account of costs generally.

(c) Pay any search fees, fees for official copies, etc.

(d) If the client has instructed a surveyor to check the property in respect of the purchase, surveyor's fees may be paid.

(e) Money may be received from the client or a third party, e.g., the bank, to meet the deposit payable on the purchase.

(f) On exchange of contracts, a deposit will be received in respect of the sale. This may be held as stakeholder, when a separate stakeholder client ledger card will be opened—it cannot be used towards the deposit payable regarding the purchase—or it may be held as agent for the seller, when it may be credited direct to the client ledger card and can be used towards the deposit payable regarding the purchase. Note that a solicitor should now account for interest on stakeholder money held, where appropriate. See **Chapter 15** on deposit interest generally.

Payment of a deposit on the purchase will be made to the seller's solicitors, either as agent for the seller, or as stakeholder.

(g) Completion statements will be sent in respect of the sale and the purchase, showing how much money will be required on completion, taking account of the deposit already paid, and any other adjustments, e.g., additional amounts in respect of carpets, fittings, etc. Note that these are merely for information— no entries will be made on the accounts until the sale and purchase are completed.

(h) A financial statement will be sent to the client, showing all the receipts and payments out in respect of the sale and purchase, together with the solicitor's bills of costs and the amount that will be due to the client, or needed from the client to complete. Note that at this stage, as the bills have been sent out, the solicitor's costs and VAT will be debited to the client ledger card. All other disbursements, receipts, etc. are entered only when actually paid or received.

(i) Any mortgage money in respect of the purchase will be received before completion and any money required from the client, if applicable.

(j) Complete the sale first, receive the net proceeds, i.e., the purchase price less any deposit paid, together with any other adjustments regarding fittings, etc.

If the deposit on the sale was held as stakeholder, the money should be transferred from the stakeholder account to the client ledger card. This should also be separately recorded on a transfer sheet or journal.

Pay out the amount needed to redeem the mortgage.

Complete the purchase. Ensure that mortgage moneys are available before paying out the amount required to complete the purchase, again less the deposit which has been paid, and take account of any other adjustments needed.

(k) Pay the estate agent's commission on sale. There should be sufficient money on client account to do this.

(l) Pay stamp duty regarding purchase, again from client account if the money is available. The rates at present are 0–£120,000 nil, over £120,000 to £250,000 1%, over £250,000 to 500,000 3%, and over £500,000 4%.

(m) Pay Land Registry fees, from client account if possible.

(n) Transfer costs and disbursements due to the firm from client account to office account.

(o) Pay any balance to the client.

14.4 Receipt of deposit on exchange of contracts

A solicitor receiving a deposit on behalf of a client may hold the deposit as:

(a) agent; or

(b) stakeholder.

14.4.1 Receipt of deposit as agent

If a solicitor receives a deposit on exchange of contracts which is to be held as agent, it is held on behalf of the client seller. To record the receipt of a deposit as agent, the solicitor will make entries in the accounts to record a receipt of clients' money on behalf of the client seller.

EXAMPLE

The firm acts for White, the seller of Whiteacre, which is being sold for £70,000. On 23 September the firm receives a 10% deposit to hold as agents.

White: sale of Whiteacre

Date	Details	Office account			Client account		
		DR	CR	Balance	DR	CR	Balance
23 Sept	Cash: purchaser's solicitor, deposit					7,000	7,000 CR

Cash account

Date	Details	Office account			Client account		
		DR	CR	Balance	DR	CR	Balance
23 Sept	White Cash: purchaser's solicitor, deposit				7,000		7,000 DR

14.4.2   Receipt of deposit as stakeholder

When a solicitor receives a deposit as stakeholder, it is not held on deposit for the client seller, or for the buyer, but held between the parties, therefore the receipt of a stakeholder deposit should not be recorded in the client seller's ledger account.

A separate account, the stakeholder account, is opened to record dealings with deposits held by a solicitor as stakeholder. The deposit is held in the stakeholder account until completion, when it belongs to the seller.

The stakeholder account only records dealings with clients' money; the money belongs to the client(s) not the solicitor.

When the firm receives a deposit as stakeholder, the following entries are made:

(a) CREDIT the Stakeholder ledger account, client column.

(b) DEBIT the Cash account client column.

Note the position where money is held on joint stake (see **11.2.4.6**).

EXAMPLE

Assume that in the example in **8.3.1** the firm receives the 10% deposit as stakeholder.

Stakeholder account

Date	Details	Office account			Client account		
		DR	CR	Balance	DR	CR	Balance
23 Sept	Cash: deposit re White sale of Whiteacre					7,000	7,000 CR

The double entry will be in the Cash account as in the example in **8.3.1**.

On completion of the sale the deposit is transferred from the stakeholder account to the client seller's account. The bookkeeping entries are those to record a transfer from one client ledger account to another.

EXAMPLE

Continuing the example, assume that completion takes place on 24 October.

Stakeholder account

Date	Details	Office account			Client account		
		DR	CR	Balance	DR	CR	Balance
23 Sept	Cash: deposit re White sale of Whiteacre					7,000	7,000 CR
24 Oct	White: transfer sheet				7,000		—

White: re sale of Whiteacre

Date	Details	Office account			Client account		
		DR	CR	Balance	DR	CR	Balance
24 Oct	Stakeholder: transfer sheet					7,000	7,000 CR

14.5 Mortgage advances

14.5.1 Acting for mortgagee and purchaser

Rule 32(6) of the Solicitors' Accounts Rules 1998 provides that a solicitor acting for a borrower and lender on a mortgage advance in a property transaction shall not be required to open separate ledger accounts for the borrower and lender provided that:

(a) the funds belonging to each client are clearly identifiable; and

(b) the lender is an institutional lender which provides mortgages on standard terms in the normal course of its business, for example, a building society or bank.

Thus, if the solicitor is acting for a buyer and a building society provides the mortgage advance, the transactions can all be recorded in the client buyer's ledger account, without the need to open a separate ledger account for the building society.

If the solicitor is acting for a buyer and a private lender, separate ledger accounts must be opened for each.

In (a) above, 'clearly identifiable' requires the solicitor to ensure that the buyer's ledger account states unambiguously the nature and owner of the mortgage advance. Care therefore needs to be taken in completing the details entry. For example, if the Branchester Building Society makes an advance of £50,000 to Smith who is purchasing Greenacre, Smith's ledger account should state, when the advance is received:

'Cash: mortgage advance from Branchester Building Society: £50,000.'

Note that the mortgage money credited to the account still belongs to the lender, not the borrower, until completion takes place.

EXAMPLE (INSTITUTIONAL LENDER)

The firm acts for Red who is purchasing Cosy Villa for £150,000. Red has obtained a mortgage advance of £100,000 from the High Finance Building Society for which the firm also acts. Red is providing the balance from his own funds. The firm receives the mortgage advance on 16 October, with the usual instruction that the cheque is not to be negotiated until completion. Red has been informed that he will be required to pay £50,517 prior to completion. He brings a cheque to the office on 17 October. Completion takes place on 18 October and on the same date the firm sends two bills of costs to Red, one for £400 plus

VAT for the conveyancing and one for £40 plus VAT for acting on behalf of the building society. The transactions will be recorded as follows.

Red: re purchase of Cosy Villa

Date	Details	Office account			Client account		
		DR	CR	Balance	DR	CR	Balance
17 Oct	Cash—you					50,517	50,517 CR
18 Oct	Cash: mortgage advance from High Finance Building Society					100,000	150,517 CR
	Cash: seller's solicitor				150,000		517 CR
	Profit costs	400					
	VAT	70		470 DR			
	Profit costs (High Finance Building Society re mortgage)	40					
	VAT	7		517 DR			
	Cash: transfer costs		517	—	517		—

EXAMPLE (PRIVATE LENDER)

In the above example assume that Red is borrowing £100,000 from Uncle Black, for whom the firm also acts. On 16 October Uncle Black pays the firm £100,000 and both give written authority for that money to be transferred and used towards Red's purchase of Cosy Villa. The transactions will be recorded as follows:

Red: re purchase of Cosy Villa

Date	Details	Office account			Client account		
		DR	CR	Balance	DR	CR	Balance
18 Oct	Cash—you Uncle Black: transfer mortgage advance					50,517	50,517 CR
						100,000	150,517 CR
	Cash: seller's solicitors				150,000		517 CR
	Profit costs	400					
	VAT	70		470 DR			
	Uncle Black: transfer costs	47		517 DR			
	Cash: transfer costs		517	—	517		—

Uncle Black: re mortgage advance

Date	Details	Office account			Client account		
		DR	CR	Balance	DR	CR	Balance
16 Oct	Cash—you					100,000	100,000
18 Oct	Profit costs	40					
	VAT	7		47 DR			
	Red: transfer sheet mortgage advance				100,000		—
	Red: transfer costs		47	—			

When this method is used the lender's costs are transferred from the buyer's account to the lender's account by making the following entries:

(a) DEBIT purchaser's ledger card office account with costs and VAT.

(b) CREDIT lender's ledger card office account with costs and VAT.

As an alternative to transferring the gross advance from Uncle Black to Red, the solicitor could have either:

(a) Transferred the net advance, after deducting costs, in which case Uncle Black's account would have appeared as follows:

Uncle Black: re mortgage advance

Date	Details	Office account			Client account		
		DR	CR	Balance	DR	CR	Balance
16 Oct	Cash—you					100,000	100,000 CR
18 Oct	Profit costs	40					
	VAT	7		47 DR			
	Red: transfer net advance					99,953	47 CR
	Cash: transfer costs		47	—	47		—

Or:

(b) Paid the net advance to the seller's solicitors out of Uncle Black's account. No entry will be made in Red's account in respect of the payment of the net advance.

14.5.2 Solicitor acting for mortgagee only

The accounting entries when the solicitor acts for the mortgagee only are:

(a) The solicitor opens an account for the mortgagee.

(b) When the mortgage advance is received, the solicitor makes entries in the mortgagee's account to record a receipt of client money.

(c) On completion, the solicitor makes entries in the mortgagee's account to record the delivery of a bill of costs to the mortgagee.

(d) On completion, the solicitor pays the net advance to the purchaser's solicitor and records this in the mortgagee's account as a payment of clients' money.

(e) Following completion, the solicitor transfers the costs from client to office account.

EXAMPLE

The firm acts for the High Finance Building Society which is making a mortgage advance of £100,000 to Red in connection with his purchase of Cosy Villa. Red's solicitors are Bagnets. The firm's costs for acting for the building society are £120 plus £21 VAT. The mortgage advance is received on 16 October and completion takes place on 18 October. Costs are transferred on 18 October.

High Finance Building Society

Date	Details	Office account			Client account		
		DR	CR	Balance	DR	CR	Balance
16 Oct	Cash—you					100,000	100,000 CR
18 Oct	Profit costs	120					
	VAT	21		141 DR			
	Cash: Bagnets				99,859		141 CR
	Cash: transfer: costs			141	—	141	—

14.5.3 Solicitor acting for buyer/borrower only

The accounting entries when the solicitor acts for the buyer/borrower only are:

(a) An account is opened for the buyer. No account is opened for the mortgagee because the mortgagee is not a client.

(b) On completion the firm records the receipt of the net advance as a receipt of client's money, in the buyer's ledger account.

(c) On completion the firm records the payment of the net advance to the seller's solicitor, as a payment of clients' money, in the buyer's ledger account.

(d) Entries are made in the cash account and the buyer's ledger account to record receipt and payment of clients' money, even if the cheque from the mortgagee is endorsed in favour of the seller's solicitor.

EXAMPLE

The firm acts for Red with regard to his purchase of Cosy Villa. Red is obtaining a mortgage advance of £100,000 from the High Finance Building Society. The solicitors acting for the building society have intimated that their costs, which are to be paid by Red, will be £120 plus £21 VAT. It has been agreed that these costs will be deducted from the mortgage advance. On completion on 18 October, the building society's cheque for £99,859 is received by the firm and a cheque for that amount is paid to Gallops, the seller's solicitor.

Red

Date	Details	Office account			Client account		
		DR	CR	Balance	DR	CR	Balance
18 Oct	Cash: High Finance					99,859	99,859
	Cash: Gallops				99,859		—

14.6 Mortgage repayment

14.6.1 Usual method

Normally a firm will treat the repayment as a normal payment out of client money.

14.6.2 Acting for the seller and a lender

Rule 32(6) of the Solicitors' Accounts Rules 1998 may not apply on redemption of a mortgage. Thus, if the solicitor acts for the seller and a lender, separate accounts will need to be opened for the seller and the lender. NB: this will be uncommon in practice.

(a) *Entries on completion.* When completion takes place the sale proceeds belong to the seller and are shown as a receipt of client's money in the client seller's account.

EXAMPLE

The firm acts for George with regard to the sale of Somehut. Completion takes place on 28 January when £140,000 is received.

George: re sale of Somehut

Date	Details	Office account			Client account		
		DR	CR	Balance	DR	CR	Balance
28 Jan	Cash: sale proceeds					140,000	140,000 CR

(b) *Costs.* The solicitor's costs for acting on the redemption will be recorded in the lender's account, although in practice they will be paid by the seller client.

EXAMPLE

The firm's costs for acting on behalf of Andover Building Society, which has a mortgage on Somehut, of £55,000, and for whom the firm also acts, are £40 plus VAT £7.

Andover Building Society: re mortgage redemption (George)

Date	Details	Office account			Client account		
		DR	CR	Balance	DR	CR	Balance
28 Jan	Profit costs	40					
	VAT	7		47 DR			

As the redemption costs will be paid by the borrower, a transfer of the costs and VAT will be made from the borrower's account to the lender's account. The transfer will be effected by making the following entries in the accounts.

(i)   DEBIT the seller's ledger account office column.

(ii) CREDIT the lender's ledger account office column.

(c) *Redemption*. When the mortgage is redeemed a transfer of the redemption money is made from the seller's account to the lender's account. The payment of the redemption money to the lender is then shown as a payment of client money from the ledger account.

EXAMPLE

The firm's costs for acting for George on the sale of Somehut are £200 plus VAT £35. The redemption figure for the mortgage is £55,000. The mortgage is redeemed and costs transferred on 28 January. On the same date a cheque is sent to George for the balance due to him. The entries in the ledger accounts for George and Andover Building Society will be as follows:

George: re sale of Somehut

Date	Details	Office account			Client account		
		DR	CR	Balance	DR	CR	Balance
28 Jan	Cash: sale proceeds					140,000	140,000 CR
	Andover: transfer mortgage redemption				55,000		85,000 CR
	Profit costs	200					
	VAT	35		235 DR			
	Andover: transfer costs	47		282 DR			
	Cash: transfer costs		282	—	282		84,718 CR
	Cash—you				84,718		—

Andover: re mortgage redemption (George)

Date	Details	Office account			Client account		
		DR	CR	Balance	DR	CR	Balance
28 Jan	Profit costs	40					
	VAT	7		47 DR			
	George: transfer redemption money					55,000	55,000 CR
	George: transfer costs		47	—			
	Cash—you (mortgage redemption)				55,000		—

14.7 Completion

14.7.1 Financial statement

Before completion of a sale or purchase on behalf of a property client, a financial statement will be sent to the client. This will show the amount which the client will have to provide for completion or the balance due to the client following completion. There is no set form of financial statement, but whichever form is used it is essential that the statement should show all moneys received from and on behalf of the client and all payments made on his or her behalf.

The following is a suggested method of presentation of a financial statement when a solicitor is acting for a client selling and buying property simultaneously.

Financial statement

To: A. Client.
Re: Sale of Blackacre
     Purchase of Whiteacre
Sale of Blackacre
Receipts:

Sale price		X	
Less payments:			
Estate agent's fee	X		
VAT on fee	X		
Mortgage redemption	X		
Costs on sale	X		
VAT on costs	X	X	
Net sale proceeds			X

Purchase of Whiteacre

Payments: Purchase price	X		
Stamp duty	X		
Land Registry fees	X		
Search fees	X		
Mortgage costs	X		
VAT on costs	X		
Purchase costs	X		
VAT on costs	X	X	

Less: Receipts			
Paid by you on account	X		
Mortgage advance	X	X	

Amount required to complete purchase	X
Less amount due from sale	X
Balance due from you before completion	X

Or: Amount due from sale	X
Less amount required to complete purchase	X
Balance due to you on completion	X

14.7.2 Exercises on financial statements

1 You act for Virgil who is selling 'Olympus' for £50,000. On 1 April you receive a 10% deposit as stakeholder, 'Olympus' is subject to a mortgage of £15,000. You receive an account from the estate agent for £600 plus VAT £105. Your costs for acting on the sale are £200 plus VAT £35. Prepare a financial statement for Virgil.

2 You act for Samuel who is buying 'The Temple' for £180,000. He is borrowing £140,000 from the building society for whom you also act. Your local search costs £75. You receive a bridging loan of £18,000 from your client's bank for the deposit. You exchange contracts and pay the deposit. You pay bankruptcy search fee £1. Your costs for acting for the building society are £80 plus VAT and these are to be paid by Samuel. Your costs are £400 plus VAT £70, the land registry fee is £90, and stamp duty land tax £1,800. Samuel's bank informs you that the interest on the bridging loan is £75. Prepare a financial statement for Samuel.

3 Black and Co. solicitors acted for Hall in respect of the purchase of a house, 10 Arden Way for £100,000 and the sale of her existing house, 25 James Street for £80,000. The mortgage repayment on 25 James Street was £40,000, and a new mortgage was taken out on 10 Arden Way for £60,000. Black and Co. paid the following disbursements, local search fee £100, estate agents' charges on the sale £1,200 plus VAT, search fee £10, land registry fee of £200. Their profit costs on the sale were £200 plus VAT, on the purchase £400 plus VAT and on the mortgage £80 plus VAT.

Draw up a financial statement for Hall, showing the amount required from her on completion.

14.7.3   Answers to exercises on financial statements

1 **Financial statement**
   To: Virgil
   Re: Sale of 'Olympus'
   Receipts:

Sale price		50,000
Less payments:		
Estate agent (inc VAT, 105)	705	
Mortgage redemption	15,000	
Costs on sale	200	
VAT on costs	35	15,940
Balance due to you from sale		34,060

2 **Financial statement**
   To: Samuel
   Re: Purchase of 'The Temple'
   Payments:

Purchase money		180,000
Stamp duty land tax	1,800	
Land Registry fees	90	
Search fees (75 + 1)	76	
Bank loan interest	75	
Mortgage costs	80	
VAT on above costs	14	
Purchase costs	400	
VAT on purchase costs	70	2,605
		182,605
Less: Mortgage advance		140,000
Balance due from you before completion		42,605

3 Financial statement for Hall
Matter : Sale of 25 James Street and purchase of 10 Arden Way

Purchase of 10 Arden Way

Purchase price		100,000	
Less mortgage advance		60,000	
		40,000	
Add			
Local search fee	100		
Search fee	10		
Land registry fees	200		
Costs on mortgage	80		
VAT	14		
Costs on purchase	400		
VAT	70		
			874
			40,874

Sale of 25 James Street

Sale price		80,000	
Less payments			
Mortgage repayment		40,000	
		40,000	
less			
Estate agents' fees	1,200		
VAT	210		
	1,410		
Costs on purchase	200		
VAT	35		
	235		
		1,645	
Net sale proceeds			38,355
Balance required from you			2,519

14.7.4 Sale completions

The solicitor's accounts must reflect all the transactions involved in completing the sale of a property on the client's behalf. The following entries will usually have to be made on the completion of a sale:

(a) Entries to record the delivery of a bill of costs to the client for acting on the client's behalf with regard to the sale.

EXAMPLE

The firm acts for Ali with regard to the sale of 'Church Cottage' at a price of £60,000. On 3 May a bill of costs is delivered to Ali in the sum of £200 plus £35 VAT. Ali's account will appear as follows:

Ali

Date	Details	Office account			Client account		
		DR	CR	Balance	DR	CR	Balance
3 May	Profit costs	200					
	VAT	35		235 DR			

(b) Entries to record the receipt of the sale proceeds from the purchaser's solicitor (i.e., entries to record a receipt of clients' money).

Continuing the example:

Completion of Ali's sale takes place on 3 May. The firm receives a bank draft for £54,000. A deposit of £6,000 was paid to the firm as stakeholders on 3 April. Ali's account will appear as follows:

Ali

Date	Details	Office account			Client account		
		DR	CR	Balance	DR	CR	Balance
3 May	Profit costs	200					
	VAT	35		235 DR			
	Cash: purchaser's solicitor on completion					54,000	54,000 CR

(c) Entries to record the transfer of the deposit from stakeholder account to the client's ledger account if the deposit was paid to the seller's solicitor as stakeholder on exchange of contracts.

Continuing the example:

Stakeholder account

Date	Details	Office account			Client account		
		DR	CR	Balance	DR	CR	Balance
3 Apr	Cash: deposit re Ali					6,000	6,000 CR
3 May	Ali: transfer sheet				6,000		

Ali

Date	Details	Office account			Client account		
		DR	CR	Balance	DR	CR	Balance
May 3	Profit costs	200					
	VAT	35		235 DR			
	Cash: purchaser's solicitor on completion					54,000	54,000 CR
	Stakeholder: transfer sheet					6,000	60,000 CR

(d) Entries to record the redemption of a mortgage.

Continuing the example:

Assume that there is a mortgage to the Timberwell Building Society on 'Church Cottage'. The mortgage of £18,000 is redeemed on 4 May. Ali's account would appear as follows:

Ali

Date	Details	Office account			Client account		
		DR	CR	Balance	DR	CR	Balance
May 3	Profit costs	200					
	VAT	35		235 DR			
	Cash: purchaser's solicitor					54,000	54,000 CR
	Stakeholder: transfer sheet					6,000	60,000 CR
May 4	Cash: Timberwell Building Society				18,000		42,000 CR

(e) Entries to record the payment of any outstanding disbursements, e.g., estate agent's fees.

Continuing the example:

Assume that on 6 May the firm pays an estate agent's charges of £705. Ali's account would appear as follows:

Ali

Date	Details	Office account			Client account		
		DR	CR	Balance	DR	CR	Balance
May 3	Profit costs	200					
	VAT	35		235 DR			
	Cash: purchaser's solicitor					54,000	54,000 CR
	Stakeholder: transfer sheet					6,000	60,000 CR
May 4	Cash: Timberwell Building Society: redemption				18,000		42,000 CR
May 6	Cash: estate agent				705		41,295 CR

(f) Entries to record the transfer of costs from client to office account and to record the payment to the client of any balance owed.

Continuing the example:

Assume that on 6 May costs are transferred and the balance remaining in client account is paid to Ali.

Ali's account will appear as follows:

Ali

Date	Details	Office account			Client account		
		DR	CR	Balance	DR	CR	Balance
3 May	Profit costs	200					
	VAT	35		235 DR			
	Cash: purchaser's solicitor					54,000	54,000 CR
	Stakeholder: transfer sheet					6,000	60,000 CR
4 May	Cash: Timberwell Building Society: redemption				18,000		42,000 CR
6 May	Cash: estate agent				705		41,295 CR
	Cash: transfer: costs		235	—	235		41,060 CR
	Cash—you				41,060		—

14.7.5 Purchase completions

The solicitor's accounts must reflect all the transactions involved in completing the purchase of a property on the client's behalf. The following entries will usually have to be made on the completion of a purchase.

(a) Entries to record the delivery of a bill of costs to the client for acting with regard to the purchase.

EXAMPLE

The firm acts for Alfred with regard to the purchase of 'Costa Bit' at a price of £45,000. On 3 May a bill of costs is delivered to Alfred in the sum of £320 plus VAT £56. The firm also acted for the mortgagee, Tall Trees Building Society, and its costs are £80 plus VAT £14. Alfred's account will appear as follows:

Alfred

Date	Details	Office account			Client account		
		DR	CR	Balance	DR	CR	Balance
200—							
3 May	Profit costs	320					
	VAT	56		376 DR			
	Profit costs: Building Society	80					
	VAT	14		470 DR			

(b) Entries to record the receipt of the balance of the purchase money from the client, if required, as shown on the financial statement.

Continuing the example:

A financial statement has been delivered to Alfred, showing a balance due from him on completion of £11,070. On 3 May Alfred pays the sum of £11,070 to the firm. Alfred's account will appear as follows:

Alfred

Date	Details	Office account			Client account		
		DR	CR	Balance	DR	CR	Balance
200—							
3 May	Profit costs	320					
	VAT	56		376 DR			
	Profit costs: Building Society	80					
	VAT	14		470 DR			
	Cash—you					11,070	11,070 CR

(c) Entries to record the receipt of the mortgage advance from the building society. Note: if the mortgage was from a private lender for whom the firm was acting, a separate ledger account would be opened for the lender and the mortgage advance would be shown as a transfer from the lender's account.

Continuing the example:

Alfred has obtained a mortgage advance of £30,000 from the Tall Trees Building Society for whom the firm also acts.

Alfred

Date	Details	Office account			Client account		
		DR	CR	Balance	DR	CR	Balance
3 May	Profit costs	320					
	VAT	56		376 DR			
	Profit costs: Building Society	80				11,070	11,070 CR
	VAT	14		470 DR			
	Cash: Tall Trees Building Society, mortgage advance					30,000	41,070 CR

(d) Entries to record the payment of the balance of the purchase moneys to the seller's solicitors.

Continuing the example:

Completion takes place on 3 May. On 3 April a 10% deposit had been paid to the seller's solicitors, Redhen and Co. The balance payable to Redhen and Co. on completion is £40,500. Alfred's account would appear as follows:

Alfred

Date	Details	Office account DR	CR	Balance	Client account DR	CR	Balance
3 May	Profit costs	320					
	VAT	56		376 DR			
	Profit costs: Building Society	80					
	VAT	14		470 DR			
	Cash—you					11,070	11,070
	Cash: Tall Trees Building Society, mortgage advance					30,000	41,070 CR
	Cash: Redhen & Co.				40,500		570 CR

(e) Entries to record the payment of any disbursements after completion, e.g., stamp duty or Land Registry fees.

Continuing the example:

On 5 May the firm pays Land Registry fees of £100. Alfred's account will appear as follows:

Alfred

Date	Details	Office account DR	CR	Balance	Client account DR	CR	Balance
3 May	Profit costs	320					
	VAT	56		376 DR			
	Profit costs: Building Society	80					
	VAT	14		470 DR			
	Cash—you					11,070	11,070 CR
	Cash: Tall Trees Building Society, mortgage advance					30,000	41,070 CR
	Cash: Redhen & Co.				40,500		570 CR
5 May	Cash: Land Land Registry fees				100		470 CR

(f) Entries to record the transfer of costs from client to office account.

Continuing the example:

Costs are transferred to office account on 7 May. Alfred's account will appear as follows:

Alfred

Date	Details	Office account			Client account		
		DR	CR	Balance	DR	CR	Balance
3 May	Profit costs	320		376 DR			
	VAT	56					
	Profit costs: Building Society	80					
	VAT	14		470 DR			
	Cash—you Cash: Tall Trees					11,070	11,070 CR
	Building Society, mortgage advance					30,000	41,070 CR
	Cash: Redhen & Co.				40,500		570 CR
5 May	Cash: Land Registry fees				100		470 CR
7 May	Cash: transfer: costs		470	—	470		—

14.7.6 Simultaneous sale and purchase

When acting for a client with regard to a simultaneous sale and purchase, entries will be made in the accounts as in **14.7.4** and **14.7.5**.

14.7.6.1 Example

Swift & Co., solicitors, acted for Gulliver in the purchase of 'Lilliput' for £350,000 and sale of 'Lagado' for £300,000 and for the Academy Building Society in respect of an advance. The following events took place.

200—

2 September	Paid search fees of £65 in respect of the purchase of 'Lilliput' by Gulliver.
9 September	Paid survey fee of £940 including VAT in respect of the purchase of 'Lilliput'.
10 September	The Academy Building Society instructed the firm to act in respect of an advance of £125,000.
15 September	Received from Yahoo Limited a cheque for £35,000, being a bridging loan in respect of 'Lilliput'.
17 September	Exchanged contracts for the sale of Gulliver's house, 'Lagado', the deposit of 10% (£30,000) having been paid to the estate agent by the buyer. On the same day contracts were exchanged for the purchase of 'Lilliput' and the deposit of £35,000 was paid to the seller's solicitor to hold as stakeholder.
24 September	Received completion statement from the seller's solicitor in respect of 'Lilliput', showing £315,000 due on completion.
27 September	Sent completion statement to the solicitors acting for the buyer of 'Lagado', showing the balance due of £270,000.

2 October	Received cheque for £125,000 from the building society. The profit costs to be charged regarding the advance are £120 plus VAT.	
5 October	Sent financial statement to Gulliver showing the balance of money required from him on completion of the sale and purchase, together with bills of costs in respect of the sale, purchase and mortgage advance. The statement includes, amongst other items, the following information:	
	Solicitor's costs on sale	£400 plus VAT
	Solicitor's costs on purchase	£600 plus VAT
	Estate agent's commission inc VAT	£7,050
	Stamp duty land tax	£10,500
	Land Registry fees	£250
	Amount to redeem mortgage	£60,500
7 October	Cheque received from Gulliver, being the balance of purchase money and payment of costs.	
12 October	Completed the sale and purchase. The amount due to redeem the mortgage is paid the same day. A cheque for £22,950 is received from the estate agents, being the deposit less their charges.	
14 October	The bridging loan of £35,000 is paid to Yahoo Limited. Gulliver has paid the interest due on the loan direct to Yahoo Limited.	
15 October	Paid stamp duty.	
25 October	Paid Land Registry fees. Transferred costs and disbursements from client account to office account.	

Draw up the ledger account of Gulliver, showing all entries necessary to deal with the above events, and prepare a financial statement, suitable for presentation to Gulliver on 5 October 200—, showing the balance due from him on completion.

Financial statement

5 October 200—
To: Gulliver
Re: Sale of 'Lagado'
    Purchase of 'Lilliput'
Sale of 'Lagado'
Receipts:

Sale price		300,000
Less payments:		
Estate agent (inc VAT)	7,050	
Mortgage redemption	60,500	
Costs	400	
VAT on costs	70	
		68,020
Net proceeds of sale		231,980
Purchase of 'Lilliput'		
Payments:		
Purchase price		350,000
Add:		
Survey fee	940	
Search fees	65	

Stamp duty land tax	10,500
Land Registry fees	250
Cost re mortgage advance inc VAT	141
Costs on purchase inc VAT	705

	12,601
	362,601
Less: Mortgage advance	125,000
Amount required to complete purchase	237,601
Less net sale proceeds	231,980
Balance required from you to complete	5,621

Gulliver

Sale of 'Lagado'; purchase of 'Lilliput'

Date	Details	Office account			Client account		
		DR	CR	Balance	DR	CR	Balance
200—							
2 Sept	Cash search fee	65		65 DR			
9 Sept	Cash survey fee	940		1,005 DR			
15 Sept	Cash: Yahoo Ltd re deposit					35,000	35,000 CR
17 Sept	Cash: deposit on purchase				35,000		—
2 Oct	Cash: mortgage advance Academy Building Society					125,000	125,000 CR
5 Oct	Costs on sale	400					
	VAT	70		1,475 DR			
	Costs on purchase	600					
	VAT	105		2,180 DR			
	Costs re advance	120					
	VAT	21		2,321 DR			
7 Oct	Cash—you to complete					5,621	130,621 CR
12 Oct	Cash balance proceeds sale					270,000	400,621 CR
	Cash: estate agent's deposit on sale less their commission					22,950	423,571 CR
	Cash: re purchase				315,000		108,571 CR
	Transfer re redemption				60,500		48,071 CR
14 Oct	Cash: bridging loan				35,000		13,071 CR
15 Oct	Cash: stamp duty land tax				10,500		2,571 CR
25 Oct	Cash: Land Registry fee				250		2,321 CR
	Cash: transfer costs and disbursements		2,321	—	2,321		—

14.8 Check list

By the end of this chapter you should be able to:

1. appreciate that a financial statement to the client should be clear, containing a full record of all receipts and payments;

2. understand the basic financial steps in a property transaction;

3. understand the difference between the receipt of a deposit as agent for the seller and as stakeholder and make the relevant entries on the accounts;

4. note the special requirements where a firm records the receipt of a mortgage advance on the borrower's/purchaser's account and make the relevant entries on the accounts;

5. make the entries required for a mortgage advance if acting for both a private lender and a borrower;

6. make the entries required for a mortgage advance if acting for the lender only, or if acting for the borrower only;

7. make the entries required for repayment of a mortgage;

8. draw up a financial statement to be sent to a client before completion of a sale and purchase;

9. make all entries required in respect of the sale and purchase of properties on behalf of a client;

10. complete the self test exercises at the end of the chapter.

14.9 Exercises on property transactions

1   Kumar and Co. act for Deakin in respect of the sale of his property, 1, Langdale Close for £180,000, and the purchase of 23, Harwood Grove, for £250,000. On 2 April the firm receives a cheque for £25,000 from Deakin for the deposit on the purchase.

On 10 April the firm exchanges contracts on the sale and purchase, receiving the 10% on the sale as stakeholder and paying the 10% deposit on the purchase. Show the entries on the client ledger account for Deakin.

Show the entries on the client ledger account for Deakin.

2   Your firm acts for Sinclair in respect of the sale of 2, Athens Avenue for £300,000 and the purchase of 1, Beech Park for £400,000. The firm has exchanged contracts on the sale and purchase. Sinclair paid the 10% deposit on the purchase and the firm received the 10% deposit on the sale as stakeholder. Show the entries required on Sinclair's client ledger account in respect of the following transactions.

1 March   The firm receives a mortgage for £150,000 from Wakefield Building Society

3 March   The firm completes the sale of 2, Athens Avenue, transferring the amount due from stakeholder account and receiving the balance of the sale proceeds. It also completes the purchase of 1, Beech Park, paying the balance of the purchase price. It redeems the mortgage on 2, Athens Avenue by paying £35,625.

3 Farrell and Co. acted for Keeble in the sale of his house 'Rosewood' for £50,000 and for the Burnley Building Society who were owed approximately £15,000 by way of mortgage on the house. The following events took place:

200—

8 May	Received cheque for £45,000 from the buyer's solicitors, being the balance of purchase moneys. The amount required to redeem the mortgage including interest is £15,325. The amount due to the building society is paid by cheque.
9 May	Mann and Co., estate agents, acting for Keeble, send a cheque for £3,590, being the deposit less their commission of £1,200 plus VAT £210.
10 May	Sent cheque for £594 including VAT to Oliver in respect of pre-sale repairs to the property.
13 May	Bill of costs sent to Keeble for £240 plus VAT.
15 May	Costs and disbursements are transferred to office account and the balance due to Keeble is paid to him.

Write up the client's ledger account for Keeble, showing all necessary entries to record the above transactions. VAT is to be calculated at 17.5%.

(Law Society Examination, revised.)

4 Your firm acts for Andrew Arbuthnot who is purchasing 'Holywell House' for £60,000 with a private mortgage of £30,000 from Lancelot Lake for whom the firm also acts. The following events take place:

2003

2 December	Pay search fee £18.
16 December	Receive cheque for £6,000 from Andrew for the deposit.
17 December	Contracts exchanged. Paid £6,000 to the seller's solicitors.
20 December	Receive completion statement from seller's solicitors showing £54,000 payable on completion.
31 December	Send statement to Andrew showing amount required for completion including:

Costs on sale: £120 plus VAT
Costs on mortgage: £40 plus VAT
Search fee: £18 already paid
Bill of costs also sent.

2004

12 January	Receive mortgage advance and Andrew's cheque for the balance of the completion money.
15 January	Complete the purchase.
16 January	Transfer costs and disbursements to office account.

Prepare the ledger accounts for Andrew and Lancelot Lake and the cash account, together with the financial statement sent to Andrew on 31 December.

5 Guppy and Jobling, solicitors, acted for Smallweed in respect of the purchase of a house 'The Badgers' and the sale of his existing house 'Chesney'. 'The Badgers' was being purchased for £180,000 and 'Chesney' was to be sold for £140,000.

200—

8 May	Paid local search fees of £50.
14 May	Instructions received from the Dedlock Building Society to act in connection with the advance to Smallweed of £28,000 regarding 'The Badgers'.
20 May	Received £18,000 from Smallweed, being the deposit on 'The Badgers'.
25 May	Exchanged contracts for the sale of 'Chesney' and received 10% deposit as stakeholder. Also exchanged contracts for purchase of 'The Badgers' and paid 10% deposit to the seller as stakeholder.
10 June	Seller's solicitors sent completion statement showing the balance of purchase money due, being the purchase price less the deposit paid.
15 June	Sent financial statement to Smallweed, showing the amount due from him on completion, together with bills of costs in respect of the sale and the purchase. Costs on sale were £280 plus VAT, costs on the purchase were £360 plus VAT, costs in respect of the mortgage advance were £80 plus VAT.
23 June	Smallweed sent a cheque for the amount shown as due on the financial statement.
24 June	Paid petty cash search fees of £10.
25 June	Received advance cheque from the Dedlock Building Society.
27 June	Completed the sale and purchase of the properties.
30 June	Paid the estate agent's charges, being £2,800 plus VAT. Paid stamp duty land tax of £1,800.
10 July	Paid Land Registry fees of £400. Transferred costs and disbursements from client account to office account.

Draw up the financial statement for Smallweed and the client ledger card.

6   Team Players & Co act for Mr and Mrs Plum in respect of the sale of their property 8, Pleasant Avenue for £450,000 and the purchase of Top Hole for £600,000. There is a mortgage of approximately £100,000 on 8, Pleasant Avenue, due to the Trusty Building Society.

  The High Flyers Bank Limited has agreed to advance £200,000 in respect of the new purchase. The bank will also assist with bridging finance in respect of the deposit due on the purchase. The balance required for the purchase will come from a bonus that Mr Plum is expecting.

200—

1 June	Local land charge search fee £100 paid.
9 June	Bridging loan in respect of the balance required for the deposit on the purchase is received in the sum of £15,000.
14 June	Contracts are exchanged in respect of the sale of 8 Pleasant Avenue the deposit of £45,000 being received as agents for the sellers. Contracts are also exchanged in respect of the purchase of Top Hole and a cheque for £60,000 is forwarded to the solicitors for the sellers who are holding as stakeholders.
20 June	A completion statement is sent to the buyers solicitors in respect of the sale of 8, Pleasant Avenue showing the balance due of £405,000 and a sum of £10,000 in respect of carpets, curtains and furnishings.

	The solicitors acting for the seller of Top Hole confirm that the balance due on the purchase will be £540,000.
21 June	An invoice is received from the estate agents acting for Mr and Mrs Plum showing the commission due to them of £9,000 plus VAT.
24 June	The firm sends bills of costs in respect of the sale and purchase to Mr and Mrs Plum. Profit costs on the purchase are £1,200 plus VAT, profit costs on the sale are £800 plus VAT. Profit costs in respect of the mortgage advance amount to £200 plus VAT.
25 June	Mr Plum sends a a cheque to cover the balance required on purchase and all costs and disbursements. The High Flyers Bank Ltd send a draft for £200,000 in respect of the mortgage advance.
4 July	Completed sale of 8, Pleasant Avenue and purchase of Top Hole. The bridging loan is repaid to the bank, together with interest of £140. The mortgage on 8, Pleasant Avenue is redeemed in the sum of £99,500. Costs and disbursements due are transferred from client account to office account.
	Stamp duty land tax of £24,000 is paid.
10 July	Paid the estate agent's commission plus VAT. Paid the Land Registry fees of £300.

Draw up a financial statement showing the amount required from Mr and Mrs Plum to complete the transactions, and show the account of Mr and Mrs Plum.

7 You act for Dinah Dobbs in the sale of 'Green Trees' and the purchase of 'Red Roofs'. The sale price of 'Green Trees' is £40,000 and the purchase price of 'Red Roofs' is £80,000. She is purchasing 'Red Roofs' with a mortgage of £55,000 from the Lendalot Building Society. 'Green Trees' is mortgaged to a private lender, her nephew Charles. You have also received instructions from the Lendalot Building Society and Charles. The following events occur:

200—	
2 August	Pay search fee £18 out of petty cash.
5 August	Receive instructions from the Lendalot Building Society in connection with the mortgage.
16 August	A bridging loan is obtained from the Mid-West Bank for £8,000 and that sum is transferred by the bank into Dinah's client account.
19 August	Exchange contracts. Receive deposit of £4,000 on 'Green Trees' as stake-holder. Pay £8,000 deposit on 'Red Roofs'.
23 August	Receive invoice from Sellalot estate agents for their commission, £400 plus VAT. The invoice is addressed to Dinah. Receive completion statement from seller's solicitors showing amount due to complete purchase of 'Red Roofs'.
30 August	Send completion statement of purchaser's solicitors showing balance of £36,000 due on completion of sale of 'Green Trees'.
2 September	Charles informs you that the amount required to redeem the mortgage on 'Green Trees' will be £10,425. Your costs will be £40 plus VAT, payable by Dinah. You ascertain from the Mid-West Bank the interest on the bridging loan is £83.
4 September	Send a financial statement together with bills of costs to Dinah showing: costs on sale £120 plus VAT, on the purchase £400 plus VAT and on the mortgage advance £60 plus VAT; Land Registry fee £175.

12 September	Receive mortgage advance, held to order until 16 September.
16 September	Complete sale and purchase. Send cheques to Charles to redeem mortgage and to the Mid-West Bank to pay the bridging loan and interest.
17 September	Pay land registry fees and estate agent's commission. Send balance due to Dinah and transfer costs and disbursements.

Prepare the financial statement sent to Dinah on 4 September and make the necessary entries in Dinah's ledger account, Charles's ledger account and the cash account to record the above transactions. VAT is assumed to be 17.5%.

8   Edward has recently retired and wishes to sell his house 'The Larches' for £250,000 and purchase 'Rose Cottage' for £140,000. There is a mortgage on 'The Larches' of £25,000. He instructs Able and Co, solicitors, to act on the sale and purchase.

The following events and transactions take place and you are required to draw up a financial statement for Edward and to show the ledger card of Edward on the books of Able and Co, making all the necessary entries to deal with the events and transactions. Both the sale and purchase should be dealt with on one ledger account for Edward.

The rate of VAT is to be taken at 17.5%.

200—

6 February	Received cheque from Edward for £200 on account of costs generally.
11 February	Local land charges search fee of £80 is paid from client account re 'Rose Cottage'.
20 February	The survey fee re 'Rose Cottage' is paid from office account, amounting to £400 plus VAT. The invoice is made out to Edward. The balance on client account is transferred to office account.
22 February	As Edward has no readily available cash for the deposit on 'Rose Cottage' a bridging loan is arranged with his bank, Village Bank PLC. The bank forward a cheque for £14,000 to be used for the deposit.
3 March	Contracts are exchanged for the sale of 'The Larches', the deposit of £25,000 being paid to Able and Co as stakeholders. Contracts are also exchanged on the purchase of 'Rose Cottage' and a cheque for the deposit of £14,000 is forwarded to the seller's solicitors, who are also holding as stakeholder.
20 March	A completion statement is sent to the buyer's solicitors in respect of the sale of 'The Larches' showing the balance due being £225,000. The solicitors for the seller of 'Rose Cottage' confirm that the balance due on completion will be £126,000.
23 March	An invoice is received from the estate agent acting for Edward, showing commission due of £4,000 plus VAT.
29 March	Bills of costs in respect of the sale and purchase are sent to Edward, being £680 plus VAT in respect of the sale of 'The Larches' and £360 plus VAT in respect of the purchase of 'Rose Cottage'.
2 April	Completed sale of 'The Larches' and purchase of 'Rose Cottage'. The bridging loan is repaid to the Village Bank PLC together with interest

of £80. The mortgage of 'The Larches' is redeemed, being £24,500, taking into account payments made and including interest due.

Stamp duty land tax of £1,400 is paid.

8 April   Paid the estate agent's commission plus VAT. Paid the Land Registry fees of £120. Transfer costs and disbursements from client account to office acccount, having received confirmation that Edward agrees the costs. Edward has also asked that the firm retain the balance in respect of the transactions until he decides where to invest it.

14.10   Suggested answers to exercises on property transactions

1   Deakin – sale of 1, Langdale Close; purchase of 23, Harwood Grove

Date	Details	Office account			Client account		
		DR	CR	Bal	DR	CR	Bal
2 Apr.	Cash—you deposit					25,000	25,000 CR
10 Apr.	Cash—deposit on purchase				25,000		—

Note that the £18,000 deposit paid as stakeholder will be credited to the stakeholder account, not Deakin's account, and then it will be transferred back to Deakin's account on completion of the sale.

2   Sinclair – sale of 2, Athens Avenue; purchase of 1, Beech Park

Date	Details	Office account			Client account		
		DR	CR	Bal	DR	CR	Bal
1 Mar	Cash—mortgage Advance Wakefield Building Society					150,000	150,000 CR
3 Mar	Transfer sheet— stakeholder deposit					30,000	180,000 CR
	Cash—balance sale proceeds					270,000	450,000 CR
	Cash—balance purchase monies				360,000		90,000 CR
	Cash—repay mortgage				35,625		54,375 CR

3 Farrell and Co.
Keeble: re sale of 'Rosewood'

Date	Details	Office account			Client account		
		DR	CR	Balance	DR	CR	Balance
200—							
8 May	Cash: sale proceeds					45,000	45,000 CR
	Cash: Burnley Building Society: mortgage redemption				15,325		29,675 CR
9 May	Cash: Mann & Co. (less commission £1,410)					3,590	33,265 CR
10 May	Cash: I. Oliver				594		32,671 CR
13 May	Profit costs	240					
	VAT	42		282 DR			
15 May	Cash: transfer: costs		282	—	282		32,389 CR
	Cash—you				32,389		—

4 Financial statement

To: Andrew Arbuthnot

Re: Purchase of 'Holywell House'

Payments: Deposit		6,000	
Balance of purchase money		54,000	60,000
Cost on purchase		120	
VAT at 17.5%		21	
Costs on mortgage		40	
VAT at 17.5%		7	
Search fees		18	206
			60,206
Less: Receipts			
Deposit paid by you		6,000	
Mortgage advance		30,000	36,000
Balance required from you before completion			24,206

Client: Andrew Arbuthnot
Matter: purchase of 'Holywell House'

Date	Details	Office account			Client account		
		DR	CR	Balance	DR	CR	Balance
2003							
2 Dec	Cash: search fee	18		18 DR			
16 Dec	Cash—you					6,000	6,000 CR
17 Dec	Cash: deposit				6,000		—
	Profit costs (purchase)	120					
	VAT	21		159 DR			
2004							
12 Jan	Cash—you					24,206	24,206 CR
15 Jan	Lancelot Lake transfer advance					30,000	54,206 CR
	Cash: completion				54,000		206 CR
	Lancelot Lake transfer costs	47		206 DR			
	Cash: transfer costs		206	—	206		—

Lancelot Lake

Date	Details	Office account			Client account		
		DR	CR	Balance	DR	CR	Balance
2003							
31 Dec	Profit costs	40					
	VAT	7		47 DR			
2004							
12 Jan	Cash—you					30,000	30,000 CR
15 Jan	Arbuthnot transfer sheet				30,000		
	Arbuthnot: transfer costs		47	—			—

Cash account

Date	Details	Office account			Client account		
		DR	CR	Balance	DR	CR	Balance
200—							
2 Dec	Arbuthnot: search fee		18	18 CR			
16 Dec	Arbuthnot				6,000		6,000 DR
17 Dec	Arbuthnot: deposit					6,000	—
200—							
12 Jan	Lancelot Lake mortgage advance				30,000		30,000 DR
	Arbuthnot				24,206		54,206 DR
15 Jan	Arbuthnot: completion					54,000	206 DR
16 Jan	Arbuthnot: transfer: costs	206		188 DR		206	—

5 Guppy and Jobling

Financial statement

To: Smallweed
Re: Sale of 'Chesney'
    Purchase of 'The Badgers'
Sale of 'Chesney'

Sale price		140,000
Less: Payments:		
Estate agent's fee inc VAT	3,290	
Costs	280	
VAT (17.5%)	49	3,619
Net sale proceeds		136,381
Less: Purchase of 'The Badgers'		
Payments:		
Purchase price		180,000
Our costs	360	
VAT at 17.5%	63	
Search fees	60	
Stamp duty land tax	1,800	
Land Registry fees	400	
Mortgage costs	80	
VAT	14	2,777
		182,777
Less: Receipts:		
Paid by you on account	18,000	
Mortgage advance	28,000	46,000

Required to complete purchase	136,777
Less: Due from sale	136,381
Balance required from you before completion	396

Smallweed: re sale of 'Chesney' and purchase of 'The Badgers'

Date	Details	Office account			Client account		
		DR	CR	Balance	DR	CR	Balance
200—							
8 May	Cash: local search fee	50		50 DR			
20 May	Cash—you re deposit					18,000	18,000 CR
25 May	Cash: deposit on sale				18,000		—
15 June	Profit costs on sale	280		330 DR			
	VAT	49		379 DR			
	Profit costs on purchase	360		739 DR			
	VAT	63		802 DR			
	Profit costs re advance	80		882 DR			
	VAT	14		896 DR			
23 June	Cash—you to complete					396	396 CR
24 June	Petty cash search fees	10		906 DR			
25 June	Cash: mortgage advance Dedlock Building Society					28,000	28,396 CR
27 June	Cash: sale proceeds					126,000	154,396 CR
	Transfer stakeholder Transfer sheet					14,000	168,396 CR
	Cash: seller's solicitors				162,000		6,396 CR
30 June	Cash: estate agents inc VAT				3,290		3,106 CR
	Cash: stamp duty land tax				1,800		1,306 CR
10 July	Cash: Land Registry fees				400		906 CR
	Cash: transfer from client to office		906	—	906		—

6 Financial statement

To: Mr and Mrs Plum

Re: Sale of 8, Pleasant Avenue

  Purchase of Top Hole

Sale of 8, Pleasant Avenue

Receipts:

Sale price	450,000
Add: Payment re carpets curtains etc.	10,000
	460,000

Less: Payments:

Estate agent's fees including VAT	10,575	
Mortgage redemption	99,500	
Sale costs	800	
VAT at (17.5%)	140	111,015
Net sale proceeds		348,985

Purchase of Top Hole
Payments:

Purchase price		600,000
Search fees	100	
Stamp duty land tax	24,000	
Land Registry fees	300	
Interest on bridging loan	140	
Costs on purchase	1,200	
VAT thereon	210	
Mortgage costs inc VAT	235	26,185
Amount required to complete purchase		626,185
Less: Mortgage advance		200,000
		426,185
Less: due from sale		348,985
Due from you prior to completion		77,200

Client: Mr and Mrs Plum

Matter: sale of 8, Pleasant Avenue and purchase of Top Hole

Date	Details	Office account			Client account		
		DR	CR	Balance	DR	CR	Balance
200—							
1 June	Cash: search fee	100		100 DR			
9 June	Cash: High Flyers Bank: deposit					15,000	15,000 CR
14 June	Cash: deposit on sale					45,000	60,000 CR
	Cash: deposit on purchase				60,000		—
24 June	Profit costs on purchase	1,200		1,300 DR			
	VAT	210		1,510 DR			
	Profit costs on sale	800		2,310 DR			
	VAT	140		2,450 DR			
	Profit costs on mortgage	200		2,650 DR			
	VAT	35		2,685 DR			

Date	Details	Office account			Client account		
		DR	CR	Balance	DR	CR	Balance
25 June	Cash—you balance due					77,200	77,200 CR
	Cash: mortgage advance					200,000	277,200 CR
4 July	Cash: balance on sale					415,000	692,200 CR
	Cash: balance on purchase				540,000		152,200 CR
	Cash: repay bridging loan plus interest				15,140		137,060 CR
	Cash: mortgage redemption				99,500		37,560 CR
	Cash: stamp duty land tax				24,000		13,560 CR
	Cash: transfer costs from client to office account	2,685	—		2,685		10,875 CR
10 July	Cash: Estate agents				10,575		300 CR
	Cash: Land Registry fee				300		—

7 **Client: Dinah Dobbs**
   Matter: sale of 'Green Trees'; purchase of 'Red Roofs' financial statement

Sale of 'Green Trees':

Receipts:

Sale price		40,000
Less: Payments:		
Estate agent's fees including VAT	470	
Mortgage redemption	10,425	
Redemption costs	47	
Sale costs	120	
VAT at 17.5%	21	11,083
Due from sale		28,917
Less: Purchase of 'Red Roofs'		
Payments:		
Purchase price		80,000
Search fees	18	
Bridging loan interest	83	
Purchase costs	400	
VAT	70	
Mortgage advance costs	60	
VAT	10.50	
Land Registry fee	175	816.50
		80,816.50

Less mortgage advance		55,000
Required to complete purchase		25,816.50
Due from sale	28,917	
Required to complete purchase	25,816.50	
Balance due to you following completion	3,100.50	

Client: Dinah Dobbs
Matter: sale of 'Green Trees'; purchase of 'Red Roofs'

Date	Details	Office account			Client account		
		DR	CR	Balance	DR	CR	Balance
200—							
2 Aug	Petty cash: search fees	18		18 DR			
16 Aug	Cash: bridging loan					8,000	8,000 CR
19 Aug	Cash: deposit paid				8,000		—
4 Sept	Costs: sale	120		138 DR			
	VAT	21		159 DR			
	Purchase	400		559 DR			
	VAT	70		629 DR			
	Costs: mortgage advance	60		689 DR			
	VAT	10.50		699.50 DR			
16 Sept	Cash: sale proceeds					36,000	36,000 CR
	Stakeholder Transfer sheet					4,000	40,000 CR
	Cash: Lendalot Building Society mortgage advance					55,000	95,000 CR
	Cash: purchase				72,000		23,000 CR
	Charles: transfer mortgage redemption				10,425		12,575 CR
	Cash: Mid-West Bank: repay loan				8,083		4,492 CR

Date	Details	Office account			Client account		
		DR	CR	Balance	DR	CR	Balance
17 Sept	Cash: Land Registry				175		4,317 CR
	Cash: estate agent				470		3,847 CR
	Charles: transfer: redemption costs	47		746.50 DR			
	Cash: transfer costs		746.50	—	746.50		3,100.50 CR
	Cash—you				3,100.50		—

Client: Charles
Matter: mortgage redemption

Date	Details	Office account			Client account		
		DR	CR	Balance	DR	CR	Balance
200— 4 Sept	Costs VAT	40 7		47 DR			
16 Sept	Dinah: transfer: redemption money Cash—you (redemption)				10,425	10,425	10,425 CR —
17 Sept			47	—			

Cash account

Date	Details	Office account			Client account		
		DR	CR	Balance	DR	CR	Balance
200— 16 Aug	Dinah: bridging loan				8,000		8,000 DR
19 Aug	Stakeholder re Dinah deposit				4,000		12,000 DR
	Dinah: deposit paid					8,000	4,000 DR
12 Sept	Dinah: mortgage advance (Lendalot Building Society)				55,000		59,000 DR
16 Sept	Dinah: sale proceeds				36,000		95,000 DR
	Dinah: purchase					72,000	23,000 DR
	Charles: mortgage redemption					10,425	12,575 DR
	Dinah: loan repayment					8,083	4,492 DR
	Dinah: Land Registry fees					175	4,317 DR
	Dinah: estate agent's fees					470	3,847 DR
	Dinah: transfer: costs	746.50		746.50 DR		746.50	3,100.50 DR
	Dinah: payment of balance					3,100.50	—

8 Financial statement

To: Edward
Re: Sale of 'The Larches'
    Purchase of 'Rose Cottage'
Sale of 'The Larches'

Receipts:

Sale price		250,000
Less: Payments:		
Estate agent's fees including VAT	4,700	
Mortgage redemption	24,500	
Sale costs	680	
VAT thereon (17.5%)	119	29,999
Net sale proceeds		220,001

Purchase of 'Rose Cottage'

Payments:

Purchase price		140,000
Search fees	80	
Survey fee including VAT	470	
Stamp duty land tax	1,400	
Land Registry fees	120	
Interest on bridging loan	80	
Cost on purchase	360	
VAT thereon	63	2,573
Amount required		142,573
Less paid on account		200
		142,373

Due from sale	220,001	
Less required on purchase:	142,373	
Due to you	77,628	

Client: Edward

Matter: sale of 'The Larches' and purchase of 'Rose Cottage'

Note transferred £77,738 to deposit 8 April

Date	Details	Office account			Client account		
		DR	CR	Balance	DR	CR	Balance
200—							
Feb 6	Cash: on account of costs					200	200 CR
Feb 11	Cash: search fee				80		120 CR
Feb 20	Cash: survey fee	470		470 DR			
	Cash transfer balance due		120	350 DR	120		—
Feb 22	Cash Village Bank: deposit					14,000	14,000 CR
Mar 3	Cash: deposit on purchase				14,000		—
Mar 29	Profit costs on sale	680		1,030 DR			
	VAT	119		1,149 DR			
	Profit costs on purchase	360		1,509 DR			
	VAT	63		1,572 DR			

Date	Details	Office account			Client account		
		DR	CR	Balance	DR	CR	Balance
2 Apr	Cash: balance on sale					225,000	225,000 CR
	Stakeholder transfer sheet					25,000	250,000 CR
	Cash: balance on purchase				126,000		124,000 CR
	Cash: repay bridging loan plus interest				14,080		109,920 CR
	Cash: mortgage redemption				24,500		85,420 CR
	Cash: stamp duty land tax				1,400		84,020 CR
200— 8 Apr	Cash: Estate agents				4,700		79,320 CR
	Cash: Land Registry fees				120		79,200 CR
	Cash: transfer costs from client to office account		1,572	—	1,572		77,628 CR

Deposit interest and interest payable to clients

15.1 Introduction

This chapter deals with the following:

1. The two methods of paying interest to clients on money held on their behalf.
2. Entries required when placing money on a special designated deposit account for a client.
3. When solicitors should pay a client interest from office account if the money has not been placed on a special deposit account.
4. Example of entries made to record interest payable to the client.
5. Earning interest on clients' money on a general deposit account.
6. Solicitor/trustees duties.

15.2 Paying interest to the client Rules 24 and 25

As solicitors often hold large sums of money on behalf of their clients for some time, in many cases they should pay interest to their clients on the sums held. There are two ways of doing this:

(1) place the sum held for a particular client on a special designated deposit account for that client (in the name of the firm) to earn interest, which will be paid to the client;

OR

(2) pay the client interest equivalent to that which would have been earned had they done so. (This will come out of office account.)

Clearly the first method will only be used if the solicitors know that the money will be held for some time. Its advantage for solicitors is that the bank will calculate the interest payable. This method may also be useful where controlled trust money is involved (see **15.2**).

The second method may be used by solicitors where they have placed a substantial part of client monies on a general deposit account, this will earn interest for the firm, and the interest will be paid into office account. The firm can then pay individual clients interest out of this. Usually a higher rate of interest will be earned on this general client account than the amount payable on the individual accounts for clients, and so the solicitors can benefit from the difference.

15.2.1 Placing money on special designated deposit account

The solicitor will ask the bank to transfer the client's money from the firm's client account at the bank to a separate deposit account in the client's name. The solicitor must account to the client for all the interest earned on this account. The money, together with interest, will be transferred back to the ordinary client account before paying the client.

EXAMPLE

The firm acts for Madden in a personal injury claim and received £50,000 in settlement of the claim on 3 September. Madden is not sure how to invest the money and on 5 September asks you to hold it for some time. The firm transfers the £50,000 to a designated deposit account.

1. The entries on the accounts will show a receipt into client account.
    Then the entries on the accounts will show a payment out of the client account, and a receipt into the deposit account.

2. Payment out of the firm's client account:

    CREDIT the Cash Account Client account.
    DEBIT the Client ledger account Client account.

3. Receipt into the firm's designated deposit account for the client:

    DEBIT the Deposit Cash Account (this will be a combined account for all the designated deposit accounts see rule 32(3)).
    CREDIT a separate Client ledger account for the deposit Client account.

Cash Account

Date	Details	Office account			Client account		
		DR	CR	BAL	DR	CR	BAL
3 Sept	Madden: settlement of claim(1)				50,000		50,000 DR
5 Sept	Madden: transfer to Deposit account (2)					50,000	—

Madden Account

Date	Details	Office account			Client account		
		DR	CR	BAL	DR	CR	BAL
3 Sept	Cash: settlement of claim (1)					50,000	50,000 CR
5 Sept	Cash: transfer to Deposit (2)				50,000		—

Deposit Cash Account

Date	Details	Office account			Client account		
		DR	CR	BAL	DR	CR	BAL
5 Sept	Madden: held on deposit (3)				50,000		50,000 DR

Madden

Held on deposit

Date	Details	Office account			Client account		
		DR	CR	BAL	DR	CR	BAL
5 Sept	Deposit cash account (3)					50,000	50,000 CR

All that has happened is that the money has been moved from the main client bank account to the deposit account, and a separate client ledger account for Madden has been opened to record this.

4. When the interest is earned the entries are:

DEBIT The Deposit Cash Account Client Account.

CREDIT Madden Held on deposit Client ledger Client Account.

Continuing the example—Interest earned on 1 December is £120.

Deposit Cash Account

Date	Details	Office account			Client account		
		DR	CR	BAL	DR	CR	BAL
5 Sept	Madden: held on deposit (3)				50,000		50,000 DR
1 Dec	Madden: deposit interest (4)				120		50,120 DR

Madden

Held on Deposit Account

Date	Details	Office account			Client account		
		DR	CR	BAL	DR	CR	BAL
5 Sept	Deposit Cash (3)					50,000	50,000 CR
1 Dec	Deposit Cash: interest (4)					120	50,120 CR

Continuing the example:

When the firm wants to pay Madden the total amount, as the deposit account will not have a cheque book, the total money held on deposit will be transferred back to the ordinary client bank account before paying Madden.

The entries for transferring the money back from deposit account are:

5. Payment out of deposit account:

CREDIT the Deposit Cash account.

DEBIT Madden Held on Deposit account client account.

6. Receipt into ordinary client bank account:

DEBIT Cash Account client account.

CREDIT Madden Client ledger account client account.

Deposit Cash account

Date	Details	Office account			Client account		
		DR	CR	BAL	DR	CR	BAL
5 Sept	Madden: held on deposit (3)				50,000		50,000 DR
1 Dec	Madden: deposit interest (4)				120		50,120 DR
	Madden held on deposit (5)					50,120	—

Madden

Held on Deposit Account

Date	Details	Office account			Client account		
		DR	CR	BAL	DR	CR	BAL
5 Sept	Deposit Cash (3)					50,000	50,000 CR
1 Dec	Deposit Cash: interest (4)					120	50,120 CR
1 Dec	Deposit Cash account (5) transfer back				50,120		—

Cash Account

Date	Details	Office account			Client account		
		DR	CR	BAL	DR	CR	BAL
3 Sept	Madden: settlement of claim (1)				50,000		50,000 DR
5 Sept	Madden: transfer to Deposit account (2)					50,000	—
1 Dec	Madden: transfer from deposit account (6)				50,120		50,120 DR

Madden Account

Date	Details	Office account			Client account		
		DR	CR	BAL	DR	CR	BAL
3 Sept	Cash: settlement of claim (1) Cash Account transfer to Deposit (2)				50,000	50,000	50,000 CR —
1 Dec	Cash Account: back from deposit (6)					50,120	50,120 CR

7. Then a normal payment out of client money to Madden can be made:

   CREDIT the Cash Account.

   DEBIT Madden Account.

Cash Account

Date	Details	Office account			Client account		
		DR	CR	BAL	DR	CR	BAL
3 Sept	Madden: settlement of claim (1)				50,000		50,000 DR
	Madden: transfer to Deposit account (2)					50,000	—
1 Dec	Madden: transfer back from deposit account (6)				50,120		50,120 DR
	Madden: balance due (7)					50,120	—

Madden Account

Date	Details	Office account			Client account		
		DR	CR	BAL	DR	CR	BAL
3 Sept	Cash— settlement of claim (1)					50,000	50,000 CR
	Cash Account transfer to Deposit (2)				50,000		—
1 Dec	Cash Account: back from deposit (6)					50,120	50,120 CR
	Cash Account—you (7)				50,120		—

Rule 32(3)(b) SAR gives an alternative to opening a separate client ledger account for the Deposit money held, the firm may have an additional column on the client ledger card recording the amount held on deposit. Using the above example the account for Madden would be as follows:

Madden Account

Date	Details	Office account			Client account			Deposit client account		
		DR	CR	BAL	DR	CR	BAL	DR	CR	BAL
3 Sept	Cash: settlement of claim					50,000	50,000 CR			
5 Sept	Cash—Account transfer to Deposit				50,000		—			
5 Sept	Deposit Cash								50,000	50,000 CR
1 Dec	Deposit Cash interest								120	50,120 CR
1 Dec	Deposit Cash transfer back							50,120		—
1 Dec	Cash Account: back from deposit					50,120	50,120 CR			—
	Cash Account: you				50,120		—			

15.2.2　Paying the client equivalent interest from office account

If the firm does not place money held for the client on deposit, then the solicitor should pay an equivalent sum under rule 24, but not if:

(a) the amount of interest calculated is £20 or less or

(b) the sum of money held does not exceed the amount shown below for a time not exceeding the period shown:

> £1,000 for 8 weeks;
> £2,000 for 4 weeks;
> £10,000 for 2 weeks;
> £20,000 for 1 week.

If a sum over £20,000 is held for less than a week, a firm need only account for interest if it is fair and reasonable to do so.

Note that there are other exceptions to the payment of interest in rule 24.

If clients have not been paid interest they may apply to the Office for the Supervision of Solicitors for a certificate as to whether interest should have been paid, and the amount payable.

If a firm pays a sum out of office account as interest to the client, a business expense has been paid. To record payments of interest, an expense account, the Interest Payable account, is opened. This is an office account only. The firm may pay the interest by a cheque drawn on office account, and send a separate cheque, drawn on client account for the money held. Alternatively the firm may transfer the interest payable from office account to client account, and pay one cheque to the client for the balance together with the interest.

EXAMPLES

A. The firm has held £10,000 for their client Floyd for one month and on 10 December pays a cheque from office account for interest of £25, together with a cheque from client account for the £10,000. Note that the interest payable will also have to be recorded on the client ledger account, office account column under rule 32(4)SAR.

1. Thus the entries to show the interest payable are:

   DEBIT the Interest Payable account Office account.
   CREDIT Floyd's Client ledger account Office account.
   Then when the two cheques are sent the entries would be:

2. Payment of interest payable:

   CREDIT the Cash Account Office account.
   DEBIT Floyd's Client ledger account Office account.

3. Payment of amount held on Client account:

   CREDIT the Cash Account Client account.
   DEBIT Floyd's Client ledger account Client account.

Interest Payable account—Expense account

Date	Details	Office account		
		DR	CR	BAL
10 Dec	Floyd (1)	25		25 DR

Floyd Account

Date	Details	Office account			Client account		
		DR	CR	BAL	DR	CR	BAL
10 Dec	Balance held						10,000 CR
	Interest Payable (1)		25	25 CR			
	Cash you: interest (2)	25		—			
	Cash you: balance due (3)				10,000		—

Cash Account

Date	Details	Office account			Client account		
		DR	CR	BAL	DR	CR	BAL
	Balance						10,000 DR
	Floyd interest (2)		25	25 CR			
	Floyd balance due (3)					10,000	—

B. If the solicitor decides to send one cheque drawn on client account, then the entries will be as follows:

1. Record the interest payable as before:

    DEBIT the Interest Payable account Office account.
    CREDIT Floyd's Client ledger account Office account.

2. Transfer the interest payable to Client account:

    CREDIT the Cash Account Office account.
    DEBIT Floyd's Client ledger account Office account.
    DEBIT the Cash Account Client account.
    CREDIT Floyd's Client ledger account Client account.

3. Pay the client the total due from Client account:
    CREDIT the Cash Account Client account.
    DEBIT Floyd's Client ledger account Client account.

    The accounts would therefore be as follows:

Interest Payable account—Expense account

Date	Details	Office Account		
		DR	CR	BAL
10 Dec	Floyd (1)	25		25 DR

Floyd Account

Date	Details	Office account			Client account		
		DR	CR	BAL	DR	CR	BAL
10 Dec	Balance held						10,000 CR
	Interest Payable (1)		25	25 CR			
	Cash transfer— interest (2)	25		—		25	10,025 CR
	Cash you: balance due (3)				10,025		—

Cash Account

Date	Details	Office account			Client account		
		DR	CR	BAL	DR	CR	BAL
	Balance						10,000 DR
	Floyd: transfer interest (2)		25	25 CR	25		10,025 DR
	Floyd: balance due (3)					10,025	—

15.3 Earning interest on clients' money on a general deposit account

As stated in **15.2** solicitors may transfer part of their client money to a general deposit account. Any interest earned on this is office money, and will be credited direct to office account. This can then be used to pay interest to individual clients, where appropriate.

When a solicitor transfers clients' money from current account to deposit account the following entries in the accounts are made:

(a) CREDIT the cash account client column.

(b) DEBIT the deposit cash account client column.

EXAMPLE

The firm has a balance of £100,000 on its client current account. The partners decide to place £30,000 of this on deposit on 9 September.

Cash account

Date	Details	Office account			Client account		
		DR	CR	Balance	DR	CR	Balance
	Balance						100,000 DR
9 Sept	Deposit cash: general deposit					30,000	70,000 DR

Deposit cash account

Date	Details	Office account			Client account		
		DR	CR	Balance	DR	CR	Balance
9 Sept	Cash: general deposit, clients' money				30,000		30,000 DR

Interest earned on the general deposit account is practice income and the firm will open an income account, the Interest Received account, to record this income.

When the bank notifies the firm that interest has been earned on the client deposit account, the following bookkeeping entries will be made:

(a) Credit the Interest Received account.

(b) Debit the Cash account office column.

EXAMPLE

On 8 May the bank credits £1,000 interest to office account on money held on general deposit.

Interest Received account/office account

Date	Details	DR	CR	Balance
8 May	Cash (general deposit)		1,000	1,000 CR

Cash account

Date	Details	Office account			Client account		
		DR	CR	Balance	DR	CR	Balance
8 May	Cash (general deposit): interest receivable	1,000		1,000 DR			

15.4 Solicitor/Trustees

If a solicitor is a trustee then under general law trustees should not profit from a trust. Either the trust money will be placed on a designated deposit account, with all the interest being paid to the trust, or the solicitor will have to account for all interest that would have been earned had the money been placed on deposit. If the trust money is paid into a general client account the solicitor must be careful not to obtain any indirect benefit from the money being placed into the client account. As the solicitor may benefit from an increased rate of interest by virtue of trust money it may be safer to place all trust money into a separate client bank account.

15.5 Check list

By the end of this chapter you should be able to:

1. understand when interest should be paid to a client;
2. understand the two methods of paying interest to clients;
3. make the entries in respect of:
   (a) the transfer to a deposit account,
   (b) the receipt of interest earned on the deposit account,
   (c) the transfer back to general client bank account,
   (d) payment to the client;
4. make the entries to show interest payable to the client;
   (a) when a separate cheque drawn on office account is sent to the client,
   (b) when the interest payable is transferred to client account before being paid to the client;

5. understand interest earned on general client deposit account is office money;

6. make the entries in respect of the transfer to general client deposit account and for the receipt of interest earned on the general client deposit account;

7. understand the additional duties imposed on solicitor trustees;

8. complete the self test exercises at the end of the chapter.

15.6 Exercises on deposit interest and interest payable

1. On 1 March Cooper asked his solicitors to hold the net proceeds of sale of his cottage, previously received by them, being £100,000, until he had taken full investment advice. The money was placed on a designated deposit account immediately, and on 1 October the sum of £102,000, including interest earned was transferred back to the client current account, before a cheque was sent to Cooper for the total. Draw up all the relevant accounts for the above.

2. A firm of solicitors acted for Booth in respect of debt collection. The firm received £14,000 from a debtor on behalf of Booth on 5 January, and Booth asked the firm to hold this until 20 March. The firm then allowed interest of £100 and paid a cheque drawn on client account for the total of £14,100 to Booth on that date.

15.7 Suggested answers to exercises on deposit interest and interest payable

1. Cooper—sale of cottage

Date	Details	Office account			Client account		
		DR	CR	BAL	DR	CR	BAL
	Balance (sale proceeds)						100,000 CR
1 Mar	Cash: transfer to deposit(1)				100,000		—
1 Oct	Cash: from deposit (5)					102,000	102,000 CR
	Cash: you (6)				102,000		—

Cooper
Held on Deposit Account

Date	Details	Office account			Client account		
		DR	CR	BAL	DR	CR	BAL
1 Mar	Deposit Cash (2)					100,000	100,000 CR
1 Oct	Deposit Cash— interest (3)					2,000	102,000 CR
1 Oct	Deposit Cash account (4)				102,000		—

Cash Account

Date	Details	Office account			Client account		
		DR	CR	BAL	DR	CR	BAL
	Cooper: balance						100,000 DR
1 Mar	Cooper: transfer to deposit account (1)					100,000	—
1 Oct	Cooper: transfer from deposit account (5)				102,000		102,000 DR
	Cooper: balance due (6)					102,000	—

Deposit Cash account

Date	Details	Office account			Client account		
		DR	CR	BAL	DR	CR	BAL
1 Mar	Cooper: held on deposit	(2)			100,000		100,000 DR
1 Oct	Cooper: deposit interest (3)				2,000		102,000 DR
	Cooper: deposit transfer back (4)					102,000	—

2. Booth account—debt collection

Date	Details	Office account			Client account		
		DR	CR	BAL	DR	CR	BAL
5 Jan	Cash: debtor (1)					14,000	14,000 CR
20 Mar	Interest payable (2)		100	100 CR			
	Cash transfer interest (3)	100		—		100	14,100 CR
	Cash you balance due (4)				14,100		—

Interest payable account

Date	Details	Office account			Client account		
		DR	CR	BAL	DR	CR	BAL
20 Mar	Booth—interest (2)	100		100DR			

Cash account

Date	Details	Office account			Client account		
		DR	CR	BAL	DR	CR	BAL
5 Jan	Booth: debtor (1)				14,000		14,000 DR
20 Mar	Booth: transfer interest (3)		100	100CR	100		14,100 DR
	Booth: balance due (4)					14,100	—

Probate transactions

16.1 Introduction

These occur when a firm acts in connection with the administration of an estate. A summary of some common financial transactions is set out below:

(a) A grant of probate or letters of administration will be required, probate fees will be paid and, where applicable, inheritance tax. It may be necessary to obtain a loan from the bank to the executors in respect of the inheritance tax payable. This may be paid direct from the loan account to the Inland Revenue, or the money may be paid into the firm's client account before payment is made to the Inland Revenue.

(b) Payments will be made regarding advertisements.

(c) Once probate has been obtained the firm will use it to collect all the assets of the deceased, for example bank account moneys, building society moneys, life policy proceeds. Some of this may be used to pay back the bank loan for inheritance tax, together with any interest due on the loan.

(d) Property belonging to the deceased may be sold, e.g., house and household contents.

(e) Debts due from the estate of the deceased will be paid, as will funeral expenses.

(f) Pecuniary legacies will be paid.

(g) The firm will charge costs (plus VAT) regarding administration and any sale of property, and transfer such costs from client account to office account with the agreement of the executors.

(h) The balance of the estate will be distributed to the beneficiary/beneficiaries, together with any interest due from the firm, either from moneys held on designated deposit or interest in lieu.

16.2 Exercises on probate transactions

1 Olde, Bayley & Co., solicitors, are instructed by the executors of Passway, deceased, to administer the estate on their behalf. The gross value of the estate amounts to £62,000 and consists of a house valued at £45,000 (subject to a mortgage of £12,000) and personalty valued at £17,000. There are various debts due by the estate amounting to £1,892. The following events take place:

7 October   Probate fees of £50 are paid by the firm's cheque.

15 October   A cheque for £16 is drawn in respect of the statutory advertisements, the cost of the local advertisement (£8) being met by a payment out of petty cash.

18 October	The balance remaining in the Standoff Building Society (£223) is paid into client account.
21 October	Proceeds of life policy received, being £5,000.
28 October	The household contents are sold and a cheque for £5,890 is received from the auctioneer. Commission of £620 had already been deducted.
4 November	Contracts for the sale of the house (£44,500) are exchanged, and a deposit of £4,450 is received by Olde, Bayley & Co., for them to hold as stakeholders.
18 November	Debts amounting to £1,927 are paid.
25 November	Paid funeral expenses £432.
4 December	The sale of the house is completed and a bank draft (£40,050) for the balance of the purchase money is received. The mortgage is redeemed by the payment of £12,367 which is inclusive of accrued interest.
11 December	A pecuniary legacy of £5,000 is paid to a legatee.
12 December	Bill of costs re sale of the house is prepared and agreed with the executors, profit costs being £440 plus VAT, and cash disbursements £20 (no VAT) are paid. Paid estate agents their commission £720 plus VAT.
16 December	Bill of costs for the administration of the estate, profit costs £520 (plus VAT) and disbursements, sent to executors, and after receiving their agreement, all moneys due to the firm from the estate are transferred to office account.
17 December	The balance of moneys now held by Olde, Bayley & Co., on behalf of the executors, is paid over to Rich, the residuary legatee, in accordance with their instructions. This includes the interest allowed on the money held by the firm on behalf of the executors of £208.

Show the client ledger card of the executors of Passway deceased. The rate of VAT is to be taken as 17.5%.

2 The firm is informed that Saturn died on 26 February, and the executors appointed in the will instruct the firm to act in the administration of the estate generally. The estate consists of a house 'Eudestar' valued at £70,000 and personalty valued at £47,500. There are various debts due by the estate (£1,500) together with a loan from an insurance company (secured on a life insurance policy) amounting to £5,000. The residue of the estate has been left to Neptune, a nephew who is in the process of buying a cottage, 'The Wild Leap', a matter which is being dealt with by the firm.

During the administration, the following events take place:

8 March	House insurance premium (£95) on 'Eudestar', now due, and the firm debits the Executors' account, the amount being transferred to the account of the insurance company, for whom the firm acts.
14 March	Probate fees of £70 are paid by cheque.
19 March	The grant is received and registered with the bank.
26 March	The amount invested by the deceased with the Constellation Building Society is, after registration of the grant, withdrawn, the balance amounting to £590 being paid into client account.

27 March	The firm draws a cheque in respect of statutory advertisements (£22), and pays £12 out of petty cash in respect of the local advertisement.
29 March	Received cheque from the Pluto Insurance Co. Ltd, for the sum of £6,342, being the net sum receivable from the company after the deduction of £5,158 in respect of the loan together with accrued interest.
1 April	Debts amounting to £1,500, together with funeral expenses of £1,000, are paid out of client account.
	The executors have agreed to an interim distribution of £4,000 to Neptune, which is transferred to Neptune's client account. The firm then sends a cheque (£4,000) to the solicitors acting for the vendor of the cottage 'The Wild Leap', for them to hold as stakeholders, contracts being exchanged the same day.
5 April	Exchanged contracts for the sale of 'Eudestar', the deposit of £7,000 having been received by the firm for them to hold as stakeholders.
12 April	Sundry fees (£3) paid from office account re the transmission of shares to Virgo, a beneficiary in the estate of Saturn, deceased.
26 April	Received completion statement in respect of 'The Wild Leap', showing £36,000 due, being the balance of purchase money. Sent financial statement to Neptune same day, showing profit costs of £280 excluding VAT (as per bill of costs attached thereto), Land Registry fees £70. Paid £10 from petty cash, in respect of bankruptcy search.
30 April	Completed purchase of 'The Wild Leap', the balance of purchase moneys being received by the firm from the Bank of Aries as a loan, an undertaking having been given that the sum would be repaid to them from the proceeds of sale of 'Eudestar'. The executors had previously agreed to this arrangement.
2 May	Completed sale of 'Eudestar', receiving a bank draft (£63,000) in respect of the balance of purchase moneys.
	Paid Land Registry fees re 'The Wild Leap'.
9 May	The firm agrees the bills of cost for the sale of the house and the administration of the estate with the executors. Profit costs with regard to the sale amount to £440 (excluding VAT), and with regard to the administration £680 (excluding VAT), together with disbursements in both cases. With the executors' agreement, a sum amounting to £36,146 is transferred from the account of the executors to the account of Neptune, and a cheque for this amount is sent to the Bank of Aries in accordance with the firm's undertaking.
16 May	All moneys due to the firm from the estate are transferred to office account.
17 May	The balance of moneys held by the firm on behalf of the executors is transferred to the account of Neptune at the request of the executors, such sum being inclusive of interest allowed by the firm of £567.
	All moneys due to the firm from Neptune are transferred to office account, the balance due to Neptune being held pending further instructions.

You are required to show the ledger accounts of:

(i) Neptune;

(ii) the executors of Saturn, deceased.

The rate of VAT is to be taken as 17.5%.

In making the necessary entries, it is important that the account in which the corresponding entry would be made is clearly identified by the appropriate entry in the details column.   (Solicitors' Final Examinations, amended.)

16.3 Suggested answers to exercises on probate transactions

1 Executors of Passway deceased

Date	Details	Office account			Client account		
		DR	CR	Balance	DR	CR	Balance
7 Oct	Cash: probate fees	50		50 DR			—
15 Oct	Cash: advertisements	16		66 DR			
	Petty cash: advertisements	8		74 DR			
18 Oct	Cash: Standoff Building Society					223	223 CR
21 Oct	Cash: life policy					5,000	5,223 CR
28 Oct	Cash: auctioneer (less commission £620)					5,890	11,113 CR
18 Nov	Cash: debts				1,927		9,186 CR
25 Nov	Cash: funeral expenses				432		8,754 CR
4 Dec	Cash: sale proceeds					40,050	48,804 CR
	Stakeholder: transfer					4,450	53,254 CR
	Cash: mortgage redemption				12,367		40,887 CR
11 Dec	Cash: legacy				5,000		35,887 CR
12 Dec	Costs: sale	440					
	VAT	77		591 DR			
	Petty cash: disbursements	20		611 DR			
	Cash: estate agent				846		35,041 CR
16 Dec	Costs: re estate	520					
	VAT	91		1,222 DR			
	Cash: transfer: costs		1,222	—	1,222		33,819 CR
17 Dec	Interest payable		208	208 CR			
	Cash transfer interest payable	208		—		208	34,027 CR
	Cash: Rich				34,027		—

2 Executors of Saturn deceased re administration of estate

Date	Details	Office account			Client account		
		DR	CR	Balance	DR	CR	Balance
8 Mar	Cash: transfer: insurance premium: client account: 'Eudestar'	95		95 DR			
14 Mar	Cash: probate fees	70		165 DR			
26 Mar	Cash: Constellation Building Society					590	590 CR
	Cash: statutory advertisement				22		568 CR
	Petty cash: local advertisement	12		177 DR			
29 Mar	Cash: Pluto Insurance Co. Ltd					6,342	6,910 CR
1 Apr	Cash: debts				1,500		5,410 CR
	Cash: funeral expenses				1,000		4,410 CR
	Neptune: transfer				4,000		410 CR
12 Apr	Cash: fees: transmission of shares to Virgo	3		180 DR			
2 May	Cash: purchaser's of 'Eudestar'					63,000	63,410 CR
	Stakeholder: transfer sheet					7,000	70,410 CR
9 May	Costs: sale	440					
	VAT	77		697 DR			
	Costs: administration	680					
	VAT	119		1,496 DR			
	Neptune: transfer			—	36,146		34,264 CR
16 May	Cash: transfer: costs		1,496	—	1,496		32,768 CR
	Interest payable		567	567 CR			
17 May	Cash: transfer: from office account in lieu of interest	567		—		567	33,335 CR
	Neptune: transfer residue				33,335		—

Neptune: re purchase of 'Wild Leap'

Date	Details	Office account			Client account		
		DR	CR	Balance	DR	CR	Balance
1 Apr	Executors of Saturn deceased: transfer					4,000	4,000 CR
	Cash: deposit re 'The Wild Leap'				4,000		—
26 Apr	Costs	280		329 DR			
	VAT	49					
	Petty cash: bankruptcy search	10		339 DR			
30 Apr	Cash: Bank of Aries					36,000	36,000 CR
	Cash: purchase of 'The Wild Leap'				36,000		—
2 May	Cash: Land Registry	70		409 DR			
9 May	Executors of Saturn deceased: transfer					36,146	36,146 CR
	Cash: Bank of Aries				36,146		—
17 May	Executors of Saturn deceased: transfer: residue					33,335	33,335 CR
	Cash: transfer: costs		409	—	409		32,926 CR

16.4 Test 1 on probate transactions

Allow approximately 1 hour to complete this test.

Tulip, Crocus & Co., solicitors, are instructed by the executors of Daffodil, deceased, to act in the administration of the estate generally. The whole of the net estate has been left to the widow of Daffodil, and consists of a house valued at £50,000 and personalty valued at £42,000. There are various debts due by the estate, amounting to £1,496, together with a bank loan of £5,000 which is secured on the house. During the administration the following events take place:

1 March	Probate fees of £50 are paid by cheque.
4 March	Grant received and registered with the bank, which transfers all moneys due by it to the deceased, amounting to £896, to the firm's bank account.
5 March	At the request of the widow of Daffodil, the executors instruct the firm to sell the house for £50,000, together with some of the contents, and, when feasible, to send a bank draft for £5,000 to a firm in Spain, which is dealing with the purchase of a villa for the widow.

8 March	Cheque drawn on a client account for £20 in respect of statutory advertisements. The cost of the local advertisement (£12) is met out of petty cash.
11 March	Proceeds of life policy (£3,500) received, together with cheque from the Pompeii Building Society for £18,000 which closes that account.
12 March	Some of the contents of the house are sold and a cheque for £3,250 is received in respect thereof.
18 March	Exchanged contracts for the sale of the house, the deposit of £5,000 having been paid to the estate agent by the prospective purchaser.
22 March	Paid the debts of £1,496 together with funeral expenses of £485.
29 March	Received cheque (£11,900) in respect of the sale of units held in a unit trust by the deceased.
12 April	Bank draft in respect of the widow's villa sent to firm in Spain, the full cost of the draft (£5,012) being charged to the firm's client bank account.
16 April	The sale of the house is completed and a bank draft (£45,000) for the balance of purchase money is received. The bank loan is repaid which, together with accrued interest, amounted to £5,340. Received same day, from estate agents, the balance of the deposit on the house, less commission of £1,150 (including VAT).
19 April	Bills of costs for the sale of the house, and for administration of the estate are agreed with the executors. The bill of costs for the sale of the house shows profit costs of £280 (plus VAT). The bill of costs for the administration of the estate shows profit costs of £600 (plus VAT) and disbursements.
22 April	All moneys due to the firm from the estate are transferred to office account.
23 April	Interest allowed by the firm of £410 is transferred to client account.
30 April	Mrs Daffodil (the residuary legatee), who is already a client of the firm, having instructed it some time previously to act for her in the purchase of a cottage, has requested that the executors pay her the sum of £2,850 on account of money due to her from the estate, this amount being the deposit on the cottage she proposes to purchase. The executors have agreed, the firm sends a cheque for that amount to the solicitors acting for the seller, for them to hold as stakeholders, the cheque being drawn on the client account.
30 April	The firm, to date, has made payments out amounting to £380 out of office moneys, in respect of the proposed purchase of the cottage.
24 May	A financial statement and bill of costs in respect of the purchase of the cottage, had been sent to Mrs Daffodil some time previously, showing the sum of £26,171 due, being the balance of the purchase price £25,650, various disbursements £380 (including VAT where relevant) and profit costs £120 plus VAT. The sum of £26,171 is transferred with the agreement of the executors, from the executors' account to the account of Mrs Daffodil, and completion then takes place. The account of Mrs Daffodil is then closed.

The rate of VAT is to be taken as 17.5%. Show the accounts of the executors of Daffodil, deceased, and Mrs Daffodil.   (Law Society Final Examination, amended.)

16.5 Suggested answer to Test 1 on probate transactions

The executors of Daffodil deceased

Date	Details	Office account			Client account		
		DR	CR	Balance	DR	CR	Balance
1 Mar	Cash: Probate fees	50		50 DR			
4 Mar	Cash: bank					896	896 CR
8 Mar	Cash: advertisements				20		876 CR
	Petty cash: advertisements	12		62 DR			
11 Mar	Cash: life policy					3,500	4,376 CR
	Cash: Pompeii Building Society					18,000	22,376 CR
12 Mar	Cash: house contents					3,250	25,626 CR
22 Mar	Cash: debts				1,496		24,130 CR
	Cash: funeral expenses				485		23,645 CR
29 Mar	Cash: unit trust					11,900	35,545 CR
12 Apr	Cash (bank draft) villa				5,012		30,533 CR
16 Apr	Cash: sale proceeds					45,000	75,533 CR
	Cash: bank loan repaid				5,340		70,193 CR
	Cash: estate agent, deposit (less commission)					3,850	74,043 CR
19 Apr	Profit costs: re sale	280					
	VAT	49					
				391 DR			
	Costs: re administration	600					
	VAT	105		1096 DR			
22 Apr	Cash: transfer: costs		1096	—	1096		72,947 CR
23 Apr	Interest payable		410	410 CR			
	Cash transfer interest	410		—		410	73,357 CR
30 Apr	Mrs Daffodil: transfer				2,850		70,507 CR
24 May	Mrs Daffodil: transfer				26,171		44,336 CR

Mrs Daffodil

Date	Details	Office account			Client account		
		DR	CR	Balance	DR	CR	Balance
30 Apr	Balance b/d			380 DR			
	Executors of Daffodil: transfer					2,850	2,850 CR
	Cash: vendor's solicitors				2,850		—
24 May	Executors of Daffodil: transfer					26,171	26,171 CR
	Cash: purchase				25,650		521 CR
	Profit Costs	120					
	VAT	21		521 DR			
	Cash: transfer: costs		521	—	521		—

16.6 Test 2 on probate transactions

Allow approximately 1 hour to complete this test.

Only Mortal & Co., solicitors, are instructed by the executors of Styx, deceased, to administer the estate on their behalf. The estate consists of a house valued at £250,000 (subject to a mortgage of around £30,000) and personalty valued at £100,000. Debts due by the estate total £15,000.

The following events take place:

5 January	The inheritance tax payable in respect of the estate amounts to £28,800 and the deceased's bank agrees to advance that amount to the executors, the sum being credited to the bank account of Only Mortal & Co. The firm then issues a cheque in favour of the Inland Revenue for the same amount.
	Probate fees of £250 are paid by the firm's cheque.
10 January	Grant received and registered with the bank, who transfer all moneys due by them to the deceased (£16,000) to the executors' loan account.
16 January	A cheque for £150 is drawn on office account in respect of statutory advertisements, and the cost of the local advertisement, being £20, is paid from petty cash.
19 January	Proceeds of sale of shares, totalling £55,000, received by the firm and £13,000 is paid by the firm to the bank for the credit of the executors' loan account (which is then closed).
29 January	The household contents are sold and a cheque for £27,120 is received from the auctioneer. Commission of £1,800 including VAT had already been deducted.
2 February	Contracts are exchanged for the sale of the house for the sum of £250,000 and a cheque for £25,000 is received by the firm as deposit, to hold as stakeholders.
20 February	Debts totalling £15,000 are paid.

26 February	Paid funeral expenses of £2,000.
4 March	The sale of the house is completed and a bank draft is received for the balance of the purchase money. The mortgage is redeemed by the payment of £30,200, which includes accrued interest.
14 March	Legacies are paid, being £10,000 to Greenpeace and £5,000 to the NSPCC.
16 March	A bill of costs re the sale is prepared, and agreed with the executors; profit costs are £600 plus VAT. The estate agents are paid £5,000 plus VAT by cheque. The amount due to the firm is transferred from client account to office account.
17 March	Elysium, the sole residuary beneficiary, who is already a client of the firm, has instructed the firm to act for her in her purchase of a house. She has asked that the executors pay her the sum of £15,000 on account of the money due to her from the estate, this sum being the deposit on the house she is purchasing. After the executors have agreed to this, Only Mortal & Co. send a cheque for this amount to the solicitors acting for the seller of the house, for them to hold as stakeholders.
21 March	A bill of costs for the administration of the estate, agreed at £800 plus VAT, is sent to the executors and after receiving their agreement, the amount due is transferred to office account.
30 March	Interest allowed of £1,500 is transferred to client account. By agreement between Elysium and the executors, the balance of moneys now held by Only Mortal & Co. on behalf of the executors, is transferred to the account of Elysium.

Show the ledger accounts of the executors of Styx deceased and Elysium, as they would appear in the books of Only Mortal & Co.

16.7 Suggested answer to Test 2 on probate transactions

Executors of Styx

Date	Details	Office account			Client account		
		DR	CR	Balance	DR	CR	Balance
5 Jan	Cash: advance bank re inheritance tax					28,800	28,800 CR
5 Jan	Cash: Inland Revenue re inheritance tax				28,800		—
	Cash: probate fees	250		250 DR			
16 Jan	Cash: Statutory adverts	150		400 DR			
16 Jan	Petty cash: local adverts	20		420 DR			
19 Jan	Cash: sale of shares					55,000	55,000 CR
19 Jan	Cash: bank loan account				13,000		42,000 CR
29 Jan	Cash: auctioneer					27,120	69,120 CR

Date	Details	Office account			Client account		
		DR	CR	Balance	DR	CR	Balance
20 Feb	Cash: debts				15,000		54,120 CR
26 Feb	Cash: funeral expenses				2,000		52,120 CR
4 Mar	Cash: balance purchase money re sale of house					225,000	277,120 CR
4 Mar	Transfer sheet: stakeholder					25,000	302,120 CR
4 Mar	Cash redeem mortgage				30,200		271,920 CR
14 Mar	Cash: legacy to Greenpeace				10,000		261,920 CR
	Cash: legacy to NSPCC				5,000		256,920 CR
16 Mar	Profit costs re sale house	600		1,020 DR			
	Customs & Excise VAT	105		1,125 DR			
	Cash: estate agents				5,875		251,045 CR
	Cash: transfer costs from client to office account			1,125	1,125		249,920 CR
17 Mar	Transfer sheet to Elysium on account				15,000		234,920 CR
21 Mar	Profit costs re admin of estate Customs & Excise	800		800 DR			
	VAT	140		940 DR			
	Cash: transfer costs		940	—	940		233,980 CR
30 Mar	Cash: Interest payable		1,500	1,500 DR			
	Cash transfer interest	1,500		—		1,500	235,480 CR
	Transfer sheet: Elysium				235,480		—

Elysium re purchase of house

Date	Details	Office account			Client account		
		DR	CR	Balance	DR	CR	Balance
17 Mar	Transfer sheet Exors Styx					15,000	15,000 CR
	Cash deposit on purchase				15,000		—
30 Mar	Transfer sheet from Exors Styx					235,480	235,480 CR

Note: the firm may consider placing moneys held for Elysium on a designated deposit account.

Further transactions

17.1 Introduction

This chapter deals with the following transactions:

1. Commission received by the firm.
2. The solicitor acting as agent for other solicitors.
3. The solicitor instructing other solicitors as agent.
4. Reducing the client's bill and VAT (abatements).
5. Dishonoured cheques on:

   (a) office account;

   (b) client account.

   Including drawing against uncleared cheques and entries required to correct any breach of the Solicitors' Accounts Rules.

6. Small transactions.

The following transactions are further examples of the operation of the Solicitors' Accounts Rules 1998, the Solicitors' Practice Rules 1990 and the Solicitors' Financial Services (Scope) Rules 2001.

17.2 Commissions

A solicitor may receive commission from a building society or insurance company for introducing business or, in the case of an insurance company, for collecting premiums.

Rule 10 of the Solicitors' Practice Rules 1990 deals with commission and provides as follows:

(a) Where a solicitor receives a commission exceeding £20, this must be accounted for to the client unless the solicitor has disclosed to the client in writing the amount or basis of the calculation of the commission or, if neither the amount nor the basis can be ascertained, an approximation, and the client has agreed to the solicitor retaining the commission.

(b) Where the commission actually received materially exceeds the amount or basis or approximation disclosed to the client, the solicitor must account to the client for the excess.

(c) Rule 10 does not apply where a member of the public deposits money with a solicitor in the solicitor's capacity as agent for a building society or other financial institution and the solicitor has not advised that member of the public as a client about the disposition of the money. So solicitors who operate building society agencies will generally be able to retain the commission paid to them by the building society.

Note also that if financial services are involved, then under s 327 of the Financial Services and Markets Act 2000 and Rule 4 of the Solicitors' Financial Services (Scope) Rules 2001, solicitors must account to clients for all commissions, i.e. there is no £20 minimum figure, subject again to the client's consent as above. The Law Society guidance states that collection of premiums is unlikely to be regarded as assisting in the administration and performance of a contract of insurance.

As a general rule, therefore, unless the solicitor has the client's prior written authority to retain commission, it is clients' money and must be paid into a client account upon receipt. Where there is no authority to retain the commission, the entries made in the accounts when it is received will be:

(a) DEBIT Cash account client column.

(b) CREDIT the ledger account of the client entitled to the commission, client column.

There is nothing in the rules to prevent the solicitor from using the commission for or towards any bill of costs delivered to the client. If the commission does not exceed £20 or if the client gives written authority for the solicitor to retain it, the commission will be practice income and an income account, the 'Commission receivable account', will be opened.

When the commission is received the following entries will be made:

(a) DEBIT Cash account office column.

(b) CREDIT Insurance commission receivable account.

EXAMPLE

The High Risk Insurance Co. pays the firm £100 for introducing its client Jones. The firm has already obtained Jones's written consent to retain the commission.

Insurance commission receivable account Office account

Date	Details	DR	CR	Balance
	Cash (High Risk)		100	100 CR

Cash account

Date	Details	Office account			Client account		
		DR	CR	Balance	DR	CR	Balance
	Insurance commission receivable (High Risk)	100		100 DR			

If a solicitor collects insurance premiums on behalf of an insurance company, then a client ledger account must be opened in the name of that insurance company.

To record the receipt of premiums, the solicitor will make entries in the accounts to record the receipt of clients' money.

EXAMPLE

The firm collects miscellaneous premiums of £500 for the High Risk Insurance Co. from non-clients.

High Risk Insurance Co.

Date	Details	Office account			Client account		
		DR	CR	Balance	DR	CR	Balance
Jan	Cash: miscellaneous: premiums					500	500 CR

When the firm charges the insurance company commission it makes the following entries in its accounts:

(a) DEBIT the Insurance company's ledger account office column.

(b) CREDIT the Insurance commission receivable account.

Continuing the example:

The firm charges the High Risk Insurance Co. £50 commission.

High Risk Insurance Co.

Date	Details	Office account			Client account		
		DR	CR	Balance	DR	CR	Balance
Jan	Cash: miscellaneous: premiums					500	500 CR
	Commission receivable	50		50 DR			

Insurance commission receivable account office account

Date	Details	DR	CR	Balance
	High Risk Insurance Co. (commission charged)		50	50 CR

When commission is to be deducted from premiums collected for the insurance company, a transfer of the commission is made from client to office account.

Continuing the example:

On 31 January commission is transferred to office account.

High Risk Insurance Co.

Date	Details	Office account			Client account		
		DR	CR	Balance	DR	CR	Balance
Jan	Cash: miscellaneous: premiums					500	500 CR
	Commission receivable	50		50 DR			
31 Jan	Cash: transfer: commission		50	—	50		450 CR

When the net premium is paid to the insurance company, entries are made in the accounts to record a payment of client money.

Continuing the example:

The net premium is paid to the High Risk Insurance Co.

High Risk Insurance Co.

Date	Details	Office account			Client account		
		DR	CR	Balance	DR	CR	Balance
Jan	Cash: miscellaneous: premiums					500	500 CR
	Commission receivable	50		50 DR			
31 Jan	Cash: transfer: commission		50	—	50		450 CR
	Cash—you				450		—

The above example is on the basis that the solicitor is taking money as an agent for a financial institution from someone who has not been advised as a client or that the solicitor has the client's written authority to retain the commission. If that were not the case and the solicitor was obliged to account to the client for commission, the commission would be shown as a transfer from the client account of the insurance company to the client account of the client entitled to the commission. No entries would be made in the commission receivable account because the firm has not received any income. So in the example below assume that the firm receives £300 from client Smith, being a premium payable to the High Risk Insurance Co. Commission on the premium totals £30. Smith has not agreed to the firm retaining the commission.

High Risk Insurance Co.

Date	Details	Office account			Client account		
		DR	CR	Balance	DR	CR	Balance
	Smith: cash premium due					300	300 CR
	Smith: transfer commission (transfer sheet)				30		270 CR

Smith

Date	Details	Office account			Client account		
		DR	CR	Balance	DR	CR	Balance
	High Risk Insurance Co.: transfer sheet (commission)					30	30 CR

17.3 Agency

17.3.1 Acting as agent

If a solicitor is instructed by another solicitor to act as agent, a client ledger account will be opened in the name of the instructing solicitor.

When a bill of costs is sent to the instructing solicitor entries will be made in the ledger account to record the delivery of a bill of costs.

If the agent solicitor allows the instructing solicitor commission/reduction in the bill, the agent solicitor's bill of costs will show gross costs less commission. VAT will be charged on the net costs.

EXAMPLE

Brown & Co., solicitors, in Newcastle, instruct the firm to represent their client Simple in matrimonial proceedings. The firm's costs for acting as Brown & Co.'s agents are £180. Commission of £20 is allowed to Brown & Co. The bill which the firm delivers to Brown & Co. will be as follows:

	£
To professional fees	180
Less: commission	20
	160
VAT (17.5%)	28
	188

The net costs and VAT on the net costs will be recorded in the instructing solicitor's account when the bill of costs is delivered to the instructing solicitors.

Continuing the example:

The entries in the firm's accounts to record delivery of the bill of costs to Brown & Co. on 2 December 2002 will appear as follows:

Brown & Co. re agency (matrimonial)

Date	Details	Office account			Client account		
		DR	CR	Balance	DR	CR	Balance
200—							
2 Dec	Profit Costs	160					
	VAT	28		188 DR			

When the instructing solicitor makes payment an entry will be made to record the receipt of the office moneys. Continuing the above example:

Assume that Brown & Co. make payment of the agency fees on 31 December.

Brown & Co. re agency (matrimonial)

Date	Details	Office account			Client account		
		DR	CR	Balance	DR	CR	Balance
200—							
2 Dec	Profit Costs	160					
	VAT	28		188 DR			
31 Dec	Cash—from you		188	—			

17.3.2 Instructing an agent

When a solicitor instructs another solicitor to act as agent, the instructing solicitor treats payment of the agent solicitor's costs as a business expense. To record the payment of agency costs, the instructing solicitor opens an expense account, the Agency expenses account.

When the instructing solicitor pays the agent solicitor's costs and disbursements, the following entries are made in the accounts:

(a) Debit the agency expenses account with the agent's profit costs. (If the agent solicitor has allowed the instructing solicitor commission, the profit costs figure shown in the agency expenses account will be the net figure, i.e., the costs actually paid.)

(b) Debit the Customs and Excise account with VAT.

(c) Debit the ledger account of the client on whose behalf the agent was instructed with any disbursements (office account).

(d) Credit the cash account office column with the total paid to the agent solicitor. *Note*: these entries are made on the date on which payment is made to the agent.

EXAMPLE

The firm instructs Burke & Hare, London solicitors, to represent its client, Knox. Burke & Hare charge £90 less commission of £10 plus VAT and have paid court fees of £20. Burke & Hare's bill is paid on 1 September 200—.

Cash account

Date	Details	Office account			Client account		
		DR	CR	Balance	DR	CR	Balance
200—							
1 Sept	Agency expenses		80	80 CR			
	VAT		14	94 CR			
	Knox: Disbursement		20	114 CR			

Agency expenses account Office account

Date	Details	DR	CR	Balance
200—				
1 Sept	Cash: Burke & Hare: re Knox	80		80 DR

The agency expenses account is a nominal expense account and therefore only has office columns.

Customs and excise account Office account

Date	Details	DR	CR	Balance
200—				
1 Sept	Cash: Burke & Hare: re Knox	14		14 DR

Knox

Date	Details	Office account			Client account		
		DR	CR	Balance	DR	CR	Balance
200—							
1 Sept	Cash: agent's disbursements	20		20 DR			

When the instructing solicitor delivers a bill of costs to the client, the agent solicitor's gross profit costs will be included. The instructing solicitor does not allow the client the commission allowed by the agent solicitor, subject to the Solicitors' Practice Rules, r. 10.

Continuing the example:

The firm sends a bill of costs to Knox, showing its profit costs as £150 plus VAT. The bill is delivered on 28 November 2002

To professional charges	150
Agent's charges	90
	240
VAT (17.5%)	42
	282
Disbursements	20
	302

The total costs (including the agent's gross fees) will be recorded as a delivery of a bill of costs by the firm to the client. No entry is made in respect of the agent's disbursements at this stage. The entry in respect of the agent's disbursements is, as we have seen, made when the agent's fees are paid.

Knox

Date	Details	Office account			Client account		
		DR	CR	Balance	DR	CR	Balance
200—							
1 Sept	Cash: agent: disbursements	20		20 DR			
28 Nov	Profit Costs	240		260 DR			
	VAT	42		302 DR			

17.4 Abatements

After a bill of costs has been delivered to the client, a solicitor may decide to reduce the profit costs.

When an abatement of costs is made, a credit note is sent to the client, showing the reduction in costs and VAT.

The solicitor will make the following entries in the accounts to record an abatement:

(a) CREDIT the client's ledger account office column with the reduction in profit costs and VAT (on separate lines).

(b) DEBIT the profit costs account with the costs abatement.

(c) DEBIT the Customs and Excise account with the reduction in VAT.

EXAMPLE

On 30 June 200— the firm delivers a bill of costs to Charles, the executor of Fred, deceased, for £600 plus VAT. After discussing the matter with Charles, the firm agrees to reduce its bill to £400 and records the abatement in its account on 31 July 200—.

Executor of Fred deceased

Date	Details	Office account			Client account		
		DR	CR	Balance	DR	CR	Balance
200—							
30 June	Profit Costs	600					
	VAT	105		705 DR			
31 July	Costs: abatement		200				
	VAT: abatement		35	470 DR			

Costs account (Office account)

Date	Details	DR	CR	Balance
200—				
30 June	Profit Costs: executor of Fred deceased		600	600 CR
31 July	Profit Costs: abatement: executor of Fred deceased	200		400 CR

Customs and excise account (Office account)

Date	Details	DR	CR	Balance
200—				
30 June	Executor of Fred deceased		105	105 CR
31 July	Executor of Fred deceased: VAT: abatement	35		70 CR

17.5 Dishonoured cheques

17.5.1 Cheque paid into office account

If a cheque paid into office account is later dishonoured, the solicitor will make the following entries in the accounts:

(a) DEBIT the client ledger account office column with the value of the dishonoured cheque.

(b) CREDIT the Cash account office column.

EXAMPLE

There is a debit balance of £235 on Peter's office account on 1 November 200— in respect of costs previously charged to Peter. On 21 November Peter pays the costs by cheque. On 26 November the firm's bank notifies it that Peter's cheque has been returned by the paying banker. To record the above transactions, the following entries will be made in Peter's account.

Peter

Date	Details	Office account			Client account		
		DR	CR	Balance	DR	CR	Balance
200—							
1 Nov	Balance b/d			235 DR			
21 Nov	Cash—you		235	—			
26 Nov	Cash: dishonoured cheque	235		235 DR			

The cash account will appear as follows:

Cash account

Date	Details	Office account			Client account		
		DR	CR	Balance	DR	CR	Balance
200—							
21 Nov	Peter	235		235 DR			
26 Nov	Peter (dishonoured cheque)		235	—			

17.5.2   Cheque paid into client account

If a cheque paid into client account is later dishonoured, the solicitor will make the following entries in the accounts:

(a) DEBIT the client's ledger account client column with the value of the cheque.

(b) CREDIT the Cash account client column.

EXAMPLE

On 4 February 200— Jane paid the sum of £200 on account of costs and disbursements by cheque. On 7 February the firm's bankers notified it that Jane's cheque had been returned. The following entries will be made in the accounts to record these events.

Jane

Date	Details	Office account			Client account		
		DR	CR	Balance	DR	CR	Balance
200—							
4 Feb	Cash—you					200	200 CR
7 Feb	Cash: dishonoured cheque				200		—

Cash account

Date	Details	Office account			Client account		
		DR	CR	Balance	DR	CR	Balance
200—							
4 Feb	Jane				200		200 DR
7 Feb	Jane (dishonoured cheque)					200	—

17.5.3 Drawing against uncleared cheques in client account

The Solicitors' Accounts Rules 1998 do not prevent a solicitor from drawing against an uncleared cheque paid into client account but, if the cheque is later dishonoured, the solicitor is in breach of the Solicitors' Accounts Rules and must make an immediate transfer from office to client account of the amount by which the client account is overdrawn.

When a solicitor has drawn on client account against a cheque which is later dishonoured, the following entries will be made in the accounts:

(a) Entries to record the dishonour of a client account cheque (i.e., those entries in **17.5.2**).

(b) Entries to record the transfer from office account to client account of the amount by which client account is overdrawn.

Note: it is not necessary to transfer the full value of the cheque which has been dishonoured unless the client account is overdrawn by this amount.

Continuing the example from **17.5.2**:

Assume that on 5 February the firm drew a cheque on client account for £55 in respect of court fees. The cheque was then dishonoured on 7 February.

Jane

Date	Details	Office account			Client account		
		DR	CR	Balance	DR	CR	Balance
200—							
4 Feb	Cash—you					200	200 CR
5 Feb	Cash: court fee				55		145 CR
7 Feb	Cash: dishonoured cheque				200		55 DR
	Cash: transfer to remedy breach	55		55 DR		55	—

Cash account

Date	Details	Office account			Client account		
		DR	CR	Balance	DR	CR	Balance
200—							
4 Feb	Jane				200		200 DR
5 Feb	Jane (court fee)					55	145 DR
7 Feb	Jane (dishonoured cheque)					200	55 CR
	Jane (transfer to client account)		55	55 CR	55		—

17.6 Small transactions

When a solicitor does work which involves only one accounting transaction—the charging of costs, for example, for drafting a will, the solicitor may open a ledger account for the client and record the delivery of a bill of costs and receipt of payment of costs in the usual way.

Alternatively the solicitor may make entries only to record the receipt of costs, as follows:

(a) DEBIT the Cash account office column with costs and VAT (on separate lines).

(b) CREDIT the costs account with costs.

(c) CREDIT the Customs and Excise account with VAT.

17.7 Bad debts

If no VAT relief is available the firm will have to write off the total amount due, including VAT. If VAT relief is available (see **13.1.2**) the VAT element can be debited to Customs and Excise account, thus offsetting the VAT due to Customs and Excise.

17.8 Check list

By the end of this chapter you should be able to:

1. understand when solicitors should account to their clients for commission received;

2. make the entries required where the commission received belongs to the client;

3. make the entries required where commission received can be retained by the firm;

4. make the entries required to charge commission and transfer commission;

5. understand the basic entries required when solicitors are acting as agent, and those made when paying other solicitors instructed as agent;

6. make the entries required in respect of a reduction (abatement) of a client's bill of costs on the relevant accounts;

7. make the entries required in respect of a dishonoured cheque;

8. make the entries required where a payment has been made from client account against a cheque which is then dishonoured;

9. note small transactions and VAT relief on bad debts.

17.9 Exercises on further transactions

1 On 3 February 200— a firm of solicitors receives a premium of £84 on behalf of the Fale Safe Insurance Co. for whom the firm acts and which currently owes the firm £16 commission due. On 20 February the net amount due is paid to the Fale Safe Insurance Co., being the gross premium received less commission of £8 and prior commission due. Commission due to the firm is transferred from client to office account. The firm is not required to account to any client for the commission. Prepare the account of the Fale Safe Insurance Co.

2 On 12 February 2002 a firm of solicitors receives £100 from its client Green on account of his pending divorce action costs. On 13 February the sum of £75 is paid out of moneys received from Green, to an enquiry agent. On 17 February the bank notifies the firm that the cheque from Green for £100 has been returned by the paying bankers. Green intimates that he will be in funds within the next two weeks. Prepare the account of Green.

3 Garnet & Co. are acting as agents in an action for the recovery of a debt, on behalf of Emerald & Co. On 3 June 2002, the agents pay an expert witness fee of £100 and court fees of £25. On 28 June 2002, the agents forward their bill of costs to Emerald & Co. showing their costs of £130 less agency commission of £10, plus VAT and the disbursements. They also send a cheque for £9,000, being the amount recovered. On 5 July, Emerald & Co. bill their client Herbert for their own costs of £110, plus the full agents' fee, VAT and disbursements. On 8 July, Emerald & Co. pay Garnet & Co., and transfer costs and disbursements from client to office account. A cheque is then forwarded to Herbert for the balance due to him.

   (a) Show the entries in the accounts for Emerald & Co. to record the above transactions.

   (b) Show the entries in the client ledger account for Emerald & Co. in the accounts of Garnet & Co. to record the above transactions.

4 You act for A who is purchasing a house:

   1 May   Receive a cheque for £6,000 for the deposit.
   2 May   Send a cheque for £6,000 to seller's solicitors.
   6 May   Bank notifies you that cheque has been returned.

   Prepare the account for A and the cash account to record the above. The cash account need not be balanced.

5 (a) On 20 January you deliver a bill of costs to Ann for £200 plus VAT £35. On 27 January you agree to reduce the cost to £160 plus VAT.

   (b) On 20 January you collect an insurance premium of £100 on behalf of Gamma Insurance Co. from Louise, since you are an agent for the Gamma Insurance Co. You retain a commission of £5, which is transferred to office account. You then send the net premium to the insurance company.

(c) On 20 January Adam sends a cheque for £500: £141 is in payment of a bill you have delivered to him and the balance is for payment to the Wilshire county court for an action which he lost. On 21 January you pay the money due to the county court. On 22 January Adam's cheque is dishonoured. On 28 January Adam brings in cash to replace the dishonoured cheque.

Show the client ledger accounts and the Cash account to record the above.

6   In the month of March the following events take place:

3 March	Receive a cheque for £3,000, the deposit on the sale of a house by your client Donald, from the purchaser's solicitor. You are to hold the deposit as agent.
4 March	Receive a bill of costs from Badlot & Co., a firm of solicitors who act as your agents, for your client Neville: profit costs £200 plus VAT, and disbursements on which no VAT is payable, £25. Neville has already paid £100 on account of costs. You send a bill to Neville showing Badlot's costs and disbursements and your costs of £200 plus VAT.
5 March	You write off the sum of £235 which has been outstanding for some time, being costs and VAT owed by Maria, who is bankrupt.
7 March	Pay Badlot's bill by a cheque drawn on office account.
10 March	Lynne, a non client, pays £90 premium due to Beta Insurance Co., for whom you act as agent. Commission due to you is currently £20.
11 March	Receive cheque from Neville in payment of his bill.
13 March	The bank notifies you that Neville's cheque has been dishonoured.
14 March	The net amount due to the Beta Insurance Co. is paid to them. Commission charged is £5.00.
20 March	You act for Daphne in the collection of a debt of £36,000. The debtor sends two cheques of £18,000 each. One cheque dated 19 March is payable to Daphne. You have already agreed your costs of £120 plus VAT with Daphne. You retain this sum and send Daphne a cheque for the balance, the debtor's cheque and receipted bill.
28 March	Complete sale of Donald's house. Receive £27,000. Redeem mortgage of £7,221 by cheque to the High Rate Building Society. Send a bill of costs to Donald for £200 plus VAT. Pay estate agents' charges of £400 plus VAT, the bill being addressed to Donald.
31 March	Donald asks you to transfer enough money from his account to settle the indebtedness of his friend Neville. After making the necessary transfer a cheque is sent to Donald for the balance due.

Show the client ledger accounts to record the above.

7   During the month of November, Teepot, Cupp & Saucer, solicitors, deal with the following events, and you are required to show all the relevant entries on the clients' ledger accounts, which are to be balanced. The rate of VAT is to be taken as 17.5%.

1 November	£6,000 is being held as stakeholder for Lemon. Cheque received (£4,000) from Peter, who is not a client of the firm, being the deposit on the sale of a house by Milko, for whom the firm acts.

	The firm is to hold the money as stakeholders. Exchanged contracts for the sale of Milko's house, and paid petty cash disbursements of £6 (no VAT) on his behalf, on the same day.
4 November	Banker's draft received (£54,000) on completion of the sale of Lemon's house, stake money of £6,000 being transferred from stakeholder account. The mortgagee of Lemon's house, Alexander, had already instructed the firm to act on his behalf in the redemption of his charge on Lemon's house, and the redemption money (£9,675) is transferred to his account. It has been agreed that the mortgagee's costs (£40 plus VAT) will be borne by Lemon. (Assume that Alexander is not an institutional lender.)
5 November	Paid by cheque the sum of £10,000 in respect of a debt which had been incurred by Lemon to Cupp, a partner in the firm, Lemon having previously agreed to this action.
	The amount due to the mortgagee of Lemon's house is paid by cheque, and the estate agent's fee (£1,200 plus VAT), is paid by the firm since the invoice was addressed to them.
	A bill of costs is rendered to Lemon, showing profit costs of £800 plus VAT.
8 November	Received cheque (£500) from Sucrose on account of costs generally. The firm writes off the sum of £70.50 (inclusive of VAT £10.50) as a bad debt, the amount having been owed to the firm by Smith since March 2000. Smith has now been adjudicated bankrupt.
11 November	The designated deposit account opened by the firm re Orange, in respect of an amount of £10,000 held by them for the period of six months, is closed, and a cheque for the sum, together with interest of £150 credited by the bank, is sent to Orange.
14 November	Cheque sent to Lemon in respect of balance of moneys held on his behalf, including agreed interest of £124. The amount due to the firm is transferred to office account and Lemon's account is then closed.
21 November	Bill of costs received from agent solicitors in connection with the affairs of Sucrose. The bill shows profit costs of £300 before allowing agency commission of £100 (excluding VAT) and disbursements of £80 (no VAT). The firm pays the agent's bill and now renders its own bill of costs to Sucrose, showing profit costs of £400 plus VAT and disbursements of £80 (no VAT). Both the profit costs and disbursements of the agent solicitors are included in the foregoing amounts.
25 November	Bill of costs rendered to Milko, showing profit costs (£320 plus VAT) together with disbursements already incurred.
26 November	Received from Sucrose, the balance in respect of the firm's bill of costs, the account then being closed.
29 November	The sale of Milko's house is completed, a banker's draft for £36,000 being received from the purchaser's solicitors. The amount due to the firm is transferred to office account, and a cheque for the balance due to Milko is sent to him.

(Solicitors' Final Examination, updated.)

17.10   Suggested answers to exercises on further transactions

1   Fale Safe Insurance Co. Ltd

Fale Safe Insurance Co. Ltd

Date	Details	Office account			Client account		
		DR	CR	Balance	DR	CR	Balance
3 Feb	Balance b/d	16		16 DR			
	Cash: premiums					84	84 CR
20 Feb	Commission receivable	8		24 DR			
	Cash—you				60		24 CR
	Cash: transfer: commission		24	—	24		—

2   Green

Green

Date	Details	Office account			Client account		
		DR	CR	Balance	DR	CR	Balance
12 Feb	Cash—you					100	100 CR
13 Feb	Cash: enquiry agent				75		25 CR
17 Feb	Cash: returned cheque				100		75 DR
	Cash: transfer	75		75 DR		75	—

3   Emerald & Co. ledger accounts

Herbert

Date	Details	Office account			Client account		
		DR	CR	Balance	DR	CR	Balance
28 June	Cash: agents					9,000	9,000 CR
5 July	Profit Costs	240					
	VAT	42		282 DR			
8 July	Cash: agency: disbursements	125		407 DR			
	Cash—you				8,593		407 CR
	Cash: transfer: costs		407	—	407		—

Cash account

Date	Details	Office account			Client account		
		DR	CR	Balance	DR	CR	Balance
28 June					9,000		9,000 DR
8 July	Cash: Garnet & Co. Agency Costs		120	120 CR			
	Herbert VAT		21	141			
	Disbursements		125	266 CR			
	Herbert transfer costs	407		141 DR		407	8,593 DR
	Herbert balance due					8,593	—

Agency expenses account Office account

Date	Details	DR	CR	Balance
8 July	Cash: Garnet & Co. (Herbert)	120		120 DR

Customs and excise account Office account

Date	Details	DR	CR	Balance
5 July	Herbert		42	42 CR
8 July	Cash: Garnet & Co. (Herbert)	21		21 CR

Profit costs account Office account

Date	Details	DR	CR	Balance
5 July	Herbert		240	240 CR

Garnet & Co. ledger cards

Emerald & Co. re agency

Date	Details	Office account			Client account		
		DR	CR	Balance	DR	CR	Balance
3 June	Cash: expert witness	100		100 DR			
	Cash: court fee	25		125 DR			
28 June	Profit Costs	120					
	VAT	21		266 DR			
	Cash: cheque					9,000	9,000 CR
	Cash—you:				9,000		—
8 July	Cash—from you		266	—			

4 **A. account**

Date	Details	Office account			Client account		
		DR	CR	Balance	DR	CR	Balance
1 May	Cash—you					6,000	6,000 CR
2 May	Cash: deposit paid				6,000		—
6 May	Cash: dishonoured cheque				6,000		6,000 DR
	Cash: transfer to correct breach	6,000		6,000 DR		6,000	—

Cash account

Date	Details	Office account			Client account		
		DR	CR	Balance	DR	CR	Balance
1 May	A: monies received				6,000		6,000 DR
2 May	A: deposit paid					6,000	—
6 May	A: dishonoured cheque					6,000	6,000 CR
	A: transfer to correct breach		6,000	6,000 CR	6,000		

5 (a) Ann

Date	Details	Office account			Client account		
		DR	CR	Balance	DR	CR	Balance
20 Jan	Profit Costs	200					
	VAT	35		235 DR			
27 Jan	Costs abatement		40				
	VAT abatement		7	188 DR			

(b) Gamma Insurance Co. account

Date	Details	Office account			Client account		
		DR	CR	Balance	DR	CR	Balance
20 Jan	Cash: premium (Louise)					100	100 CR
	Commission	5		5 DR			
	Cash: transfer		5	—	5		95 CR
	Cash—you				95		—

(c) Adam account

Date	Details	Office account			Client account		
		DR	CR	Balance	DR	CR	Balance
20 Jan	Balance			141 DR			
	Cash—you		141	—		359	359 CR
21 Jan	Cash: Wilshire county court				359		—
22 Jan	Cash: dishonoured cheque	141		141 DR	359		359 DR
	Cash: transfer to correct breach	359		500 DR		359	—
28 Jan	Cash—you		500	—			

Cash account

Date	Details	Office account			Client account		
		DR	CR	Balance	DR	CR	Balance
20 Jan	Gamma insurance: premium				100		100 DR
	Gamma insurance: transfer commission	5		5 DR		5	95 DR
	Gamma insurance: balance of premium					95	—
	Adam	141		146 DR	359		359 DR
21 Jan	Adam: Wilshire county court					359	—
22 Jan	Adam: dishonoured cheque		141	5 DR		359	359 CR
	Adam: transfer to correct breach		359	354 CR	359		
28 Jan	Adam:		500	146 DR			

6 Donald account

Date	Details	Office account			Client account		
		DR	CR	Balance	DR	CR	Balance
3 Mar	Cash: deposit					3,000	3,000 CR
28 Mar	Cash: completion					27,000	30,000 CR
	Cash: High Rate Building Society				7,221		22,779 CR
	Profit Costs	200					
	VAT	35		235 DR			
	Cash: estate agent				470		22,309 CR
31 Mar	Cash: transfer to Neville				395		21,914 CR
	Cash: transfer costs		235	—	235		21,679 CR
	Cash—you				21,679		—

Neville account

Date	Details	Office account			Client account		
		DR	CR	Balance	DR	CR	Balance
4 Mar	Balance					100	100 CR
	Profit Costs	400					
	VAT	70		470 DR			
7 Mar	Cash: agents disbursements	25		495 DR			
11 Mar	Cash—you		395	100 DR			
	Cash: transfer		100	—	100		—
13 Mar	Cash: dishonoured cheque	395		395 DR			
31 Mar	Cash: Donald		395	—			

Maria account

Date	Details	Office account			Client account		
		DR	CR	Balance	DR	CR	Balance
5 Mar	Balance			235 DR			
	Bad debts		200				
	Customs and Excise		35	—			

Beta Insurance Co. account

Date	Details	Office account			Client account		
		DR	CR	Balance	DR	CR	Balance
10 Mar	Commission due	20		20 DR			
	Cash: premium					90	90 CR
14 Mar	Commission	5		25 DR			
	Cash: transfer commission		25	—	25		65 CR
	Cash—you				65		—

Daphne account

Date	Details	Office account			Client account		
		DR	CR	Balance	DR	CR	Balance
	Profit costs: agreed fee	120					
	VAT	21		141 DR			
20 Mar	Cash: debtor					18,000	18,000 CR
	Cash: transfer		141	—	141		17,859 CR
	Cash—you				17,859		—

Note: the other cheque for £18,000 payable to Daphne could have been shown on the account by way of a memorandum entry.

7 Teepot, Cupp & Saucer

Milko

Date	Details	Office account			Client account		
		DR	CR	Balance	DR	CR	Balance
1 Nov	Petty cash: disbursement	6		6 DR			
25 Nov	Profit Costs	320		326 DR			
	VAT	56		382 DR			
29 Nov	Cash: sale proceeds					36,000	36,000 CR
	Stakeholder: transfer: deposit					4,000	40,000 CR
	Cash: transfer: costs from client to office account		382	—	382		39,618 CR
	Cash—you				39,618		—

Lemon

Date	Details	Office account			Client account		
		DR	CR	Balance	DR	CR	Balance
4 Nov	Cash: sale proceeds					54,000	54,000 CR
	Stakeholder: transfer: deposit					6,000	60,000 CR
	Alexander: transfer: redemption				9,675		50,325 CR
	Alexander: transfer: redemption costs	47		47 DR			
5 Nov	Cash: Cupp				10,000		40,325 CR
	Cash: estate agent	1,200		1,247 DR			
	Profit Costs	800					
	VAT	350		2,397 DR			
	Interest allowed		124	2,273 DR			
14 Nov	Cash: transfer interest	124		3,397 DR		124	40,449 CR
	Cash: transfer: costs		2,397	—	2,397		38,052 CR
	Cash—you				38,052		—

Alexander

Date	Details	Office account			Client account		
		DR	CR	Balance	DR	CR	Balance
4 Nov	Profit Costs	40					
	VAT	7		47 DR			
	Lemon: transfer: redemption					9,675	9,675 CR
	Lemon: transfer: redemption costs		47	—			
5 Nov	Cash—you				9,675		—

Sucrose

Date	Details	Office account			Client account		
		DR	CR	Balance	DR	CR	Balance
8 Nov	Cash—you					500	500 CR
21 Nov	Cash: disbursements paid	80		80 DR			
	Profit Costs	400					
	VAT	70		550 DR			
26 Nov	Cash—you		50	500 DR			
	Cash: transfer: costs		500	—	500		—

Smith

Date	Details	Office account			Client account		
		DR	CR	Balance	DR	CR	Balance
8 Nov	Balance			70.50 DR			
	Bad debt		60				
	Customs and Excise VAT		10.50	—			

Orange

Date	Details	Office account			Client account		
		DR	CR	Balance	DR	CR	Balance
	Cash account: back from deposit					10,150	10,150 CR
	Cash: you				10,150		

Orange

Held on deposit

Date	Details	Office account			Client account		
		DR	CR	Balance	DR	CR	Balance
	Balance						10,000 CR
	Deposit interest					150	10,150 CR
	Deposit cash: transfer back				10,150		

Stakeholder account

Date	Details	Office account			Client account		
		DR	CR	Balance	DR	CR	Balance
	Balance					6,000	6,000 CR
1 Nov	Cash: Milko					4,000	10,000 CR
4 Nov	Lemon: transfer				6,000		4,000 CR
29 Nov	Milko: transfer				4,000		—

Revision exercises and questions on solicitors' accounts

18.1 Introduction

This chapter contains the following questions on solicitors' accounts:

Set 1 These questions require a statement of the principles or rules involved.

Set 2 These questions require a statement of the principles or rules involved and the entries on the accounts.

Two long questions requiring you to make entries in a series of transactions.

18.2 Revision questions

Explain how a firm of solicitors should deal with the following. You should state the principles/rules involved. There is no need to state the debit and credit entries involved.

1 The firm is dealing with a probate matter and the deceased's bank agrees to advance £20,500 to the executors in respect of inheritance tax. A loan account is opened by the bank for the executors and a cheque for £20,500 is drawn by the executors, payable to the Inland Revenue, and handed to the firm of solicitors.

2 The firm has held the net proceeds of sale of a house on behalf of its client David for the past two months. David now asks for the net proceeds, totalling £10,000, to be sent to him.

3 The firm has referred investment business work for its client Fred through a stockbroker, who splits the commission on sales and purchases of shares with the firm of solicitors. Can the firm retain the commission?

4 Jane, a client, owes the firm £940, being £800 re costs and £140 re VAT. Seven months after the bill was delivered the firm writes off the debt.

5 The firm receives cash of £600 on behalf of its client Clarke in settlement of a claim. Clarke has asked that the firm pay this cash over to Boswell in payment of a debt due from Clarke to Boswell.

6 The firm acts for Ruby, a partner in the firm, and her friend John, who is a legal executive in the firm. They are selling a cottage and purchasing a larger house in town. The firm receives a cheque for £30,000 to hold as agent for the seller.

7 The firm has received commission from the Welsh Widowers' Insurance Company in the sum of £300. This is in respect of £150 in respect of commission payable for collection of

a premium from a non client, and £150 payable in respect of commission received in respect of another client, Susan.

8 The firm receives a cheque for £400 on general account of costs from their client Ian. A disbursement of £415 (no VAT payable) is paid by the firm on behalf of Ian.

9 The firm receives a cheque for £770 from their client Lisa. This is in respect of the firm's bill for £400 plus VAT, which had been sent to Lisa, and counsel's fees of £300 (no VAT) which have not yet been paid.

18.3 Suggested answers to revision questions

1 No entries need be shown on the solicitors' accounts at all, as the loan account at the bank belongs to the executors and not the firm. The cheque is made out to the Inland Revenue, so it does not belong to the firm and it should merely be forwarded to the Inland Revenue.

2 As £10,000 has been held for two weeks or more, here two months, then the money should have been placed on a designated deposit account to earn interest for David. The proceeds plus the interest should be paid to him. See Rule 24(1). If the money has not been placed on a designated deposit account for David then the firm should pay an amount at least equivalent to the amount that would have been earned. Interest payable will come from the firm's office account.

3 Generally Rule 10 Solicitors' Practice Rules 1990 applies to commission earned relating to clients. Solicitors should account to clients for any commission received of more than £20 unless, having disclosed the amount in writing to the client they have the client's consent to retain it. However if investment business is involved then under the Solicitors' Scope rules 2001 solicitors should account for all commission, subject to client consent as in Practice Rule 10.

4 As the debt is at least six months old the firm may claim bad debt relief. Thus the amount of £800 will be recorded as a bad debt, and the VAT of £140 can be debited to the Customs and Excise account, thus reducing the VAT payable to Customs and Excise.

5 Although normally a firm of solicitors must pay money received on behalf of a client into a client bank account, under r. 17(a) of the Solicitors' Accounts Rules 1998, where money is received in cash and is without delay paid in cash in the ordinary course of business to the client or on the client's behalf there is no need to pay into the client bank account. The firm can therefore pay the money to Boswell. However, entries must be made on the accounts showing the receipt and payment out of client money. Take care re money laundering.

6 Although money received on behalf of partners in the firm is not client money Rule 13 Note (xii) where the money is received on behalf of a partner together with a non partner then the money will be client money and as this is held as agent for the seller, it can be recorded on a client ledger card for Ruby and John.

7 See as stated in **Answer 3** above. It may retain the commission of £150 in respect of the non client. It must account to Susan, however, for the £150, unless she has been advised in writing and has agreed that the firm may retain the commission. Note that the Law Society consider that collection of premiums is not likely to be regarded as assisting in the administration and performance of a contract of insurance.

8 The £400 on general account of costs should have been paid into client account Rule 13 Note (i)(d). The firm cannot pay the total disbursement of £415 from client account

Rule 22(5). Although it would be technically possible for the firm to pay two cheques, one for £400 from client account and one for £15 from office account, this would seem odd, and the better course would be to pay £415 from office account, and then transfer £400 from client account. It is also possible for the firm to advance money to fund the payment under r. 15. It may be necessary to ask the client for further funds if these are needed for other disbursements.

9 This is mixed office/client money Rules 19 & 20. The sum of £470, being £400 plus VAT £70, is office account money. The remaining £300 should be held on client account until counsel's fees are paid. The cheque may be split or, more usually, the whole amount paid into client account, and then £470 transferred to office account within 14 days. Alternatively the entire sum may be paid into office account and counsel's fees paid or the money transferred to client account by the end of the second working day following receipt (Rule 19).

18.4 Self-assessment questions

Decide whether the following transactions should be dealt with through client account or office account, and show the entries that would be made on the accounts.

1 A solicitor receives £400 on general account of costs from Janet.

2 A solicitor receives £470 as an agreed fee in respect of work to be done for Harold. The firm has not yet sent a bill to Harold.

3 The solicitor holds £200 on general account of costs from Ethel. An enquiry agent is paid £150 (no VAT is payable).

4 The firm is acting for one of the partners, John, in respect of his sale of a flat in Mersey Quays. The sale price of £54,000 is received on completion from the purchaser's solicitors.

5 The firm is acting on behalf of one of its employees, Patsy, in respect of the sale of a house. Sale proceeds are received in the sum of £90,000.

6 The firm is acting for one of its partners, Jane, together with her husband in respect of the sale of a house. Sale proceeds are received in the sum of £150,000.

7 The firm has £80,000 on general client account. The office account is overdrawn at the bank. A disbursement of £50 has to be paid on behalf of their client Brian, who has not yet sent any money on account of costs.

8 The firm sent out a bill to Anthony for £800 plus VAT £140. Counsel's fees are due but not yet paid in the sum of £600. Anthony sends a cheque for £1,540.

9 The firm receives £5,000 in respect of Derek's sale of 'The Gables', to hold as stakeholder.

10 The firm receives £6,000 in respect of Mary's sale of 8, Beaumont Square, to hold as agent for the seller. The sum of £5,000 is paid out in respect of her purchase of 10, Bloxham Road.

11 A cheque made out to client James for £300 is received by the firm.

12 The firm receives £60 cash on behalf of their client Cecil. Later that day the cash is handed to Cecil who has called into the office.

13 The firm receives a cheque for £450 on behalf of Barbara which is then endorsed over to her.

14 A cheque is received made out to the firm for £9,000 in respect of a debt due from Agnes to their client Joe.

15 The firm sent out a bill of costs for £800 plus VAT to their client, Tim. The firm later agreed with Tim to reduce the bill to £600 plus VAT.

18.5 Suggested answers to self-assessment questions

1 Money on general account of costs is client money and must be paid into client account (see r. 13).

Janet

Date	Details	Office account			Client account		
		DR	CR	Balance	DR	CR	Balance
	Cash—you on account of costs					400	400 CR

Cash book

Date	Details	Office account			Client account		
		DR	CR	Balance	DR	CR	Balance
	Janet: on account costs				400		400 DR

2 An agreed fee is office money and must be paid into office account (r. 19(5)).
So:

(a) CREDIT Harold client ledger card office account.

(b) DEBIT the cash book office account.

3 The £200 on general account of costs would have been paid into client account. As this money is available, and VAT is not involved, the enquiry agent can be paid from client account.

Ethel

Date	Details	Office account			Client account		
		DR	CR	Balance	DR	CR	Balance
	Cash—you on account of costs					200	200 CR
	Cash: enquiry agent				150		50 CR

Cash book

Date	Details	Office account			Client account		
		DR	CR	Balance	DR	CR	Balance
	Ethel: on a/c costs				200		200 DR
	Ethel: enquiry agent					150	50 DR

4 Client's money does not include money to which the only person entitled is the solicitor himself or herself or, in the case of a firm of solicitors, one or more of the partners in the firm: see the notes to r. 13. The money cannot be paid into client account; it must be held on an office account in the name of John.

John

Date	Details	Office account			Client account		
		DR	CR	Balance	DR	CR	Balance
	Cash: sale proceeds		54,000	54,000 CR			

Cash book

Date	Details	Office account			Client account		
		DR	CR	Balance	DR	CR	Balance
	John: re sale	54,000		54,000 DR			

5 Patsy does not fall within the exception in **Answer 4** above: she is a client and the money will be paid into client account on her behalf. So:

(a) CREDIT Patsy client ledger card client account.

(b) DEBIT the Cash book client account.

6 Provided Jane's husband is not a partner in the firm, the money is again client money: see **Answer 4** above, i.e., Jane is not the only person entitled. So:

(a) CREDIT Jane and husband client ledger card client account.

(b) DEBIT the Cash book client account.

7 Although there are sufficient funds on client account to pay the disbursement, as the firm is not holding any money on behalf of Brian, the payment cannot be made out of client account, it must be made out of office account. See r. 22(8), which makes it clear that money drawn cannot exceed the total held on account of the client. So:

(a) DEBIT Brian client ledger card Office account.

(b) CREDIT the Cash book office account.

8 A solicitor may only pay money into office account in respect of, *inter alia*, 'costs', which excludes counsel's fees which have not yet been paid. On the assumption that no VAT is payable in respect of counsel's fees in this case then £940 is office money, and £600 is client money. The cheque may be split, i.e., £940 paid into office account and £600 into client account, or all the money may be paid into client account, and then £940 transferred to office account within 14 days or all the money may be paid into office account and then either counsel's fees paid or transferred to client account, within 2 working days see r. 19.

Entries where the money is split:

Anthony

Date	Details	Office account			Client account		
		DR	CR	Balance	DR	CR	Balance
	Costs	800		800 DR			
	VAT	140		940 DR			
	Cash—you		940	—		600	600 CR

The cash book would be debited £940 on office account, and debited £600 on client account.

Entries where the money is paid into client account and then transferred:

Anthony

Date	Details	Office account			Client account		
		DR	CR	Balance	DR	CR	Balance
	Balance re costs and VAT			940 DR			
	Cash—you					1,540	1,540 CR
	Cash: transfer costs		940	—	940		600 CR

Cash book

Date	Details	Office account			Client account		
		DR	CR	Balance	DR	CR	Balance
	Anthony				1,540		1,540 DR
	Anthony: transfer costs	940		940 DR		940	600 DR

9 The money does not belong to Derek until completion of the sale. It must be paid into stakeholder account, a client ledger card, client account. So:

 (a) CREDIT the stakeholder account client ledger card client account.

 (b) DEBIT the Cash book client account.

10 As this money is held for Mary it may be paid into her client ledger card, client account and used in respect of the deposit payable on the purchase.

Mary: Sale 8, Beaumont Square; purchase 10, Bloxham Road

Date	Details	Office account			Client account		
		DR	CR	Balance	DR	CR	Balance
	Cash deposit: agent for vendor					6,000	6,000 CR
	Cash deposit on purchase				5,000		1,000 CR

The other entries would have been to debit the cash book client account with £6,000, and to credit the cash book client account in respect of the deposit paid on purchase, i.e., £5,000.

11 As the cheque is made out to the client, it cannot be paid into the solicitor's bank accounts, whether office account or client account. No entries need be made on the accounts, although a note may be made if required.

12 Although the rules do not require this money to be paid into client account at the bank, client's money has still been received and then paid out.
    Receipt:

    (a) CREDIT the client ledger card of Cecil client account.

    (b) DEBIT the cash book client account.

    Payment out:

    (a) DEBIT the client ledger card of Cecil client account.

    (b) CREDIT the cash book client account.

13 Again this money need not be paid into the firm's client bank account. However, the receipt of client money, and payment out of client money, should be recorded on the accounts. The entries would be as in **Answer 12** above, on Barbara's client ledger card and the cash book re £450.

14 As the cheque is made out to the firm it can be paid into the firm's bank account. The money is received on behalf of Joe and is client money. So:

    (a) CREDIT Joe's client ledger card client account.

    (b) DEBIT the Cash book client account.

15   **Tim**

Date	Details	Office account			Client account		
		DR	CR	Balance	DR	CR	Balance
	Profit Costs	800		800 DR			
	VAT	140		940 DR			
	Abatement		200	740 DR			
	VAT		35	705 DR			

Profit costs account Office account

Date	Details	DR	CR	Balance
	Tim: bill of costs		800	800 CR
	Tim: abatement	200		600 CR

Customs and excise (VAT) account Office account

Date	Details	DR	CR	Balance
	Tim: bill of costs		140	140 CR
	Tim: abatement	35		105 CR

18.6   Test on further transactions

Allow approximately 1 hour to complete this test.

Harriet, Peter and Alex are solicitors, and they deal with the following events:

2 January	Brown pays cash (£104) to the firm, who act as agents for the Nonpay Insurance Co. Ltd. Commission currently due to the firm on that agency amounts to £43. The firm is not liable to account to any client for the commission.
3 January	Paid by cheque the sum of £2,000 on behalf of Black, and received later the same day from Black, a cheque for £1,500 in partial satisfaction. The balance is to be paid from the proceeds of the sale of his house, which will be received within a few days' time.
7 January	Received cheque, in respect of the sale of Black's house, amounting to £22,634, being the balance of purchase money. The sum of £2,500 is transferred from stakeholder account the same day. The firm also acts for the mortgagees of Black, the Savall Building Society, and £7,436 is sent to that company to redeem the mortgage. The bill of costs is sent to the building society. The costs of redemption of Black's mortgage (£20 plus VAT) are to be borne by Black.
10 January	Bill of costs sent to Black (£240 plus VAT).
13 January	Pink repays a personal loan of £1,000 made by Peter, a partner in the firm.
15 January	The firm acts for Yellow in a court action, having already paid the counsel's fee of £100 plus VAT (the principal method was used). The firm had appointed local agents, and their bill showed profit costs of £120, less agency commission £20, plus VAT. Bill of costs is sent to Yellow, showing profit costs of £220 (including agents' profit costs) plus VAT.
16 January	Grey pays £200 on account of her pending divorce action costs, and petty cash disbursements of £16 are paid in respect of this on the same day.
17 January	The net amount due to the Nonpay Insurance Co. Ltd is paid, being the gross premium received (£104) less commission of £15 and prior commission due (£43).
20 January	Received amount due from Yellow.
22 January	Paid enquiry agent, on behalf of Grey, the sum of £40 (no VAT), the cheque being drawn on client account.
24 January	The bank notifies the firm that the cheque from Grey has been returned unpaid by the paying bankers.
29 January	The sum of £1,000, which has been held on behalf of Blue for some three months, is repaid to Blue, together with agreed interest of £40. The payment is made by means of a cheque drawn on client account. The money has not been deposited in a designated deposit account.

Write up the client's ledger accounts, showing all relevant entries. All accounts are to be balanced. The rate of VAT is to be taken as 17.5%.

(Law Society Final Examination, updated.)

18.7 Suggested answer to test on further transactions

Nonpay Insurance Co. Ltd

Date	Details	Office account			Client account		
		DR	CR	Balance	DR	CR	Balance
2 Jan	Balance due	43		43 DR			
	Cash: Brown					104	104 CR
17 Jan	Commission	15		58 DR			
	Cash—you					46	58 CR
	Cash: transfer: commission		58	—		58	—

Black

Date	Details	Office account			Client account		
		DR	CR	Balance	DR	CR	Balance
3 Jan	Cash	2,000		2,000 DR			
3 Jan	Cash—you		1,500	500 DR			
7 Jan	Cash: purchaser's solicitors					22,634	22,634 CR
	Stakeholder: transfer					2,500	25,134 CR
	Cash: Savall Building Society: redemption				7,436		17,698 CR
10 Jan	Profit Costs	240		740 DR			
	VAT	42		782 DR			
	Costs (mortgage redemption)	20		802 DR			
	VAT	3.50		805.50 DR			
13 Jan	Cash: transfer: costs		805.50	—	805.50		16,892.50 CR

Yellow

Date	Details	Office account			Client account		
		DR	CR	Balance	DR	CR	Balance
15 Jan	Balance			100 DR			
	Profit Costs	220					
	VAT (17.50 + 38.50)	56		376 DR			
20 Jan	Cash—you		376	—			

Grey—divorce

Date	Details	Office account			Client account		
		DR	CR	Balance	DR	CR	Balance
16 Jan	Cash: you					200	200 CR
	Petty cash: disbursements	16		16 DR			
22 Jan	Cash: enquiry agent				40		160 CR
24 Jan	Cash: returned cheque				200		40 DR
	Cash: transfer to correct breach	40		56 DR		40	

Blue

Date	Details	Office account			Client account		
		DR	CR	Balance	DR	CR	Balance
29 Jan	Balance						1,000 CR
	Interest payable		40	40 CR			
	Cash transfer interest	40				40	1,040 CR
	Cash: you amount due				1,040		—

Note: an account is not opened for Peter as he is a partner in the firm and it would be in breach of the Solicitors' Accounts Rules 1998 to pay the money received from Pink into client account.

18.8 Test on ledger accounts including VAT

Allow approximately 1 hour to complete this test.

Except where specifically referred to in the questions, taxation (including VAT) should be ignored.

Bread, Butter and Honey are solicitors, and they deal with the following events:

3 April	Paid £23.50 (including VAT £3.50) by cheque drawn on office account, in respect of the reproduction of documents. The invoice is made out to the client, Phantasia, for whom the firm are acting in a tax matter before the special commissioners.
4 April	Received banker's draft for £49,500 from the purchaser's solicitors, being the balance of purchase money re the sale by Smith of his house 'Figleaf'. On the same day the sum of £19,500 is sent by cheque to the mortgagees of the property, in full payment of the amount due to them.
7 April	Logger, Hedd and Co., the estate agents acting for Smith, send cheque to firm for £4,235, being the deposit on 'Figleaf' less their commission.
8 April	Received the sum of £300 from Phantasia on account of costs generally.

11 April	The firm acts for Jones in the collection of a debt due to her, amounting to £5,000. The debtor sends two cheques for the debt, each cheque being for the sum of £2,500 and dated 16 May and 16 June, respectively.
14 April	Sent cheque for £587.50 (including VAT £87.50) to A. Builder in respect of pre-sale repairs to 'Figleaf'. The invoice was addressed to the firm.
28 April	Paid fee of £235 (including VAT £35) to E. X. Pert, a witness who appeared on behalf of Phantasia. The payment was made out of client account.
29 April	Bill of costs sent to Smith (£300 plus VAT).
5 May	Paid from client account £94 (including VAT) in respect of transcripts obtained on behalf of Phantasia.
9 May	Profit costs and disbursements are transferred from client account to office account in respect of Smith.
20 May	Bill of costs in respect of tax matter is rendered to Phantasia, showing profit costs of £700 plus VAT.
16 June	Received cheque in settlement of Phantasia's account with the firm.
17 June	Bill of costs for £60 plus VAT delivered to Jones.
20 June	Both cheques from the debtor of Jones, having been presented and met, the total amount due, after deduction of costs but inclusive of interest allowed by the firm (£22), was paid over to Jones. It is the practice of the firm to record all interest payments made by the firm on the client's ledger account. The amount due to the firm is transferred from client to office account.
30 June	The firm allows interest of £250 for Smith, before paying the total due from client account.

You are required to show the ledger accounts of Phantasia, Smith and Jones, recording all the above transactions. The rate of VAT is to be taken as 17.5%.

(Law Society Final Examination, updated.)

18.9 Suggested answer to test on ledger accounts including VAT

Phantasia

Date	Details	Office account			Client account		
		DR	CR	Balance	DR	CR	Balance
3 Apr	Cash: production of documents	23.50		23.50 DR			
8 Apr	Cash—you					300	300 CR
28 Apr	Cash: E. X. Pert				235		65 CR
5 May	Cash: transcripts				94		29 DR
	Cash: transfer	29		52.50 DR			
	Cash: transfer					29	—
20 May	Costs	700					
	VAT	122.50		875 DR			
16 June	Cash—you		875	—			

Smith

Date	Details	Office account			Client account		
		DR	CR	Balance	DR	CR	Balance
4 Apr	Cash: purchaser's solicitors					49,500	49,500 CR
	Cash: redemption				19,500		30,000 CR
7 Apr	Cash: estate agent (less commission)					4,235	34,235 CR
14 Apr	Cash: A. Builder	500		500 DR			
29 Apr	Profit Costs	300					
	VAT	140		940 DR			
9 May	Cash: transfer: costs		940	—		940	33,295 CR
30 June	Interest payable		250	250 CR			
	Cash transfer interest	250		—		250	33,545 CR
	Cash—you				33,545		—

Jones

Date	Details	Office account			Client account		
		DR	CR	Balance	DR	CR	Balance
16 May	Cash: debtor					2,500	2,500 CR
16 June	Cash: debtor					2,500	5,000 CR
17 June	Profit Costs	60					
	VAT	10.50		70.50 DR			
20 June	Interest payable		22	48.50 DR		22	5,022 CR
	Cash: transfer	22		70.50 DR			
	Cash: transfer		70.50	—	70.50		4,951.50 CR
	Cash—you				4,951.50		—

INDEX